All for a Bottle of Whisky

Reed's Maritime Library

All for a Bottle of Whisky

Ralph von Arnim

SHERIDAN HOUSE

This edition published 2001 by
Sheridan House Inc.
145 Palisade Street
Dobbs Ferry, New York 10522
www.sheridanhouse.com

Copyright © 2001 by Ralph von Arnim

First published in Great Britain 2001
by Thomas Reed Publications

A Cataloging-in-Publication record of this book is available
from the Library of Congress, Washington, DC.

Edited by Alex Milne
Series Consultant Tony Brunton-Reed
Design & Layout by C E Marketing
Produced by Omega Profiles Ltd.
Printed and bound in Great Britain

ISBN 1-57409-139-5

INTRODUCTION

FIRST A WARNING to anybody who is about to cast off for a long voyage. Cruising under sail is highly addictive and it will revolutionise your idea of life. But it is deeply worthwhile and it is never too late to begin.

It was an illusion to believe that I could sail from Asia to Europe in one year. I then convinced myself that a sabbatical year at sea must last 24 months. The maintenance and repair of a cruising yacht eats away enormous amounts of time, especially if the yacht happens to be made of wood. In any case, it would be impossible to ignore and sail past all the beautiful places along the way. A paramount rule for cruising, as I found out, is to have time; this is more than a luxury, it is in fact a safety issue.

Many things in life that we had previously regarded as perfectly normal were now seen from a totally different perspective. We developed a much higher respect for the forces of nature, and we found ourselves wondering why people in the western world worry so much about petty problems.

For my companions and myself, this voyage was a sensational experience. We were driven by the search for adventure and by curiosity. Encounters with people and cultures, many of which were historically connected to Europe, were an ideal foundation for the planning of the voyage. We travelled in slow motion and yet lived life in the fast lane. I was also lucky in sharing these experiences with a light-hearted group of people; many people we met along the way commented that *Ryusei* was a happy ship.

Our adventures fade into insignificance against the long history of seafaring; however, I still believe that our experiences are worth writing down. In this way, those who dream of cruising under sail can share and enjoy our voyage without actually having to break free from their obligations ashore.

Fair winds!

DEDICATION

To John MacNab

PART I

Cramalott Inn

July 1995, Grand Bruit, Newfoundland

THICK FOG WRAPPED ITSELF around us like a wet blanket; it was icy cold and *Ryusei* was pitching heavily in a rough sea. We were bitterly regretting having left the harbour of Petites on the south coast of Newfoundland. Heavy weather had kept us there. Then, because the wind had lessened and the forecast sounded good, we set sail. We had become used to the fog during these past few months but today it was extremely thick so that Norman, the ever-helpful boat-builder, had piloted us out to sea in his fishing boat. We had chosen a longer but safer route, as the seas were breaking on the bar in the harbour entrance. This alone should have been reason enough to turn back, but now it was too late. Norman had been swallowed by the fog and we were at sea. Without him, it would have been impossible to find our way back through the rocks into the tiny harbour. There was nothing now but to shape a course for the harbour of Grand Bruit, which had been recommended to us. This short hop of only 22 miles should be possible even in foul weather, or so we thought.

On board were Malley, Elizabeth and myself. My female shipmates came from the United States. We had met in Maine, and now they were game to sail across the Atlantic to Scotland with me. For the sake of this adventure, Malley had taken a holiday from both her work and her fiancé, and Elizabeth was taking a break from university to sail to Europe and Africa.

As if it wasn't bad enough already, the wind died on us. Our sails were flapping and the boom crashed from side to side because the sea had not yet quietened down. The storm, caused by a low from the Caribbean, had finally passed. We lowered the sails and started to motor. The ship's motion was by now so violent that all of us suffered from sea-sickness. Next, one of the ties holding the radar reflector broke. The metal cylinder swayed wildly and was smashing against the mast, threatening to destroy itself in the process. I had no choice but to climb the mast, secured by a life-line and the spinnaker halyard, to try to fix the radar reflector back in place. As soon as I was back on deck, Malley called "There must be a ship behind us. I can see a blip on the radar!"

"This looks as if she is on collision course" I said after we had watched the signal for a few moments. "It is a big blip, meaning a big ship, and she is bearing down on us fast!" I took the helm while Elizabeth sat in the companionway and monitored the radar. Malley and I stared back into the fog. All of a sudden we saw the vague shape of a ship's bow, about two hundred metres away. It passed us far too close and then vanished in the fog ahead. "At least we are not the only ones out here in this lousy weather" I said, in a feeble attempt to cheer us up.

Soon we were facing our next problem. Should we risk entering the harbour in this poor visibility? We studied the chart together. My gut feeling was that we ought to head out to sea and safety, but as the boat was rolling and pitching like a drunken cork on the waves, I decided to give it a try. "If we find the island in front of the entrance and identify the approach buoy on the radar, we can make it" I said. Using the GPS, echo-sounder and radar, we inched towards the rugged coast. The seas were now even rougher with the decreasing depth. Elizabeth concentrated on the radar, but finally said "Ralph, there are so many signals that I just can't identify anything – no buoy, not even the island."

"That must be because of the huge waves, but if we increase the filter, we won't be able to find the buoy. Let's just keep our eyes and ears wide open so that we can see or hear the waves breaking ashore!" I called back. Tension was high, as we knew that the area was infested by rocks and shallows.

We were saved by Malley's sharp eyes. "Breaking water ahead!" she cried. Then I saw white water too, both ahead and to one side. In an instant reaction, I gave full throttle ahead and pulled the helm hard over, turning us back in our tracks. We then slowly motored eastwards, in the hope of locating the island. The confusion grew as we did not find anything.

Again we came dangerously close to the breakers, again we turned back. By now we were completely relying on our senses and instinct. Malley kept a sharp look-out, while Elizabeth strained her ears and kept an eye on the depth sounder. I was able to see the radar screen in the companionway from my position at the helm. I had become used to countering tough situations on board with humour, but now our lives were at stake and it was difficult to suppress a rising sense of fear. It was in this moment of desperation that we saw the approach buoy behind the breakers. At the same instant, the freighter which had passed us earlier suddenly appeared near the shallow bank, but on the opposite course. "They must be even crazier than us" Elizabeth called.

As we rounded the bank, we came between the buoy and the island. The waves crashed onto the rocks with a thunderous roar, and visibility was worse than miserable. The radar was as good as useless in such a tight space. Very slowly we approached the still invisible harbour. "Breakers ahead, to port and to starboard!" the look-out cried. Then, just when we were in the narrowest part of the passage, and when we should have run back out to sea, the bows of a ship appeared. The captain stood on the open bridge and waved down to us. In the next instant, the ship was gone again – a hair-raising encounter. We had only just escaped a collision.

We carried on and compared the coast's profile with the chart. Norman had warned us that we would only see the entrance when we were already as good as inside. A gap of about one hundred metres appeared in the rocks. Was this the right spot? We could see nothing in the fog, but the thunder of the breaking waves was as loud as ever. I took a deep breath and a risk, and steered *Ryusei* towards the gap. Moments later we were in sheltered waters, and a wooden pier with a small hut on it emerged from the mist.

We had made it! With weak knees we stepped ashore and fell into each other's arms, full of joy. The air was filled with sound. As we looked around, we could just about make out the fringes of a small bay. Wooden huts stood on the shore and in the middle of this tiny hamlet a waterfall cascaded down from the rocks. This is where the name Grand Bruit, meaning 'big noise', originated.

As we wandered through the little community, the romantic and unworldly atmosphere was enhanced by the mist. We began a conversation with one of the fishermen. When we told him about our adventurous entrance, he just smiled and gave us a knowing look. The fishermen know these waters like the backs of their hands and find their way even in the densest fog. As we walked on, we came to a small cabin with a sign over the door saying 'Cramalott Inn'. "This is where we all meet each evening for a drink" another fisherman told us.

We came back later in the evening. Everyone brought along their own drinks and snacks. The cabin had a small gas stove and a refrigerator. It was a tiny place, very warm and completely packed with people. It was then that we realized the meaning of the name.

Many of the guests were stranded here. Two days ago, a wedding had taken place in Grand Bruit. Due to the bad weather, the ferry had ceased to run and now the wedding guests were caught out here. There was much laughter when we told our tale of how we had arrived. They were able to laugh because it had all come to a happy ending but in fact we should have stayed in Petites until the weather improved.

The ship which had passed us twice during our dramatic approach turned out to be the supply ship for the gold mine in the next bay, Cinq Cerf Bay. Because of the heavy swells they could not land there and had to turn back to Port aux Basques.

The Cramalott Inn had neither TV nor radio. Conversation consisted almost entirely of telling jokes and spinning yarns. The walls were decorated with caricatures and silly quotes. One of them was 'If assholes could fly, this place would be an airport!' The cabin shook with roars of laughter when Elizabeth said "And if we assholes could fly, we would at least see the sun above the fog!"

Naturally, tales of fishing were high on the agenda, so I told them how we had poached a lobster. "This was when we sailed through the large salt water lake of Bras d'Or in Nova Scotia. Quite by chance, we anchored close to a lobster pot. It was unusually hot and despite the cold water we went snorkelling. As I dived down to the lobster pot, I found a big lobster sitting in there.

"Could we use a lobster for dinner?" I asked Elizabeth and Malley when I surfaced.

"Yes, of course" they replied.

So I dived again. As I was about to open the pot, the lobster attacked with his two big claws. Quickly, I closed the pot again and re-surfaced. In the Cramalott Inn, I performed a pantomime of the lobster's attack which was greeted with laughter.

I then reasoned that I would never be able to catch the beast with my bare hands alone and dived again, this time taking the harpoon with me. Again, the lobster attacked. Gasping for air, I came to the surface once more. "Where is our dinner?" the ladies mocked me. There was nothing for it. I took a deep breath and vanished again. The mockery was worse than the claws of the beast. I opened the pot and shot the harpoon between his eyes. This calmed him down somewhat, but now the harpoon had become entangled with the ground tackle of the pot. I had to dive several times more before I could finally hand over the booty to my expectant ladies. "The poor fisherman has to have some kind of compensation" we then decided. So we put a five-dollar bill with a letter into a clear plastic bag. In the letter we wrote "Dear fisherman, I, the lobster, have tried in vain to chase off the poacher with my claws. Please find enclosed a compensation for my disappearance!" I then deposited the watertight bag inside the pot. We were a bit apprehensive, as we knew that both the Americans and the Canadians shoot at poachers without much hesitation.

I ended this story with the words "Can you imagine the fisherman's face when he found five dollars instead of his lobster?" My listeners yelled with laughter and continued to imitate the attacking lobster.

Later in the evening, I was faced with a question that was not easy to answer in a few words. "Tell us about your voyage. How did you come to sail here?"

By now, the alcohol had loosened my tongue and so it was during this night in the "Cramalott Inn" that I began to tell the tale of my adventures.

Bingo

"He looks just like a monkey!" These apparently were the words which welcomed me into this world. Thirty-two years later, I was working in a steel factory in China. My interpreter, Mr Liu, was always curious about foreigners, whom he called 'long-noses'. "When were you born?" he asked. "December 1956" I replied, and he clapped his hands in delight. "So then you are a monkey, too, just like myself. We are the best. We are the monkey-kings!"

He was, of course, talking about the Chinese horoscope with its zodiacs. According to the legend, Buddha once invited all the animals to come to him. Those who did come were honoured by having a year dedicated to them. In balance, the animals gave their characters to those humans who were born in the relevant year.

Asia threatened to become my permanent home because of my profession. Moreover, an Asian lady called Lisa had conquered

Portrait of Ralph by Sabine von Arnim

my heart. We were both stressed by our jobs, surrounded by others
wore themselves out until they died of heart attacks.

"Will we ever reach the age where we can live our dreams?"
we asked ourselves in one romantic night under the full moon.

Lisa, originally from Singapore, had studied oceanography and economics in America. She loved the sea but now worked as a broker for a bank. I was an engineer selling steel factories in the Far East. Both our jobs were extremely demanding. We could not spend much time together, but we shared a dream – to sail across the oceans of the world and also to leave Asia. I missed the seasons and the familiar surroundings of home; after five years in Asia, my goal was Europe. Lisa tended more towards the United States, but the general direction was the same.

I would never have dared to set off on my own, but with a partner – Bingo!

Singapore, September 1992.
The search

The romance of wood

We had an old motor boat which we used from time to time to flee from the sophisticated life in Singapore. With Seth, Lisa's faithful dog, we spent many nights on lonely beaches or in abandoned kellongs (fishing shelters built out over the water on stakes) on Malaysian or Indonesian territory. Here, we dreamed of freedom and our future.

However, our boat trips also allowed us to have a good look at all the cruising yachts which were anchored in Singapore. Consequently, we met some of the cruising people – the legendary Vincent Goudi on his British pilot cutter *Amulet*, for example, and the French family who circumnavigated with their triplets. We then met the Australian Graeme Ireland; he lived alone on his 52-foot yacht *Nefertiti* but always had attractive lady crews. He also knew the local yachting scene like no-one else. Graeme became the godfather of our project and without him we would have been stranded well before our departure.

Graeme soon introduced us to the world and art of cruising, of which Lisa and I knew precious little. He also helped me study the details of yachts which brokers were sending from all corners of Asia and from as far afield as Australia and New Zealand. Not one of these boats was right; they were too big, too small, too ugly, too run-down or too expensive. At least this search helped me to formulate an idea of what kind of boat I was really looking for. "A classic yacht, built of wood or fibreglass, but not of metal" is what I, as the specialist in this material, said.

Graeme was hesitant about wood; he had once owned a wooden boat and knew the problems. On the other hand, wooden boats are generally cheaper to buy because of their higher maintenance costs, and they are something special. A wooden boat is alive, breathes a pleasant atmosphere and brings the romance back into sailing.

In November, Graeme called us. He was sailing from Singapore to Phuket in Thailand with an old friend. "Why don't you come and join us next weekend?" he suggested. "Some fresh air and a bit of practical experience will do you a world of good. Besides, there is a suitable yacht for sale right here!" We jumped at the chance and had a wonderful sailing weekend.

The yacht in question was an attractive and well-equipped cruiser. Just to be sure, I had another look a week later. The price was tempting, so I called the owner, with an unaccustomed feeling of nervousness, and made my offer. It is difficult to describe what happens inside a person who is about to commit himself totally with mind and soul to a floating object – especially if one has never before actually lived on a boat.

"I'm sorry" the owner said. "Yesterday, I promised the boat to a couple who are in real trouble. Their own yacht has sunk due to a fire in the galley. It would be impossible to break my word, although your offer is higher than theirs!"

This made me realize how closely the floating community of live-aboards stick together.

La Cigale, **Hong Kong**

In my disappointment I had another long look at all the offers I already had at home. I had already spoken to a broker in Hong Kong about a classic Sparkman & Stephens yawl. "Yes" he confirmed on the telephone "the boat is still on the market" and added "She is built of the rare wood, Tasmanian Huon pine. She must be one of the prettiest boats in this part of the world. I will send you more details".

At the end of November, during a business trip to Korea, I had the opportunity of a stop-over in Hong Kong. The place was overwhelming. On leaving the terminal building, I was instantly drowned in a sea of bustling activity. The streets are bursting with people and business activities know no bounds. A whirlwind of images is thrown at the visitor: a sea of people, unknown languages, exotic scents, colourful shops and much more. Thousands of red and gold signs in Chinese script dangle above the streets, advertising heaven knows what, creating a tunnel-like effect. Amidst all this mayhem the double-decker trams rumble past, looking like the famous London buses on rails.

I took the ferry from Kowloon to Hong Kong Island, where I met the friendly broker David Westerhout. He summed up his impression of Hong Kong in a few words. "You can tell by the ever-growing sky-scrapers how active this tiny state is. During the last decade, they have sprung up like mushrooms. But China's ambitions are clearly illustrated by the fact that the building of the Bank of China towers way above all others. What happens when the British leave Hong Kong is anyone's guess."

David showed me around a couple of boats which were for sale, but having seen the boat with the romantic name *La Cigale* (meaning 'The Cricket'), I had no eyes for any other boat. It was as if I had tasted the best wine at the beginning – a clear case of love at first sight.

Her elegant lines surpassed all other boats. She was narrow (10 foot 6 inches) for her length (51 foot including bowsprit) and her wooden masts gave her a graceful air. The varnished cabin and the teak decks conveyed a feeling of warmth. No unnecessary frills spoilt the perfect harmony of this yacht. A classic ship full of romance, one to dream with. Apparently, there was only one drawback; she had none of the gear necessary for long voyages, as she had previously only been sailed in the coastal waters around Hong Kong.

David's elaboration on the pros and cons of classic wooden yachts fascinated me so much that I nearly missed my ongoing flight to Korea, where I was meeting up with my European boss to visit an important client. Had I missed the flight, we probably would have sailed much earlier!

During a second visit, Lisa got to know *La Cigale*, and she was as enthusiastic about her as I was. Shortly afterwards, we agreed on a price. In February 1993, we opened a bottle of champagne on the terrace of my house in Singapore. The first step was made and, in our minds, we were already at sea.

"Where will we be sailing – around the world?" Lisa asked.

"No" I replied, "everybody does that nowadays. Let us just sail in big zigzags towards Europe; it should be possible to do that in a year."

As is usual upon purchasing a yacht, I had made the deal subject to a survey. I was an engineer, but knew little about boats, so I hired a surveyor with a proven track record in wooden boats.

We had agreed that I would be present for the second part of the survey, on the 5th of March, when she would be hauled out of the water. After a sleepless night in the Airport Hotel, I took a taxi to the Hebe Haven Yacht Club early in the morning. It was a grey, miserable morning. There she was, high and dry. With a pounding heart, I sneaked around her hull. Then a voice woke me out of my dreams.

"Are you the gentleman who is buying this boat?"

I turned around and faced a weathered character who was accompanied by a young Chinese lady. "Yes" I replied, hesitantly.

"In that case, let me introduce myself. I am Captain Gardner and this is my assistant, Miss Wu. We have surveyed this yacht thoroughly. But before we continue, we should talk about matters over a coffee."

Upon hearing these words, a slight feeling of dizziness descended on me. We ordered coffee in the Yacht Club and, without further ado, Captain Gardner explained the serious faults he had found, helped by some drawings and photographs. David, who arrived a little later, pulled a long face when he saw the devastating surveyor's report.

"Ralph, this is a shock" he then said. "Even if you were still determined to buy her under these circumstances, I as a broker would not allow you to set your and Lisa's lives at risk with this boat!"

"Let me summarize" the expert said without mercy. "*La Cigale*'s backbone is soft and full of rot in various places, as are at least half of her planks, which would have to be replaced. The boat would need a total refit if you wanted to take her on a long voyage. This would be an expensive undertaking which would take at least one year, and with an old boat like her you can never be sure what other defects would be found once the work was under way. You are lucky that you had her surveyed. On the surface, she looks fine. But you would have been in for an unpleasant surprise. In heavy weather or when colliding with driftwood, the hull would almost certainly open up and she would sink like a stone."

This was it – the end of a dream. We certainly had no wish to take avoidable risks, or to spend our sabbatical with a restoration project. All we wanted was to sail off towards the horizon and forget about the stresses of our professional lives. What should be so complicated about that?

Of course, Graeme had warned us beforehand "Sailing is full of imponderables. Wind, weather, your mood or any other event can change your plans. Take your time! You are entering a different world!"

We had lost a ship without even having put to sea, but we had won a new friend in David. Together we vowed that whichever ship would take us on our voyage, she would sail under the flag of Hong Kong, the place of our first love.

Ryusei

The Big Day

One of my neighbours in Singapore was an Englishman who had chartered a boat with his girlfriend in Thailand. Both were afterwards so much taken by sailing that they wanted to buy a yacht. Later, when I told them about my mishap in Hong Kong, they said "Ralph, why don't you come over to us. We have a whole pile of yachts' details, all of them for sale, which have been sent by a broker in Thailand. We have decided not to buy a boat after all."

We studied the documents that same evening. The description of one boat stood out from the rest. Not only was she of an exceptionally beautiful design, but she already had all the necessary gear for long voyages.

Her name was *Ryusei*; she was a Sparkman & Stephens Sloop, overall length 44 feet, built in 1966 in Japan. Full details are in the appendix.

Ryusei is a sister to the Sparkman & Stephens Yacht *Firebrand*, which once won the Admiral's Cup. The yacht was built in one of Japan's best yards for a Japanese owner. After successfully participating in the South China Sea Race in 1966, she dominated the local racing scene for many years. With the changes to the International Offshore Rule (IOR), her career as a racing yacht came to an end. In 1982 an American who was then living in Japan bought the yacht, refitting her for cruising around the Far East.

When I phoned him, the broker in Thailand confirmed that she was still for sale. Lisa and I did not lose a moment. That same weekend, we flew out to Phuket, a popular holiday island in south-west Thailand. In the bar "Latitude 8" in Ao Chalong on the southern tip of Phuket, we met John, an Australian broker who had settled here. I thought that after *La Cigale*, no other boat would ever take my fancy again. Thankfully, this turned out to be wrong. After having a good look at *Ryusei*, we were both convinced that we had found the right ship at last. This boat fulfilled all needs of a serious cruising yacht. The size was right, and she made a very solid impression.

"*Ryusei* is ready for the sea" John said. "All you need to bring along is your tooth-brush!"

That same day, we also met Raudi, who is the head of the amateur radio net for cruising people in the Far East. He told us that *Ryusei*'s owner, Ron Brandon, had arrived in Phuket three years earlier with his Japanese wife.

"But nearly all marriages break up in Thailand" Raudi said. "The temptations are simply too much!"

The couple separated. Ron was a Vietnam veteran who had lived in Japan for many yearsIn Thailand, he lost all sense of reality. But after a while, he found his feet again and then set up a company in Phuket. Three years ago, he had also left *Ryusei*. The abandoned ship had since been on the market and under the care of the broker, who had so far been unable to sell her due to the high asking price.

The temptations and prostitution which Raudi had mentioned were overly evident, especially in Phuket. Sex has become a means of survival for humans in need; many young women need it to live on and support their families, and the men are simply led by their desires – clearly demonstrating which is the weaker gender.

Back in Singapore, we both returned to our work routines, but *Ryusei* never left our thoughts. We asked Graeme and David Westerhout for advice. Apart from the fact that this was again a wooden boat, they were optimistic. After all, anybody who knew *Ryusei* immediately started to rave about her sailing abilities. And a broker in England, a specialist in wooden ships, found the offer to be attractive, as long as the boat lived up to the specification. "In which case" he told me, "you will not lose money on her once back in Europe".

So the Big Day arrived. I rang the broker and discussed the price. Shortly afterwards, I had her owner on the line. After much haggling, we agreed on a price of 88,000 US dollars, subject to survey, with 10 percent being paid as a deposit.

Instead of behaving a bit more humbly this time around, we again opened a bottle of champagne and let our thoughts wander off into the distance. However, this time we were really sure that we had found the right boat and that we would be able to buy her without too many complications.

Preparing for our departure

The turbulence started with buying the boat. The broker demanded payment of the deposit into his account in Singapore, the owner wanted it in his account in Hong Kong. Also, the handing over *Ryusei* should take place in international waters, to avoid the high sales tax in Thailand. For the survey, we chose a local expert instead of flying Captain Gardner out from Hong Kong. We agreed that *Ryusei* should be hauled out at the end of March and that we would meet in Phuket to settle the whole affair.

We were so sure that all was going to be fine that Lisa and I even handed in our notice at work. As Lisa was dealing with important clients at her bank, she was immediately given leave from her work. Things were not as easy for me. I had worked loyally for my firm for seven years and did not want to let them down. After handing in my notice, I stayed on for the three months required by the contract.

At the same time, I wrote letters both to my father in Germany and my mother on Mauritius in which I tried to explain my decision to leave and go sailing for a year. My father answered

"Dear son, I am not sure if breaking off a promising career so abruptly is a wise move. To be honest, I was quite disconcerted after reading your letter, so I allowed myself a large whisky. I then read it for the second time and was still quite disturbed, so I had another whisky. I then read the letter a third time and regretted the fact that I am no longer young enough to accompany you on your voyage".

My mother was worried about the sailing part of our plan, although she fully understood my motives for having a break from the career. I later heard that she had spoken to a friend of hers whose son was already leading the cruising life. Her friend's response was "Sailing itself is nothing to worry about, but be prepared for the fact that Ralph will not be the same person after this voyage. A long voyage under sail does change people, but not for the worse!" This comforted her a little.

Complications

I arrived in Phuket one morning in April. The night before, I had not slept well and dreamt of yachts eaten away by rot and woodworm. Graeme, who had agreed to help me, met me at the airport. His expression made it clear that there was trouble ahead. After an unusually short greeting, he said "Bad news. We have to think about the whole thing once more. But first, have a look at the surveyor's report in the marina."

In the Blue Lagoon Marina, the owner, the broker and the surveyor, Andy Dowdon, were waiting for us. I only had eyes for *Ryusei*, as I was seeing her out of the water for the first time. She had a massive hull with a three-quarter keel and clearly classic lines. Then, Andy handed over his report. It was sobering, to put it mildly.

The transom, the last frame and supporting knees had rot. This also meant that the backstay did not have a secure fitting. The glass laminate on the deck had many cracks, through which rainwater had penetrated to the wood underneath, which was now rotten in places. The stainless steel standing rigging had to be renewed, some terminals were split. The antifouling paint was falling off in places and had to be renewed completely.

However, his report also held some positive things. Taking her age, 27 years, into consideration, this wooden boat was in good condition. This meant that she had been well maintained over the years. She had an extremely large inventory for cruising. All in all, she was built to a high standard.

Summarizing his report, he warned us "All rotten parts have to be replaced. You will risk losing the mast if you don't repair the transom and last frame as well as the chain plate for the backstay."

"Sh★t!" I cried in desperation. But Graeme was calm and pragmatic and suggested that we should have lunch while looking at the options. I had lost my appetite, but we agreed to meet the broker and the owner again in the afternoon. The main questions Graeme and I discussed were: who could undertake the work, how long would it take and how much would it cost? With his experience in both yacht repair and the work ethic in Thailand, Graeme said "It is no use pretending otherwise. Even if all goes well, the repairs will take two months. You would have to negotiate a substantial reduction in price. If you ask me, I would not buy her!"

But he had not reckoned with my stubbornness. *Ryusei* was, apart from *La Cigale*, by far the best yacht we had seen. I was prepared to fight for her. After lunch, we went to a specialist who would hopefully do the necessary repairs. He also thought that the work would take about two months and gave us a rough idea of the money involved.

Graeme and I then worked out the reduction in the purchase price for *Ryusei*. The yard had quoted around 12,000 US dollars. To this, we added 5,000 dollars for unforeseen extras and 3,000 dollars for travel costs and other expanses.

I thought these figures were a bit high, but Graeme insisted "Ralph, believe me! The cost of a refit always ends up higher than the original quote. Also, you lose some of your valuable time, as you were only going to take one year off in the first place. Either the price goes down by 20,000 or you should forget *Ryusei*."

This was the bitter truth, but I had to face it. So I planned a strategy for the next meeting with the owner who was, after all, a hardened businessman, confident in negotiating both with western and eastern adversaries. I chose attack as my route of negotiation.

When we met, I came straight to the point "Ron, I am sure that none of us knew about the true state of your boat. It came as a shock, as I had now hoped to have found the right boat for my sabbatical year. We want to sail for a year and not spend time on a refit. On the basis of the survey, I have to withdraw my offer to buy."

Ron was upset. "I know my boat inside and out. The surveyor is over-dramatizing things. All repairs can be made within a few weeks!"

"The yacht has been at anchor for three whole years, and has obviously suffered from neglect. In your sales offer it said: Ready to go – with the tooth brush only. This is not the case, so I cannot buy her" I replied. After a little pause, I continued "I might possibly still consider buying her, but I hesitate to tell you the price; you would probably regard it as an insult. However, let me know if you are interested." With these words, Graeme and I left Ron and his broker alone in the room to discuss the situation.

Some minutes later, Ron came to me and asked to speak to me alone. He probably hoped to be able to deal with me more easily if I were without Graeme. "Well, what did you decide?" I asked.

"I would like to know what price you are offering to pay" Ron said.

"I did warn you. Maybe I should forget about the whole thing here and now. The price I would pay for *Ryusei* as she is now: 20,000 dollars less than the original price."

Ron was outraged. But I remained firm and explained how we had arrived at this figure. I also mentioned that, even with this reduction in price, I would still be losing time. If I left my departure too late, I would miss the season for the Red Sea. In effect, I would be the loser in this deal. I told him that I was only considered buying *Ryusei* because I liked her so much.

After a great deal of squabbling, we came to the conclusion that I would pay 69,000 instead of the original 88,000 dollars. The money was due, in the form of a cheque, upon reaching the duty-free island of Langkawi and the handing over of the ship's documents. I would be paying for the cost of the refit beforehand. I was taking a risk here, as the yacht did not belong to me while the repairs were being made, but I wanted to supervise the work myself. If everything went disastrously wrong, I would be losing my deposit plus the cost of the refit. But in affairs of the heart, rational decisions are rare. Especially so, if the object of desire is a classic sailing yacht.

After this turbulent argument with Ron, we all met again and I announced our agreement. The broker had a fit when he heard the new price. He said to Ron "But I will have my commission on the original 88,000 dollars."

"No" Ron replied angrily. "Your commission is based on the price, as agreed."

"Which means 10 percent on 69,000?"

"No, as agreed and not one cent more!"

Both got into a heated argument about the commission. They called each other liars and cheats, until Ron exploded "I warn you, nobody can call me a liar without consequences!"

I could already see the drawn knives, knowing that Ron was a hard-boiled Vietnam veteran. Apparently they had agreed on a flexible commission. If *Ryusei* had been sold for 100,000 dollars, the broker would have had 10 percent. With 110,000 dollars, this would have increased to 11 percent. But with the price now standing at 69,000, he would only get a meagre 6.9 percent. The broker argued that he had been unable to sell the boat for three years due to the high asking price and that he would not even cover his costs with this commission. He then tried to involve me.

"The commission is strictly an affair between broker and seller" Graeme stated flatly.

As the situation was threatening to get out of hand, I offered a compromise. "Calm down. Disregarding your original agreement, I am willing to pay half of the difference between 6.9 and 10 percent, if Ron will pay the other half."

But Ron growled back "I don't care what you do, Ralph, but we have an agreement. I am paying 6.9 percent and not one cent more." With this, the discussion ended.

In the bar "Latitude 8" we had a drink to calm down. Graeme was well known here among the crowd of cruising folk. Everybody knew that I was hoping to buy Ron's boat. Also, the result of the survey was by now common knowledge. We discussed the next steps. Unfortunately my work was eating up nearly all my time. I already had a meeting scheduled in Switzerland for the next day. Graeme, on the other hand, had lots of time. He was happy that he could help friends and enjoyed a bit of excitement, so he promised to check out *Ryusei*'s papers and to get the refit under way. He also agreed to fly out to Phuket every one or two weeks to check the progress while the work was being done. I would pay him his airfares and other expanses.

That same evening, I flew to Singapore, packed my suitcase and continued on to Zurich with Lisa. In less than 24 hours we had covered the distance which we were planning to sail in one year.

As soon as we arrived in Europe, I received a fax from the broker. He was complaining bitterly that the deposit for *Ryusei* had not been paid into his account. As my money had already been parked in Hong Kong, from the deposit originally paid for *La Cigale*, I had found it easier to transfer it into Ron's account in Hong Kong. I also deemed this to be more secure, as neither the broker nor the seller had their domicile in Thailand. I had heard in the meantime that both of them had to leave Thailand every three months solely to get a new visa for another three months. The broker now threatened "If I do not have the deposit in my account within the next 14 days, I will report the sale to the local authorities!"

I immediately called Ron. After all, we shared a mutual interest. He wanted to sell, I wanted to buy. We would not bow to blackmail. We agreed to officially call off the sale due to all these complications. Unofficially, we would continue as planned.

I also received a message from Graeme. He had found someone who would do the work. He also asked me to call the authorities in Guam, USA, to find out if the yacht was registered in Ron's name. At least this worry was unfounded. The man in the shipping register confirmed that a Mr Brandon was the owner of the yacht *Ryusei*. He also mentioned that the entry in the register had expired one year ago. Finally, he asked me about the whereabouts of Mr. Brandon, but I gave no answer to that. I had enough problems already.

The trip to Europe was, for me, purely business. After only a few days in Zurich I had to visit clients in Korea. Lisa, who had already finished her job at this time, decided to visit friends in the south of France. It was the beginning of April, the best time for Provence. As I would not be returning to Singapore for two weeks, I even encouraged her to stay on. As a joke, I also warned her about the charm of the French.

It was not until three weeks later that we finally saw each other again. I was under enormous pressure: leaving my job but still finishing projects there, the work on *Ryusei*, the imminent move on board and financial stresses all racked my nerves. Only the prospect of going to sea soon kept me going.

The launching

Refit

Graeme had found a British boatbuilder in Phuket to do the job on *Ryusei*. As time was of the essence, we had to concentrate on the most important items. These were the repair of the transom and the last frame, the repair of the deck and the soft wood underneath the glassfibre sheathing, the re-caulking and painting of the hull and the varnishing of all wood on deck with seven layers. As we had feared, we discovered even more trouble; the upper part of the bow also had some soft spots, where rainwater had penetrated the wood. So all fittings on the bow had to be removed, the planks had to be unfastened at the front end and the entire upper part of the stem replaced. Again, a time-consuming affair.

Graeme flew to Phuket a few times to oversee the repairs and to encourage the boatbuilders to work faster. We could not afford to loose any more time. With *Ryusei*'s draft, the marina at the end of a winding river could only be reached at spring tides, and the last possible date for our departure was the 13th of May.

Graeme, Lisa and I arrived in Phuket with a week to spare, but new trouble was waiting for us. The stereo set and the binoculars with in-built bearing compass had been stolen from the yacht. Then the broker appeared and announced "If you buy *Ryusei* and Ron does not pay my commission, I will take it from the boat!"

"*Ryusei* is strictly Ron's affair" I countered. "We are only here for a holiday."

To be on the safe side, we hired a guard to keep a watchful eye on the boat. I then seemed to have another reason for sleepless nights. Lisa had been behaving strangely since her return from France; she appeared indifferent and aggressive. I hoped that this was only a passing phase and put it down to the pressure under which we found ourselves. I tried to avoid all possible conflicts, as we had enough on our plates already with all the endless preparations for our voyage. Then we had problems with the yard. The deck had been repaired but, when Graeme and I hosed it down, we noticed a steady trickle of water running into the quarter berth next to the electrical panels. Immediately, we made a temporary repair. The varnishing was another concern, as regular showers announced the arrival of the Monsoon season. However, we enjoyed a special moment when the panel with *Ryusei*'s new home-port on was screwed on to her transom. It now said "*Ryusei*, Hong Kong".

The countdown was on. The broker's threats kept us on our toes, wondering what tricks he or the authorities would try to stop us. As a blind, we announced that we would launch *Ryusei* on the 13th and sail on the 15th.

Handing her over

As we by now knew only too well, the previous owner was a clever American businessman, and his hard businesslike style was being supported further by the cunning of the Asian. He had started a small company which then rapidly progressed to become the leading importer for meat and sausages into Phuket. He now needed cash for further expansion of the company, hence the sale of *Ryusei*.

Ron had insisted that, when he handed over of the ship's documents, I should pay the balance in bank cheques. He then asked if these cheques could be cancelled, and if they were valid. I gave him the number of my bank in Europe. The branch manager explained to him that he had made out two cheques to the combined value of 52,000 US dollars in the name of Ron Brandon. He also mentioned that international bank cheques could, by definition, always be cancelled, and that a letter of credit would be needed to prevent subsequent cancellation. Ron digested this piece of information with obvious dislike. He would have loved to change the cheques into a letter of credit there and then, but that was impossible. He then insisted that we should present the cheques to the manager of his bank in Phuket, so that they could be verified.

A short while afterwards, we sat in the office of the local bank manager. He eyed the cheques in wonder; presumably he had never before seen these kind of sums made out. At last, he declared that these papers did indeed look like cheques, but only his superior in the head office in Bangkok could verify them beyond doubt. This procedure would take at least another week, because of the approaching public holidays.

Furiously, I said to Ron "So far, I have done everything you have demanded. Now you are about to move the goal-posts once more. If this does not stop here and now, I will let the whole thing fall through!"

Upon my outburst, Ron gave way marginally and suggested that the cheques were to be deposited in his safe until the handing over of the boat. I immediately smelled foul play and answered, fuming, "These cheques are made out in your name. Nobody else will be able to cash them. Under no circumstance will I hand them over until I have a signed contract and the ship's documents in my hands!"

As the day of our intended departure drew nearer, Ron announced that he would not be able to sail with us to Langkawi, which is where we had agreed that the handing-over would take place. He claimed that he had no time for this short 24-hour trip due to his business commitments, and invented all sorts of excuses not to come along. During dinner, Graeme, Lisa and I held counsel. "Why isn't he coming now?" I asked. "There's something fishy going on here!"

"Perhaps he's afraid that the broker will take revenge on his possessions while he is away" Graeme suggested.

"Or does he think that we'll feed him to the sharks on our way across?" Lisa added, laughing.

Time was a major problem now; there were only three days left before the last possible date for leaving the marina. We decided to run the risk of taking over *Ryusei* in Phuket, but only if Ron would drop the price even further.

The next day, I confronted Ron with our decision. We had yet another bitter argument, but in the end we reached an agreement. On the following day, he would clear out *Ryusei* and also finally hand her over. The next day, we marched from one official body to the next: immigration, customs, harbour master. Ron asked if he could see the latter by himself, without us. Minutes later, he emerged from the office, a big smile on his face. We then stopped at a bank, where he presented the clearance documents. As he had been living in Thailand, he had been required to put down a deposit for the boat; the clearance documents now enabled him to redeem this deposit.

The final handing over took place in the garden of Ron's firm. Under the shadow of a tropical tree, all documents were spread out on a table. The contract, according to David a watertight document, was signed by Ron and myself, while Graeme and Lisa signed as witnesses. I handed out the cheques and received the ship's papers and the clearance documents in return.

Countdown

I was walking on air. After all the setbacks of the past days and weeks I could hardly believe that we were about to sail. A bottle of wine helped to soothe the nerves. Graeme then brought me back down to earth. "Ralph, we have to prepare the boat. If we miss tomorrow's tide, we'll be stuck here for at least another three weeks!"

The countdown was on. We were frantically busy for the rest of the day. In the meantime, my brother Axel had arrived. He was hoping for a relaxing sailing trip. Had he known of all the work which was in store, he would probably have stayed at home. As it was, he helped as best he could. He had the tough job of filling up with 400 litres of water and 300 litres of diesel, all of which had to be carried up to the boat in canisters. The remaining deck repairs were finished and the yard was working feverishly on their defective travel-lift. The manager of the marina had promised that they would launch us the following morning. If they had not been so worried about their reputation as a marina, the repair of the travel-lift would probably have taken many weeks with the usual working pace of the Thais.

We checked out of the hotel and moved on board the following morning. There was a lot to do and we were still not familiar with the boat. Only an experienced yachtie like Graeme could keep his nerve under this sort of pressure. Calmly, he checked all systems on board, at least as far as this was possible with *Ryusei* still parked high and dry. Axel and Lisa stowed away provisions and cleaned the ship, which had been left in a mess by the boatyard people. Even as the travel-lift was lifting *Ryusei* into the air, Graeme and I were still busy installing electronic navigation gear and the new steering compass on the wheel pedestal.

Time was running out and the flood rising. High water was to be at 13.50 hours, and the manual chains clanked as the boat was lowered into the water at 13.00. Graeme and I buried our heads in the engine compartment, where I was reading out the manual check-list for Graeme who was checking all the systems. Suddenly, there was a short and sharp jolt, but we ignored it and continued with the motor. A few days before, we had changed all filters and the fuel system would have had to be bled. If the engine would not start now, we'd be trapped in the marina. Fortunately, after a bit of stuttering, the engine sprang into life – what a relief! We left without any further delay.

The open sea lay three miles down a shallow, winding river. No sooner had we left the marina when we were aground, in spite of the pilot we had taken on board, who allegedly could smell the channel. It was then impossible to get off under our own steam, and a slight panic raised its head as the flood had already reached its highest level. Help came from the yard foreman, who arrived in a high-powered inflatable and towed us off. Half a mile further, we were aground once more. We came to realize that either our pilot was a fool or, on this particular day, he was having severe problems with his channel-smelling nose. Thankfully, this time we managed to come off, although tension remained high until at last the sea opened out in front of us. It seemed like a new world – the world of freedom!

Not much later, my brother revealed something which makes my hair stand on end even now. "Remember the jolt when *Ryusei* was launched? You two, Graeme and Ralph, were below deck busy with the engine, while Lisa and I helped with the slings of the travel-lift. When we were nearly in the water, one of the shackles holding the slings opened – we fell into the water, but luckily only the last few centimetres or so!" It was mind-boggling to imagine what would have happened if the shackle had given way while we were still higher up in the air, especially with all of us on board! I really don't know if this was accident or not.

It appeared that we finally had luck on our side but, without Graeme's help, all the luck in the world would have been useless.

The lucky star
The yard foreman came alongside in his inflatable, relieved us of our unfortunate pilot and wished us bon voyage. He displayed a happy grin – he knew about our past problems and was glad to see the whole thing had come to a happy ending.

For the first time, we made sail and set a course for Phi Phi Island. *Ryusei* was piercing the waves in silence and we were in jubilant mood.

Even the normally cool Graeme was euphoric. He was back in his element, steering a fine yacht under full sail. "I have seldom sailed a boat which has such a good feeling about her" he claimed. Lisa called out "Just take a look at the wonderful dragon in our sail!" In surprise, we looked up. And there he was: a red dragon was stitched into the upper part of the mainsail.

It was then that we grasped the meaning of the name *Ryusei*; it is a Japanese word which means Dragon-Star. The dragon was the boat's coat of arms but, in contrast to European mythology, the dragon is a positive creature in the Asian world. As we philosophised about the name, someone remarked "I hope the dragon will not show us his claws!"

"No" was the reply "I think that the dragon–star will be our lucky star!"

The majestic rocks of the islands Phi Phi Island and Phraya Nak glowed warmly in the setting sun. It was a purely magical moment and we decided to continue on through the night.

We had just finished our supper when we heard strange noises from below decks, culminating in the exclamation "Oh, sh★t!" My brother emerged red-faced from the companionway. "The toilet isn't working!" We had omitted to check the heads, so Graeme and I now looked into the problem. A particularly disgusting task lay ahead. We dismantled the toilet, transformed the once cosy cockpit into the toilet repair workshop and took everything apart, then cleaned, glued and reassembled the whole affair. This took time and patience and I was not holding back on swear-words. It seemed as if, after the magical lucky moment, the dragon had indeed flashed his claws at us.

The Lake of the Pregnant Maiden

We crossed the border into Malaysia during the night and reached the island of Langkawi. We thought that our problems lay behind us at last and so decided to hang around one more day in these beautiful waters instead of setting off immediately. Graeme knew these waters so well that he did not even need a chart. He directed us into a lagoon which was surrounded by steep cliffs. We anchored and celebrated with a gala dinner, which we finished just before a tropical thunderstorm passed overhead. The rain was as strong as hail; we used it as a shower and a welcome opportunity to cool off.

A little further, we reached another anchorage between two islands. On one of them, Dayang Bunting, is the famous 'Lake of the Pregnant Maiden', which has volcanic origins. According to an ancient myth, bathing in this lake would boost our fertility. We had to dive in, we decided, even though the lake was high up in the mountains. Only my brother complained, as we had, in our jubilant mood, already finished all beer on board and he would now not have any fuel for the difficult ascent. By chance, I found one last bottle in the depths of our fridge and hid it away at the bottom of my rucksack.

With sweat pouring off us after the long uphill march, we finally reached the lake, tore off our clothes and jumped in. I hid the bottle beneath the little jetty. When the others were resting in the sun on the jetty, I said "Let's dive for the secret treasures of this lake!" A moment later, I reappeared with the bottle in my hand. Lisa and Graeme, who had known my little scheme, bent over backwards, laughing. Axel was astounded and believed at first that some previous visitor had left the beer until he recognized it as one of our bottles. We shared this last beer, wishing for eternal fertility.

Rowing back to our boat, we passed another anchored yacht which had arrived in the meantime. Before we could count to two, we were in the midst of an ecstatic welcome. The newcomers turned out to be two old friends of Graeme, and they invited us all on board for drinks and supper.

The lake had definitely displayed its magical powers: fertility in the form of food, drinks and hospitality.

Greetings from Thailand

After a quiet and restful night, we sailed on to Kuah, the main town on Langkawi, to complete our entry formalities. Graeme had yet another tip for us greenhorns: "When dealing with the authorities, dress up a bit – never arrive in dirty T-shirts and shorts. Imagine that you want to sell them something. Also, patience and stubbornness are the priorities when dealing with officialdom!"

Togged up, we presented our papers in a new, neat folder at the harbour master's office. The harbour master glanced at our clearance paper from Thailand, shook his head and said "Sorry, but you will have to return to Thailand."

"What?" I said, flabbergasted.

"This document is forged" he replied calmly. "It has already been used once before to enter Malaysia. On the back of the document you can see my stamp and my signature from 1990. Although the correct date is entered on the front, it is impossible for me to accept it as it is. You will have to return and get new papers in Thailand."

We were speechless. Eventually, Graeme said "But we know each other; over the last few months I have been here with my own boat twice." The harbour master appeared to acknowledge this; someone with an impressive sun-hat like Graeme's was indeed not easily forgotten! "Please listen to us," he continued, "my friend here has just bought this boat in Thailand. These are the only documents which he received from the former owner. There are no other papers."

The harbour master stayed firm; we let the time slip by patiently. Trying to hide my inner anxiousness, I repeated what

Graeme had just said in other words and implored him to make a special exception to the rule this time. Perhaps it was the familiar, honest face of Graeme or the fact that the harbour master's lunch break was drawing closer. With a loud sigh, he finally gave way, cleared us in and said good-bye with the words "But get lost quickly!"

We aired our anxieties over lunch. "This crook has double-crossed us again" Lisa exclaimed, and Axel added "At least now we know why Ron refused to sail with us to Langkawi. He must have known about the defective toilet and other things too – by now, we would definitely have thrown him over board!"

Graeme steered us back into good spirits. He raised his beer and gave us the toast "Welcome to Malaysia!" The wonderful food also served to dampen our anger, and I even had a bright idea for getting even and taking revenge. "Remember how worried Ron was about the possibility of the cheques being cancelled? On my return to Singapore tomorrow, I will cancel the one for 2,000 dollars!"

We then started planning the passage to Singapore. Graeme suggested sailing by day only as far as Kuala Lumpur and stopping there for a week. "Firstly, I have to check my own boat in Singapore, and secondly we will probably need a rest by the time we arrive in Kuala Lumpur. At this time of year, we will encounter headwinds all along the Straits of Malacca."

As I had to return to my official work in Singapore the next day, Lisa, Graeme and my brother would sail on without me.

Headwinds

When I returned to the boat from a business trip to Taiwan, Lisa was again upset and agitated. Due to the strong headwinds, they had had to motor nearly all way to Port Klang near Kuala Lumpur. Conditions could not have been much worse. Axel had returned to Europe as planned, and Graeme was on his own boat in Singapore. In an attempt to soothe Lisa, I said "Despite all this, I would much rather have been on board with you than having to negotiate with clients!"

Unfortunately, two days later I had to leave again for yet another business trip. Before leaving, we agreed with Graeme that we would sail the last hop to Singapore the following weekend. Just before my departure, the underlying conflict with Lisa became much more apparent. "Think positive" I said to myself, hoping that things would return to normal as soon as we were both living permanently on board.

Fate has many surprises in store, as I was to find out upon my return to the boat. Apparently, when she stayed in the south of France, Lisa had fallen in love with a French guy. On top of this had come the sudden realization that sailing is not always pleasant. The combination of the two must have driven her to pack her bags and take a plane rather than a sailing boat back to Europe.

On the last leg to Singapore, which I now sailed only with my dear friend Graeme, we again had strong headwinds but in my misery I did not notice much.

How Lisa and I could have lost each other just as we were so close to achieving our mutual dream remains a sad mystery. Maybe, for her, the difference between dream and reality was too wide to be bridged. The pressures of the last few months had made me blind, otherwise I might have seen the alarm signs.

With hindsight, however, we can now both be glad that our paths did diverge before the big voyage.

Singapore

Arrival and memories

As we approached Singapore, the shipping increased and more and more planes flew overhead. Then we saw skyscrapers and cranes looming over the horizon. There was no doubt that this was Singapore. It is a small island, off the southern tip of the Malaysian peninsula, which achieved independence in 1965 after a racial conflict. Originally, Moslems inhabited Malaysia, then Chinese emigrants arrived and settled where they found work. Soon, the harbour towns of Penang and Singapore became dominated by the Chinese. The Malaysian government in Kuala Lumpur feared the Chinese influence, so they released Singapore. A Chinese by the name of Lee Kuan Yew took charge and ran Singapore with the efficiency of a businessman and the hard hand of an old sea captain; those who did not comply with the new ways got locked up in prison.

Three million people now live in Singapore. Seventy-seven percent of them are Chinese, the rest being mainly of Malaysian and Indian descent. The common languages are English, Mandarin Chinese, Malay and Tamil.

As we sailed along the Singapore coast we saw industrial harbours, shipyards, steel factories, skyscrapers, a vast ocean of houses and the airport. Hundreds, if not thousands, of ships were anchored there and the air was filled with a constant stream of jets, landing and taking off. In less than 30 years, Singapore has risen to become the main commercial centre in Southeast Asia, a pearl amongst her chaotic neighbours. There probably is no port, and no airport, in the world which is more efficient. Everything is organized perfectly. This is where I had lived, or rather where I had my base, with my flat and the office. Selling steel works, I spent most of my time travelling – my clients were everywhere on that side of the globe, from China to New Zealand, and most of them were Chinese.

In Indonesia, Malaysia, the Philippines and Thailand the economies are mainly run by a Chinese minority. These people have risen from the lowest to the highest social levels purely by determination and diligence. Their money is invested in the education of their children, and no school in the world is too expensive for them. Talking business with them demands a high degree of flexibility. While it takes quite a while before a conversation finally touches business matters with the older patriarch type, the younger generation, often educated in America, will come straight to the point, saying for example "Cut the bullshit, let's talk business!"

I witnessed incredibly fast development in Singapore even during my few years there. On my first visit, I stayed in the Raffles Hotel. It was in a desolate state then; I shared my room with a brigade of cockroaches, and the floorboards squeaked in the grubby 'Long Bar', with ventilators churning lazily below the ceiling. Even so, the atmosphere was superb, especially when seated in one of the wicker chairs with a cool 'Singapore Sling' in hand! Five years later, the place had undergone a complete transformation. It now had the sterile luxury of the typical business hotel, as found anywhere around the globe. This is called progress and we are not supposed to moan about it but, for me, it was another reason to sail back home.

The yacht moorings and marinas are located by the roads between Singapore and the Malaysian mainland. We picked up a mooring next to Graeme's boat, *Nefertiti*, off Changi Point and the NatSteel marina.

Work

The weeks following my return to Singapore were exhausting. My job demanded full attention up until the very last minute, while I also had to organize the big move on board and sort out various jobs on the boat. Diving into activity was a perfect therapy for me, helping me to overcome the loss of Lisa.

With the help of Graeme I drew up a list of jobs that would have to be done before we could embark on our planned shake-down cruise along the Malaysian east coast. The main items were as follows: (i) New toilet. I chose a Lavac; it was said that this one would rarely block up and could even cope with bricks! (ii) Instruments. Both the echo sounder and the speedometer were defective and out of date, so I replaced all instruments. (iii) Anchor windlass. All cruising sailors agreed that we would need a hydraulic or electric anchor winch, with a manual back-up, as we would have to anchor a lot. We replaced the manual windlass with an electric one. (iv) High pressure deck pump. A water pump to hose down the decks and the anchor chain seemed useful to us. (v) Radar. We knew that a radar was essential in the southern and northern regions with frequent fog and busy shipping lanes. I chose a small radar with a slim LCD display and a range of eight miles. (vi) Sun awning. Severe skin diseases are a danger in the tropics, which is why we fitted *Ryusei* with a completely new awning. (vii) Sails. All sails were inspected, and repaired where necessary. I also bought a new spinnaker. (viii) Varnishing. The wooden toe-rail and all wooden parts on deck had to be varnished several times – time-consuming job but a must for classic wooden yachts. (ix) Standing rigging. Corrosion and cracks in the terminals showed that the shrouds had to be replaced. However, none of the professional riggers could tell us how to dismantle the lower and cap shrouds without lowering the mast first. The quotes for this work seemed astronomical to me. "An engineer can do anything" I thought, and tried to undo the shrouds myself with huge spanners. This proved to be a frustrating endeavour. Dangling on the mast in a bosun's chair, I wrapped my legs around the spar and used both hands on the spanner and hammer. I needed a third hand to hold onto the mast, as the wash from passing ships rocked *Ryusei*. Even when two of us went up the mast, we failed. In the end, we gave up and decided to replace the shrouds in South Africa, despite the risk.

Balance
The cost and time involved in a refit are frightening for someone buying a boat for the first time. I had underestimated both by far. Without the survey, it would have been even worse. The total cost in the case of *Ryusei* was as follows (all in US dollars).

Purchase of *Ryusei*
Price negotiations reduction	from $98,000 to $88,000	
Further reductions due to the negative survey	($19,000) = $69,000	
Further reductions for handing over in Thailand	($3000) = $66,000	
Cancelled cheque	($2000) = $64,000	
Overall reduction was thus ($24,000)		
Nett purchase price	$64,000	

Refit costs
Costs incurred before departure from Singapore (Repairs, new gear and related travel expanses)	$22,000
Further refit costs incurred in South Africa (Thailand and Singapore refits had been incomplete because of the time pressure)	$15,000
Refit total	$37,000

Totals for the first year
Purchasing *Ryusei*	$64,000
Total refit cost	$37,000

Grand total
Overall cost for purchase and refit	$101,000
[Total time spent on repairs and maintenance	7 months]

Ryusei *with cruising spinnaker*

The new crew

One evening I called my friend Guillaume in Paris. We had known each other since we were boys, when we had learnt to sail dinghies together. Now I told him about the planned voyage and my crew problem; he was really excited "Great!" he exclaimed "I've just given up my job and need a break. When do you want me — tomorrow?" A week later he arrived in Singapore, complete with canvas bags and guitar.

When I had said farewell to my former boss in Zurich, I met an old acquaintance, Hilde, and she did not know what to do in her holidays, so I invited her along for our shake-down cruise in Malaysia.

The pressure was on again a week before our departure. It was time for me to pay the bills. In front of my bank in the city of Singapore, I was stopped by a young man. I was in such a rush that I nearly shoved him aside, when he asked me "Do you speak English?"

"Yes" I replied, impatiently.

"Do you know your way around here?"

I was losing too much time. "Of course" I said. "Where do you want to go?"

"Can you tell me where to find the yacht club?"

This was unexpected – here, amongst the skyscrapers of the financial district.

"It's at the other end of town" I replied. "But if you have a little time, I can take you there." The backpacker, who was called Luke, said he had the time.

As we were talking, the mobile phone rang in my pocket. The removal firm was waiting in front of my house to fetch the last few boxes. We stormed through the bank at lightning speed, drove to my house, then rushed to my office to pick up the mail and finally, after a hair-raising race through the thick traffic of Singapore, arrived at the yacht club. Luke must have thought that he had fallen into the hands of a lunatic!

However, once all bills were paid and all work for the day was finished, Guillaume and I sat down at the bar of the Changi Yacht Club with Luke. It transpired that he was South African and was looking for a trip on a sailing boat. Guillaume and I liked him, so we offered to take him along on the first leg of our journey.

"I can even sail" Luke promised. Of course, anybody who was looking for a passage on a yacht would say that.

My last day at work was the 30th of June. My friends and former colleagues gathered in a restaurant which offered a superb view of the bay beneath, and even of *Ryusei* as she swung on her mooring. As a symbol for all the troubled waters which lay behind me, I had hoisted *Ryusei*'s trysail between two palm trees. For me, this was a party of mixed feelings. An intensive time in Asia was ending and my life was taking a completely new direction.

Amazed, some of my friends stared down at the yacht and said "You want to sail home in that nutshell? Are you completely crazy?"

Shake-down cruise

Night passage
The island of Tioman lies to the south-east of the Malaysian peninsular, surrounded by another 63 smaller islands. The natural beauty of these islands and their proximity to Singapore made them an ideal goal for our shake-down cruise.

We planned to set off around mid-day in order to reach Sibu on the east coast of Malaysia the following morning. Perhaps because of our nervousness, we did not have the boat ready in time.

Hilde had arrived, and there were now four of us on board: Hilde, Luke, Guillaume and myself. We went on board Graeme's *Nefertiti* for a last briefing. I was uneasy, as my previous experience with yachts was limited to three trips. Guillaume was uneasy too. He had already experienced an all too dramatic situation on board a yacht. The professional skipper of the sailing school where he was then taking a course had made a navigational error while the boat was on a passage across the English Channel. During the night they hit rocks and sank within minutes. In his agitation, Guillaume had had difficulties in unclipping his safety harness from the sinking yacht and was nearly dragged down with her.

Only Luke and Hilde were calm, Hilde because she knew no better and Luke because he had a wealth of offshore experience, although we did not yet know about this at the time.

"Shouldn't we postpone our departure until tomorrow?" we kept asking.

"I will never get rid of you if you always postpone until tomorrow. Don't worry, it'll be all right!" said Graeme, laughing.

We then studied the chart and Graeme said "If you want to be really safe, perhaps you should sail outside the island of Mungging. I'd take the shorter route myself, between island and mainland, but of course I've already done it a few times. Even on a dark night you can see the rocks and, if in doubt, you can use your radar."

Before we left, we agreed on the ham radio frequency on which we would communicate at set times with Graeme.

The sun disappeared behind Singapore as we sailed away from Changi Point. The peace was shattered by the turbines of countless jets which continuously left Changi airport. For us, they sounded like farewell fanfares. Night descends quickly in the tropics and soon we were sailing in the dark, leaving the lights of the city behind us.

Luke and Guillaume tore me from my navigation as they called me on deck. "Look" they called "There are quite a few boats which are approaching us fast. I think we are on a collision course!" After my eyes had adapted to the darkness, I could make out about ten high-speed boats coming towards us. I was just about to start the engine, in case we would have to do any abrupt manoeuvres to avoid them, when they were all around us, zigzagging wildly. We were bewildered.

"What on earth is going on? Are they completely mad?" Luke shouted in his strong South African accent. Then one of them came so close that we could identify it despite the darkness. It was a naval landing craft. We were in the middle of a naval exercise. The proximity to Malaysia and Indonesia is regarded as a high risk by Singapore, so they have a tough little military force which is constantly out on manoeuvres. Our boat must have seemed to them the ideal object for some training. Thankfully, they disappeared as quickly as they had arrived.

Island of the dangerous passage

Around midnight, we closed in on the straits described by Graeme.

"Do we really want to sail through there?" Guillaume asked nervously.

"Of course!" said I. "If Graeme can do it, so can we. Plus we have our radar!"

The wind was very light, so we planned to motor-sail through the strait. Tension built up when we found we could only see the island on the radar. Eventually a big black shadow suddenly loomed up to starboard. The sea became choppy, which indicated the presence of a tidal stream. I had just increased the engine revs to improve steering when the engine gave one last cough and died. We were in a state of shock, but Luke reacted instantly "Quick! Let's unfurl the genoa and prepare the anchor!" Guillaume and I handled the sails while Luke went forward to unlash the anchor. Very slowly, we picked up speed in the fickle breeze, but the current was setting us dangerously close to the island. "Stand by with the anchor in case we get closer!" I shouted to Luke, but we did just manage to scrape past after what seemed like an eternity.

Between Thailand and Singapore, the engine had not failed once. "Why does it have to happen at the worst possible moment?" we asked ourselves. The reason, as we soon discovered, was simple; even the best engine in the world will not run without fuel.

"But we filled up before leaving!" Hilde pointed out. *Ryusei* has two diesel tanks. We had only filled up one, and had wrongly assumed that they were interconnected.

In the early hours, the wind increased and we sailed on a fine beam reach under full canvas. Ironically, *Ryusei* was now heeling over so hard that the diesel from the second tank spilled out through the vent, directly on to Luke's hiking boots. These boots already carried the stench of the whole of Asia. The odour now rose to previously unknown heights with the addition of the diesel. We seriously contemplated throwing the boots over the side there and then, but Luke begged and pleaded, so we were merciful and temporarily parked them out of range.

We reached the island of Sibu during the afternoon. We could hardly wait to anchor in front of the main resort on the north tip of the island. After only a casual glance at the chart, I went for the direct route around the north tip. We were relaxing in the cockpit when I saw the water changing ahead, both in colour and wave pattern.

"Luke, it looks a bit strange there. Why don't you go forward to keep an eye on things" I suggested. No sooner had he arrived at the pulpit when he shouted "Go about! Go about now!" while wildly gesticulating to starboard. I pulled the rudder hard over and *Ryusei* smartly rounded up through the wind, her sails flapping. As we were heading back out towards the open sea, Luke came back and said "We nearly ran aground on a rock there!" Shocked, I had another close look at the chart. There it was, one rock lurking just beneath the surface. My carelessness had nearly brought disaster.

We then kept a respectful distance from the shore and shortly afterwards anchored off the resort. In the bar we made conversation with the manager and mentioned our near disaster. He nodded knowingly and said "Not long ago, another yacht ran onto that rock. She was saved, but only with a lot of luck."

He then asked "Do you know the meaning of the island's name, Pulau Sibu?" We did not, so he explained "It literally means island of the dangerous passage!"

With my friends laughing, I said "This should serve as a warning. We'll give the island a really wide berth on our way back!"

The sirens of Sibu

The evening sun spilled a soft reddish light over the thatched cottages and the palm trees along the beach. Then there were the anchored yachts behind the coral reef. Even the best travel brochure could not have topped this idyllic image. The open hut housing the bar had straw mats and piles of cushions on the floor. We lounged happily on these cushions and took in the intense, flaming colours of the sunset. The short trip from Singapore to Sibu had already brought us together as a team. In this idyllic spot our cares were far behind us and we defined our mutual goal: to have fun.

At this moment, four attractive Chinese girls came into our cosy hut. Our seafaring hearts jumped at the sight of these beauties. They ordered drinks and sat down next to us on the cushions and it did not take long for us to engage in animated conversation. Our new acquaintances came from Singapore and wanted to spend a weekend away from personal and professional problems. Before we returned on board for the night, we invited them for a sail the next day.

Under a blazing sun we made sail and steered for a nearby uninhabited island. The giggling of our guests died down as *Ryusei* came alive and heeled over. The motion and noises of a boat under sail always have something frightening about them for the complete novice. After a short and beautiful sail, we anchored in front of a dazzling white beach and went ashore with snorkelling gear and picnic bags. We joked and laughed and flirted. While one of the girls definitely had her eye on Luke, Guillaume and I remained a bit more detached in order not to hurt Hilde and her standing as our crew.

The weather gods apparently disapproved of our boisterous party. Just as it was getting comfortable, huge black clouds loomed over us. In all haste we made back to the boat and upped the anchor just as the first gusts and showers came down. *Ryusei* surged away under full canvas in a rising sea, and our guests again grew silent. Luke's new girlfriend turned green and spent the rest of the trip bent over the guard-rails. Happily, we reached our sheltered anchorage before sea-sickness could claim more victims. The girls came alive again as soon as they had solid ground underneath them. We spent the remaining time at the starting point of our little excursion, in the beach bar. After a couple of tropical cocktails we found ourselves engaged in a wild pillow battle. What the hell – we were young and out of the public eye!

We stayed together until deep in the night, discussing the meaning of life, partnerships and sailing. We were so absorbed that we did not notice the absence of Luke, his lady and our tender. Later, Luke explained "I was just showing her around the boat!" We grinned and said "Yes Luke. And we all believe you!"

It was a sad and somewhat emotional farewell on the following morning. We saw them off, our 'Sirens of Sibu', onto a little ferry which took them back to the mainland.

Island to island

That same day we set sail and headed for the island of Aur, 30 miles north-east of Sibu. The wind was 15–20 knots and came from the south-east, so we enjoyed some relaxed sailing. We experimented with different sails and got to know the feel of the boat. We also checked the new instruments, calibrated the anemometer and tried the autopilot at different settings. We began to realize just how complex a fully equipped sailing yacht is. Our shake-down cruise could only be the very beginning of a long, steep learning curve, but Ryusei felt solid and dependable. The hull sliced through the waves without losing momentum. I was reminded of what I had read about the design philosophy of Sparkman & Stephens. They designed offshore racing yachts which were fast, seaworthy and comfortable.

Ryusei's speed only became apparent in a fresh breeze. In light airs, our heavy equipment became a handicap. Anyway, we were so engrossed in handling the boat that time flew by and we thought that we had made a fast passage to Aur.

The following morning, I awoke to beautiful singing. Puzzled, I climbed on deck and found Hilde. "As an opera singer, I have to keep my vocal chords in training, even on holiday!" she explained. I had no problems with that, but was a bit worried about our crystal glasses. It was a musical morning: Guillaume had gone ashore and played his guitar on the beach.

As we sat down to breakfast, Luke said "With all these good sounds, we'll probably get the perfect breeze today!"

"Or catch a huge fish" I added, as we had earlier seen a large marlin jump close to the boat.

For the next couple of days we cruised in a leisurely manner from island to island. One of them was Bebi Kechil, which had been the scene of a sad chapter in the history of Asia; 15,000 Vietnamese refugees had been kept there for a long time, herded together on less than a square mile.

Another island was Babi Besar, which has a few private homes. We anchored and spent an afternoon on the beach, where we met Betty. She was an eccentric, nature-loving lady of Chinese descent from Singapore, and regularly spent her spare time on the island. She invited us to her beach hut for a sundowner. This is a ritual that goes back to colonial times. The landowners would meet at sunset, discuss current affairs and enjoy a couple of drinks in the process.

It started to blow and rain as soon as we had returned on board for dinner. Heavy on-shore gusts howled through the rigging. We let out all our remaining chain and settled down. Below, we watched a video. The TV and video were luxuries that came with *Ryusei*, but we soon got rid of them. When cruising in search of adventure, the last thing one needs is a TV.

The morning arrived in brilliant sunshine. As we gathered in the cockpit for a breakfast of fresh coffee and tropical fruit salad, the boat which had been anchored next to us the previous night returned. Her skipper came alongside in his dinghy and explained that he had slipped his anchor during last night's gale and that it was now lying on the bottom. He asked us if we could help him to retrieve it.

"As long as we get a cool beer afterwards, we're ready for anything!" we replied. At last we had a proper reason to use our diving gear, and we soon found his ground tackle.

"You were lucky that the wind didn't increase further" he told us. "These gusts often come with hurricane-force winds, which have been the end of many boats. You should always leave the anchorage in an onshore gale like that!"

Pulau Tioman

Tioman is the largest island off Malaysia's west coast. Allegedly, she ranks among the ten most beautiful islands in the world. She has a striking profile with a mountain range and the peak of Gunung Kayang, which is more than 1000 metres high. Dense tropical woods spill down the mountains, while the coast is made up of black rocks and white sandy beaches.

Due to this natural beauty and a convenient geographic location, the island has now been developed into a centre for tourism. In the process, the last natural reserves have been destroyed. Traditional fishing craft became ferry boats, the jungle had to make way for the airport, small hamlets grew into villages, garbage now lines the beaches and romantic coves are spoilt by ugly hotels. The sea is also suffering. More garbage, raw sewage, over-fishing, anchoring on top of coral reefs and diving souvenir hunters are all destroying this unique under-water world. Natural beauty draws tourists and, when they arrive, the beauty is destroyed; this seems to be one of the very sad laws of the modern world.

As we were supposed to be on a shake-down cruise, we also had to sail once in a while. In a light breeze we reached the village of Juara on Tioman's east side. We liked this isolated place so much that we stayed for three days. Guillaume was missing his privacy on board, so he escaped to a little beach hut which he rented. It even had a shower, which in turn was much appreciated by the rest of us. From here, we went for long hikes up into the nearby mountains. Once, we found a wonderful cascade, under which we cooled ourselves down; tropical heat can be very pleasant, but not continuously. I was longing for Europe.

Shots in Indonesia

On *Ryusei*, we had a complete ham radio set but not the license to run it. My friend Graeme put it this way: "The radio is important for emergencies and general communication. Many cruising people have no license. In our ham radio circles, such people are known as pirates. A licensed radio operator risks loosing his license if he speaks to a pirate. However, the laws are not taken very seriously in this part of the world. Just stick to a few basic rules." He then also added "You get nowhere if you only act as the law would have it!"

He then helped us to invent a license number. As we later realized, nearly all radio pirates use Panama as the country for forged licenses.

During our shake-down cruise we were in contact with Graeme in Singapore every morning and kept him informed about our adventures.

It was over the radio that we heard about some other friends, a Canadian couple, who had sailed to the Indonesian archipelago of Anambas, about 50 miles east of Tioman. These islands were said to be even more beautiful and much less developed, and originally we had planned to sail there with them. We did not get an entry permit and, while we remained in Malaysia, they decided to sail to Anambas anyway.

After a rough and exhausting passage, they had anchored in the first available bay. Shortly afterwards, they were woken by rifle shots. A boat with rough-looking men in semi-military uniforms had come alongside. They had fired into the air to wake our friends. They then boarded the yacht and turned it upside down but luckily they only took alcohol and cigarettes. Our Canadian friends were of course deeply shocked and felt even more vulnerable without a permit. They immediately set sail and returned to Malaysia.

Return passage

Time flew by and we had already spent more than two weeks in the islands. When we left Sembilang in a flat calm under power, we were alarmed by a squeaking noise from the bilges. We soon found the reason; the shaft lock, which prevents the fixed propeller from turning when under sail, was defective. The bearing was already glowing red hot. There was no choice but to dismantle the shaft lock altogether if we wanted to continue using the engine. It took us an hour of sawing and hammering to remove the fitting, and from now on we had to tie a rope around the shaft to stop it from rotating when sailing.

We killed the engine soon as a little breeze sprang up. We sailed over smooth water towards a familiar island. We just could not withstand the temptations of Sibu, despite our vow to give it a miss on our way back. The same afternoon, our anchor splashed into the clear water in front of the resort. We joined the manager and a few fellow sailors for cold beers in the beach bar, but Luke's attention was arrested by two young ladies at the bar. We then lost sight of him until our departure – the 'sirens' again.

Burial at sea

Again, we had a heart-breaking farewell from Sibu. We sailed one afternoon, planning to arrive in Singapore the following day. We were tacking into a pleasant breeze from the southeast when the time had come for an act of great importance.

"Luke, is it time to throw your stinking boots over board?" Guillaume suggested.

"No" Luke replied in panic. "Impossible! I've walked all the way across Asia in them!"

"For three weeks now we've tolerated the foul smell of your diesel-impregnated boots" Guillaume replied mercilessly. "We've tried everything. For days on end, we've towed them behind the boat. We then let them cook in the sun, and even the fresh mountain cascade had no effect. Our three noses are in the majority against yours. But we will offer them a proper burial!"

"You have my deepest sympathy in advance!" Hilde said, laughing.

Luke saw that he had no choice and gave in. At once, activity filled the boat in preparation for the burial. The Malaysian flag was flown at half-mast. The boots were tied together and weighted. Drinks were served and melancholy music was played. We then gathered along the rail, drinks in hand, while Luke gave his faithful old boots a valedictory speech. Then they flew into the sea.

During the evening, the weather deteriorated. Life became uncomfortable as we pitched heavily into the oncoming seas. For the first time, Hilde was sea-sick and stayed in the cockpit.

"Neptune's angry with us for the stinking gift!" Luke claimed. "We'll all have to pay dearly for that!"

Guillaume was not discouraged by the foul weather and decided to bake a cake. As he was about to crack the eggs into the dough, a huge wave threw the boat on her side, catapulting the eggs onto the cabin sole. The flour followed an instant later and the floor boards looked as if they were covered in snow, but Guillaume, our heavy-weather cook, did not give up and managed to bake his cake.

We passed the infamous straits off the southern tip of Malaysia during the early hours, accompanied by a heavy thunderstorm. Rain drummed down on us like hail, but this time we remained unruffled. Our shake-down cruise thus found a happy ending, although we were tempted to dub it 'break-down cruise' instead because of the various gear failures.

Farewell

"Partir, c'est mourir un peu!"

Bound for Scotland
We had a big party on our return to the Changi Yacht Club. Despite our lack of experience, we had found our way back to the port of departure and, disregarding some minor problems, both the ship and her crew had coped well with this first trip.

Graeme was really euphoric; in the meantime, he had sold his boat and agreed to deliver it to Australia. As crew he had enlisted two of his girlfriends, putting him into even higher spirits. He had tried for some time to sell his boat and build a new, larger one. "A man needs a new project from time to time," he would say.

This was the right kind of atmosphere for me to contemplate my own project. "The voyage must have a beginning and an end somewhere," I thought. Splitting up with my partner had changed a lot, but it had not changed my plan to sail back to Europe within one year.

"And what happens, when you arrive?" people asked me time and time again. "I shall cross that bridge when I come to it" was all I could reply.

We then concentrated on some basic decisions: to finally set the date of departure and decide on the route we would be taking. The latter was largely determined by the fact that I wanted to visit my family on Mauritius en route. "If you sail via Mauritius, you'll miss the winds in the Red Sea for the north-bound passage, as you only have southerly winds in January and February" said Graeme. "Also, you'll have the Monsoon against you from Mauritius to Djibouti. It's more than unwise, in fact it's outright stupid, to try and sail against the prevailing winds and against nature!" So, in the end, we decided to take the route of the old sailing ships, around the Cape of Good Hope. The current south-easterlies meant that we would normally have sailed through the Straits of Malacca towards Thailand. However, after all the recent trouble, we did not want to return to Thailand under any circumstances. Instead, we decided to sail through the Sunda Straits, the passage between Java and Sumatra, into the Indian Ocean.

Later in the evening, I had an idea. "Hey guys, haven't you always said that there has to be a purpose to every voyage?" I suddenly shouted, startling my listeners. "Well, I've found one.

Many years ago I was hiking on the island of Arran in Scotland with a friend. In our backpacks we had some sandwiches and a bottle of whisky. We ate the sandwiches and drank a wee dram, as they say there, to encourage us up the next steep hill. In the end we had to lighten our ballast, so we buried the bottle of whisky as a ration for the future. The bottle's still there. So the plan is to sail to Europe to retrieve that bottle of whisky from the island of Arran!"

My little speech was greeted with laughter and merriment. "You crazy bastard" they said. "We can have the whisky here and now — there is no need to sail that far!" And they called the waitress to bring a round of whisky.

That same evening, Graeme and I decided to set sail at the same time, at the end of August: Graeme with his two ladies to Australia, us to Scotland. 'Us' was initially only Guillaume and myself. Luke wanted to return to South Africa and Hilde had to fly back to Switzerland as her holidays were ending.

Three men in a boat

Our shake-down cruise had made it clear that it would be much safer to sail with three rather than just the two of us. I asked Guillaume if he would agree to taking Luke along.

"Of course" he said. "In fact, I was going to suggest the same thing. I think he's a great character and knows a lot about sailing!"

So I asked Luke. "Originally, you were only going to stay for a few days. Now you've been on board for four weeks. Why don't you come along and sail with us back home to South Africa?"

"Great!" Luke was overjoyed. He had more reason to be happy about this turn of events than just the prospect of the sailing trip. One year ago, he had disappeared from South Africa to Asia because he wanted to evade the national military service. Neither he nor his parents were overly excited by the prospect of him being killed as a soldier in a civil war, which many people in South Africa were expecting, due to the elections coming up. On a sailing boat, he could return home without being detected as a deserter.

I laughed when I heard his story. The parallel to my own history was unbelievable. After finishing school, 17 years ago, I had travelled to South Africa for exactly the same reason — although I had not been very successful because when I returned to Germany I still had to join the army. What an incredible twist of fate it had been for us to bump into each other in the financial district of

Singapore. From now on, we were a team: Guillaume, Luke and I, three men in a boat.

Storm

After our return from our island cruise, the telephone never stopped ringing in the Changi Yacht Club. We were becoming unpopular, as nearly all the calls were for us – to be precise, mostly for Luke who had to settle his personal affairs. His romance on Sibu had not been without the natural consequences. Completely downcast, he told us one evening that his married Chinese girlfriend was pregnant by him. She and her husband had been trying in vain for two years to have a baby and now, after one adventure with Luke, she was pregnant.

"What are you going to do?" I asked.

"We'll meet tomorrow and discuss the situation" Luke said. Morally, I felt we were all in the same boat. "Let me know if you need any help. We are one team now!" In an attempt to crack a joke, I added "If the worst comes to the worst, we will have to sail under the motto 'three men and a baby in a boat'!"

But the four girlfriends had already come to a decision even before Luke met his woman. She wanted an abortion. She had decided to separate from her husband anyway, and Luke's European genes would have led to great friction in a traditional Chinese family.

Abortions are not unusual in Singapore, where a strict family planning policy was introduced long ago. Some years before, the press had publicized the one-child-family with the slogan "one is enough". In the following years, the economic situation and with it the family planning policy changed, and the new slogan was "have two or more – if you can afford it!" Local humour slightly changed the gist of this as the men were now claiming that this referred to the number of wives instead of the number of children.

But all this gave us little consolation. We were left with a bad conscience and a bitter taste. It seemed as if our lives had been caught in a severe gale.

Insurance and registration

To sail to Europe must be a highly dangerous affair. This is the conclusion we came to when trying to insure the boat. I had another, expensive, survey made for an insurance company. It was not until afterwards that I learnt that the insurers regarded the risk as too high anyway. They did not want to insure a classic wooden boat or our planned route around the Cape of Good Hope, quite apart from our lack of experience. I was so angry at the hypocrisy of the insurers, feigning interest at first, that I vowed to sail without insurance cover. After all, it was in our own interest to keep the risk as low as possible, and no insurance in the world can do anything about one's own stupidity.

The original plan to have *Ryusei* registered in Hong Kong also met with difficulties. David had found out that a leisure yacht can only be registered in Hong Kong if she is actually there. He tried to calm me down on the telephone "With the correct forms and your French passport, it should be possible. I will tell the official that *Ryusei* is afloat in one of the far away derelict corners of the harbour, and they will be too lazy to come and check. It will take a little time and, until then, you will have to sail with the original American registration."

However, Guillaume just had finished the wooden plate with the beautifully engraved home port of 'Hong Kong' on it. So we decided to bolt that to our transom anyway, regardless of what our papers said. Graeme agreed with us, saying "Nobody has ever checked my transom against my papers. If you have a complaint, just tell them that the new registry is under way but will still take a little time!"

Packing and provisions

In a letter to my family, I described our intended route and the last preparations. 'You cannot imagine what it means to provision a boat for several months. It can only be compared to preparing at least ten normal holidays at the same time. Amongst many other things, we stowed away 700 litres of water, 600 litres of diesel, 150 litres of petrol, 200 cans of beer, 60 bottles of whisky, 30 bottles of wine and 40 litres of milk. Not to mention case upon case of basic victuals such as rice, noodles, fruit, vegetables and a million other things. There is so much to pack that we have already postponed our departure by a week. The boat is technically well prepared, but we are nervous, nevertheless.

'As I have already written , we will be sailing south along the coast of Sumatra until we reach the Sunda Straits between Java and Sumatra. From there, we will head for Chagos, which people say is a little paradise in itself. The entire voyage including several stopovers will take about 50 days, meaning that we will probably arrive in Mauritius at the end of October. Please do not worry if you receive no news from us for a while...'

For our entertainment on board, we bought books and music. We all had different musical tastes, so we ended up with classical music for Guillaume, pop for Luke and South American music for myself.

In the book shop, Luke asked me "By the way, is there a bible on board?" My answer was negative but I had to agree that every ship must have its ship's bible. We were surprised that we could not find a bible in Singapore's largest book store. The lady told us "Bibles are sold next door, in the bible shop!"

There, they had about one thousand different bibles. All languages, all versions, and all sizes one could possibly imagine. When we simply asked for a bible, we were confronted with the question "How much do you want to spend?"

"We just need a very simple bible in the English language" I answered, and Guillaume added "If possible, waterproof, please. We are going to sail around the world with it!" The lady shot him a very curious glance but then produced a suitable bible for us.

Doubts

In the days before our departure, I found myself thinking more and more about my time in Asia and asked myself over and over again if I had chosen the right course. I had an uneasy feeling. Was it fear? Surely. Then I remembered a similar situation. Five years ago I had been sent to start up a steel factory in China, while I was still quite inexperienced in my job. The noise, the dust, the heat of the liquid steel and the glowing sparks were unforgettable. I then had similar feelings before my first negotiations as a vendor of whole steel works. One thing I had learnt from these experiences – jump in at the deep end and then swim for your life.

My time in Asia had left its mark. When I was finished with the project in China, aged 33, I had for the first time experienced chest pains. A successful professional career can be addictive and then alarm signals from an exhausted body can be ignored – at least this was the only explanation I could find for the fact that so many of my colleagues had died far too young of heart attacks.

This and other things reinforced my decision to return home in a leisurely manner. Those who go to work in Asia or Latin America are often regarded as no longer suitable for re-integration in Europe after five years. Consequently, most of them stay abroad until they retire. This could also have been my fate if I had stayed on in Asia.

I was really missing the seasons and the cultural sphere in

which I had grown up and I did not want to stay away forever. Despite all my sympathy towards the Asian people I was still a foreigner.

I was aware that returning home by boat held many disadvantages. Sailing is known to be one of the most expensive, uncomfortable, slow and dangerous ways of travelling, but the lure of adventure and the whole romance of it were all too great and simply outweighed the rational arguments. It seemed as if I was entering a new dimension, with a new concept of time, which demanded a great deal of peace and leisure. I remembered the words of a friend, "He who sails without enough time is asking for trouble!"

Sailing with sufficient time is only feasible for someone who is financially and personally independent, and who is willing to accept a break in his professional career. These being the case in my situation, and also taking into account my love of sailing and watersports, my way was clear. Of course, doubts remained, but they did not change my decision to set sail.

Singapore to Chagos

Departure with difficulties:
30.8.93 from 1°23'N/103°58'E

We had found many reasons to postpone our departure for a few days. Finally the day arrived when I declared "Tomorrow we shall sail, come what may!"

That morning, Guillaume and Luke disappeared quickly on a secret mission. Cast down, they returned to tell me that we would have to stay yet another day. I was about to explode when Guillaume explained the reason. "It was supposed to have been a surprise. We have ordered a special cake for our ceremony on crossing the equator, but forgot that today is Sunday and that the cake shop is closed. So we will have to wait until tomorrow!" They were both firmly of the opinion that we could not sail without the cake, but I was determined to set sail. "We'll sail today! Even if it is only for a mile until we anchor again!"

We therefore came to anchor very shortly after setting off, in a detached bay of the island of Pulau Ubin north of Singapore. We spent the remainder of the day doing odd jobs around the boat. I again studied the planned route, drew courses onto the charts and noted the distances and bearings on a slip of paper. I also programmed the waypoints into our GPS. Graeme came along in his dinghy to spend a last evening with us, and our conversation, fuelled by a couple of beers, carried on well into the night. His own crew, for his imminent trip to Australia, had now increased by one to three ladies.

"You will be pampered like a Persian pasha" we prophesied, but we did not envy him; we were happy to sail without female companions after our problems.

Early the next morning, we returned to our original anchorage off the NatSteel marina. The weather was oppressive and hazy. As we were only going ashore briefly to fetch the cake, we left *Ryusei* on a short length of chain and went to the nearby Changi village by tender. The moment we entered the cake shop, a hefty gust blew along the streets and rain drops announced an oncoming thunderstorm. Luke was quick to react "Ralph, I think I'd better get back to the boat. Who knows if our anchor will hold in this weather. I'll pick you up later at the Changi Yacht Club!"

Impatiently, we waited with our equatorial cake on the yacht club landing for Luke. When he finally arrived, he was rather keyed up. "Just imagine! Our boat had drifted – I found her at the other end of the bay. Our friend Geoff was on board. He had seen *Ryusei* slip after the first gust and jumped into his dinghy to follow her. He made it just in time, boarded her and let out all the chain, otherwise she would have ended up on the rocks at Changi Point!"

Fortunately, Geoff knew his way around *Ryusei*; he had even helped us to install the windlass. With his typical humour, his only comment was "Your impatient boat wanted to leave Singapore on her own because her crew couldn't get ready for departure!"

This hint was big enough. We stowed away the cake, said good-bye to our friends and upped the anchor. Ship's bells and fog horns were sounding as we sailed out and away.

The Batam adventure

For the last time, we heard the jets taking off from Changi airport droning overhead. They would reach the goal of my journey within 12 hours. How long it would take me was uncertain. After all, it had 'only' been eleven months from my first thoughts about sailing home until this day of departure. Solemnly, we took down the Singapore courtesy flag and hoisted the Indonesian one. We then had one long, last glance at Singapore's impressive skyline.

The Indonesian island of Batam, ten miles south of Singapore, is a popular place for day trips, as one can buy duty-free cigarettes and alcohol there – our main reason to land there too.

"You could waste half a day with the clearance procedure into Indonesia. It's better to anchor secretly on the remote northeast coast, where they are building a holiday village, and take a taxi to the nearest duty-free shop!" is what a friend had advised us.

Our approach towards Batam was not without apprehension, as 'secretly' also meant 'illegally'. We anchored about a mile off, and Luke and I went ashore in the inflatable.

"This is going to be fun" Luke said morosely, after we had already walked a considerable distance. Suddenly, a car full of people approached us and stopped when we flagged them down. As soon as the driver heard of our plan, he let all the others get out and took us on board. We were a bit surprised, but he calmed us down "They all live only a mile from here." He could smell business, as he knew what we didn't – the main village of Sekupang was much further away than we had anticipated, and it was just before 18.00 that we stopped in front of the duty-free shop, which was about to close.

"Hurry up if you still want anything" the shop keeper told us.

As they did not accept any credit cards, we could only buy half the amount we had wanted. At least our cash was still good enough for six cases of Tiger Beer and two cases of whisky. Luke also bought tobacco and cigarette papers for himself and Guillaume.

Night had already fallen when our driver finally dropped us off again at our far-flung bay. We carried our booty to the inflatable and pushed it out through the muddy water. The darkness was complete and navigation became a challenge, especially as the water was so shallow that we grounded the propeller of the outboard several times. Just as we had reached open water, a large motorboat came towards us. We feared that it might be the coastguard and sped away to hide behind a small island. Tension grew as we waited for them to move on.

"If they catch us now, we'll end up in jail" Luke whispered.

"Don't be silly!" I tried to be reassuring. "All they can do is charge a fee for illegal entry. Besides, it could also be a fisherman!"

After a while, the enemy disappeared and we finally returned back on board. "Where have you been all this time?" Guillaume exclaimed. "I was getting seriously worried!"

But he surprised us with a delicious dinner and while we wolfed down the huge steaks with ratatouille we told him of our adventures. After the moon had risen above a completely calm mirror-like sea, we motored off southwards towards the equator. We were so keyed-up that sleep was impossible.

Equatorial celebration at 0°00'/104°30'E

Early in the morning a breeze sprang up, but of course it was against us, on the nose. We motor-sailed on, close-hauled. A current was running against the wind and created a confused sea. Around noon we reached the narrow passage south of the island of Pasirgagah. Our chart had been surveyed over 50 years ago and showed a depth of 15 metres. Luke climbed up to the cross-trees to spot any shallows. The current was now running at over four knots and the water was white with the breakers. It was hair-rising, but we came through unscathed and shortly afterwards crossed The Line. After some meticulous eye-ball navigation, we found an anchorage behind the island of Botot, only half a mile from the equator, in a completely sheltered bay surrounded by thick mangroves. The peace was heavenly. This was part of an extensive archipelago called Lingga, east of Sumatra and 115 miles south of Singapore.

Under a full moon, we celebrated our equatorial Christening. Classical music and a grand dinner made this evening unforgettable. For dessert, we had champagne and our equatorial cake. The world now lay at our feet and we felt that we could sail anywhere on the globe. We were free and full of optimism.

Sunda Straits

We allowed ourselves a day's rest. Then we removed some weed from the propeller, checked our emergency equipment and upped the anchor.

Luke was poised on the pulpit to spot the reefs, which were all around us but usually easily detected by the colour of the water. The problem in our case was the overcast sky, which made this eye-balling very difficult. While I was at the helm, Luke suddenly shouted out. There could only be one reason for this, and in a reflex I pulled back the throttle from slow ahead to full astern. The engine roared and I anxiously waited endless seconds for the keel to touch. It took half an eternity until our heavily laden boat finally stopped and then slowly started to move astern. Still agitated, Luke reported "A coral reef – because of the bad light, I saw it much too late. It was about one metre below the surface and I could see it disappear under the boat. It's a miracle that we didn't hit it!" Again, Luke's sharp eyes had saved us. In my imagination, I could already see the unflattering headlines "Stranded on the equator!"

Soon afterwards, we sailed towards Banka, helped along by a strong current. A thunderstorm started to brew overhead and, moments later, we were engulfed in lightning and deafening thunder. One lightning bolt struck the water with an enormous roar close by and we went rigid with fear. Thankfully, the weather calmed down towards evening, and we rushed along on a broad reach under full sail touching seven knots. After the narrow escapes of the day, we allowed ourselves a large whisky at sunset and as Luke had saved us from grounding he was awarded a double ration. Afterwards, the moon came out and the mood was on for romantic dreams. On nights such as these, we all looked forward to our night watches.

To add to our delight, we had a perfect contact over the radio with Raudi in Phuket. Like many other cruising folk, we continuously reported our position and where we were heading for. Graeme also came on air, congratulated us for passing the equator and wished us "Fair Winds". As he was about to sail with his three ladies, we ended our conversation with the somewhat ambiguous sentence "Keep it up!"

The wind died down again during the following night. At four in the morning, during my watch, the high-pitched engine alarm suddenly pierced the stillness. The main fan belt had broken, the water pump had stopped and the 'cooling' water was already boiling. Swearing, Guillaume and I replaced the belt, and half an hour later we were under way again.

"Don't worry, a bit of overheating never harms a robust diesel" Graeme said soothingly on our next radio call. As was to be expected at this season, we mainly encountered headwinds. This region, remote from the shipping lanes, is also infamous for piracy so at night we sailed without navigation lights. People had also advised us to use the radar, but the moon gave enough light as it was, although I did have a dreadful shock when another unlit vessel crossed our bows in the dead of night.

We now enjoyed wonderful sailing. Close-hauled in 14–20 knots of breeze we reached some good speeds, although Luke wrote in his diary '*Ryusei* heels over as soon as someone farts. We eat, sleep and sh*t at an angle of 45 degrees!'

We only reached deeper water near the Sunda Straits. Located between the islands of Java and Sumatra, this is the gateway to the Indian Ocean. Our pilot had warned us about strong cross-currents, but with the help of the GPS and manual bearings we had no problems. After a truly memorable passage, we anchored in the harbour of Marek on Java that evening. During our usual sundowner, we reflected on Indonesia.

With nearly 200 million inhabitants, this is one of the most densely populated countries in the world. A cruising sailor could spend an eternity among her 13,000 islands. Sumatra is one of the largest islands, roughly four times as big as Java, although two thirds of all Indonesians live on Java. This is also the political and economic centre.

During my Asian years I witnessed how incredibly fast this economy is developing. Cheap labour draws companies from all over the world, but it is also creating a social time-bomb. The Chinese, for example, have control of over 70 percent of the economy, although they only make up three percent of the population. In the western part of Java there is a centre for heavy industry which I knew well, as the company I worked for had provided parts of the Krakatau Steel works.

Steel Hell

In Marek, we were welcomed by my former agent Karel and other business partners at Krakatau Steel. They did not want to miss the departure of the daring Mr von Arnim for anything.

That evening, Karel invited us to dine with a few friends of his. One of them turned out to be the chief harbour master of the district, who promised me that we could do as we pleased. If any official – of which there are many in Indonesia – should cause us trouble, we would only have to call him. Allies like that are worth their impressive weight in gold in a country where bribery is common practice and openly referred to as the 'second income'.

His charming wife wanted to know all about our adventures and finally said "After your voyage, you will have to sell your yacht to us. My husband and I have been dreaming of such an adventure for a long time!"

As I had promised my shipmates, Karel took us on a tour of Krakatau Steel. They were impressed, to put it mildly, and Luke wrote in his diary 'The sight of this monstrous set-up was extraordinary. I could hardly believe how huge the furnaces were. The people working here wore helmets and fireproof clothing. In the furnace, in which the pig iron is converted into steel, the sparks flew in all directions. The temperature inside the furnaces is said to be 1600 degrees Celsius. The heat in the factory buildings was indescribable. It was like a visit to hell. We also saw the continuous casting machines which Ralph's former company had provided. Here, the liquid steel is poured in at the top. The steel emerges from the bottom as red-hot strands, which are then cut and rolled out in the rolling mill.'

After this visit I invited Karel, his two assistants and my Indonesian business friends from Krakatau Steel for lunch to the intimate Café de Paris. During the previous years, we had been here frequently. The chief engineer commented on my departure as follows. "After all business has been closed, you now flee out to the open sea and leave us to languish in the steel hell. I would love to come along, but I am afraid of the sea." And this from a man who, as a steel engineer, has one of the most dangerous professions.

Dancing on the volcano

Thirty miles east of Merak are a few islands with a doubtful reputation. These are the remains of the volcano Krakatau, which erupted in the year 1883 and partly destroyed itself in the process. This was the biggest eruption in recent times. The explosion reduced the island by two-thirds and had the mind-boggling energy of 2000 Hiroshima bombs. A massive tidal wave, up to 40 metres high, devastated large areas and was even felt in the English Channel. The explosion could be heard from Perth to Sri Lanka, and 40,000 people lost their lives in the inferno. Since 1928, Krakatau has been showing new signs of activity with submarine eruptions and the emergence of a new island. This is called Anakrakata (the son of Krakatau) and has so far reached a height of 200 metres. There had been fresh rumblings in the previous months, and only a short while ago two American tourists were killed in a minor eruption. All ships had been advised to keep at least five miles off.

However, we were here for the thrill. We reached the islands in darkness. In our excitement, we fantasized that we could smell the sulphuric acid. Guillaume, who was at the helm, had to wear a protective outfit in the form of the breathing unit of our diving gear and a saucepan lid, just in case there were any volcanic rocks flying about. We found a rather exposed anchorage off Anakrakata, so the rolling swell and the nagging fear of the volcano gave us a restless night. At dawn, we were faced with an awe-inspiring picture. Four steep-sided islands surrounded us and Anakrakata had smoke trailing from its peak.

Shortly afterwards we landed on a pitch-black beach. A frozen lava stream reached down to the water not far away. The flanks of the volcano were covered in ashes and sharp boulders. Large rocks were strewn about in little craters. It was obvious that they had fallen from a great height, following an eruption; it must have been this sort of rock fall that killed the two Americans.

Guillaume dons protective gear in case

Luke and I wanted more. We were going to climb up to the smoking summit. Perhaps not a wise decision, but one does not often have an opportunity like this. Guillaume stayed behind and said that in case of an emergency, at least one of us should be able to fetch help. As Luke and I ascended, we heard deep rumblings, which heightened the thrill. Closer to the summit, the rocks beneath our feet grew hot. Foul smelling fumes came from little crevices; the heat and the stench were incredible. At last, we stood on the edge of the crater. An infinite ravine vanished into nothingness below, while the sides were crusted with yellow sulphur. Smoke drifted up from the depths where, invisible to us, the lava was boiling. Never before or since have I felt the slumbering forces of nature so intensely as on the summit of that volcano.

After a fortifying meal on board we raised our anchor and sailed out towards the Indian Ocean. The relief at having survived this little adventure made the prospect of our first ocean passage less daunting. Climbing the volcano had touched us more deeply than we were prepared to admit.

The Indian Ocean

Slowly, the mass of land was lost behind the horizon as the depth of the ocean gradually increased. According to the chart, we would sail over the Sunda Deep, one of the deepest parts of the world's oceans. The thought of having several miles of water beneath our keel made us shudder. But the fringe of the continental shelf held an abundance of fish and marine life. Entire schools of flying fish regularly sped away from our bows, and we were escorted throughout the afternoon by dolphins, some of which even turned somersaults in the air. We took this as a farewell gesture from Southeast Asia.

It wasn't until sunset that a little breeze sprang up. This was the first indication of the south-east trades. We killed the engine and made sail, suddenly surrounded by a soothing silence. The sea was easy and we were certainly not thinking of the proverbial 'calm before the storm'. However, the night then gave us a taste of what was in store, with squalls of up to 35 knots. The first squall hit us under full sail and *Ryusei* promptly went out of control and performed a Chinese gybe. Thankfully, the preventer on the main saved us from the worst, but the Genoa wrapped itself around the forestay and gave us a lot of trouble.

These conditions revealed our lack of experience. Only Luke

knew anything about sailing in heavy weather. Anyone who is only half familiar with the South African coast knows why. From now on, I let Luke have the last word in situations like these. We were all in the same boat and all wanted to reach our destination. Rank, age and social background do not count in these circumstances and it would have been outright dangerous if I, with my limited experience, had insisted on the captain's right to decide.

The second day

The wind was SSE 20 knots and the weather overcast. Our speed was 7 knots, reaching with the main and genoa up.

At dawn we saw some of the huge waves which we would have to deal for the first time. Not only were they massive, but they also travelled at an astounding speed. Often I thought that one wave would swallow us, but the yacht always rose above it at the last moment, like an elevator, so that we ended up on top of the crest with an exalting view all around. Immediately, we would be speeding on downhill into the trough and staring at the next approaching blue-grey wall of water in awe. From time to time, a sea would break with a thunderous roar. This was unlike anything that I had ever experienced before. I now sensed the meaning of 'being in the hands of nature'.

"Why are the seas so huge around here?" Guillaume asked. I recited what I had read earlier. "Waves are made by the friction between the wind and the water's surface. Wind speed and the fetch, which is the distance over which the wind can affect the water, determine the speed and height and frequency of the waves. Depth and currents also have a prominent influence, but in this case it is the trade winds which blow freely over very long distances that create these big seas."

We still had 1843 miles to go to Chagos. Sailing was fun, as we were on a broad reach and surfed down the waves in 20 knots of wind. Alas, the fun ended below decks. The ship rolled madly and everything which was not glued, nailed or wedged firmly into place joined forces in the creation of a hellish concert. Melons and pumpkins rolled back and forth across the cabin and it took a long while until we had stowed everything in more or less secure places. Our boat was heavily loaded, involving areas above the waterline, and we thought this was one reason for the exaggerated rolling. We were carrying stores for two to three months, two dinghies, two outboard engines, diving gear including a compressor, and full water and diesel tanks. In addition to all this, we even had rows of canisters of water and fuel lashed on deck.

Cooking now required all the talents of an acrobat. As Guillaume was preparing lunch, a large packet of rice fell victim to gravity and distributed its contents all over the cabin sole.

For the evening, the wind whipped up to 30 knots. We did not want to be caught out again carrying too much sail, so we reduced down to the storm jib alone. Now it was at least possible for the autopilot to steer, although the reduced sail area also meant that we were rolling even more, which somehow dampened our spirits.

At dusk, we drew lots for the watches at night. We also introduced the following rules. Whoever is on watch has to stay in the cockpit and wear a safety harness. If he has to go on deck for some reason, he must wake one of those off-watch first. None of the two sleepers below would probably notice if the person on watch fell over board. And this was our greatest fear. We also banned the usual male practice of peeing over the side. It is a fact that many drowned sailors are found with their flies open...

The fifth day

The wind at 12.00 was ESE, 15–20 knots, the sun was shining, the main was double-reefed and we had the genoa up. We had again had a rough night. The seas were confused, the wind gusting and we often had to steer by hand, achieving frightening speeds. The autopilot had to work hard to keep on course, which varied between a broad reach and running dead downwind. However, we were satisfied as long as we were only roughly on course.

During our early-morning radio call with Raudi and Graeme we were able to report a record run of 187 miles from noon to noon. This was also partly due to the south equatorial current which helped us along with an extra knot.

Our radio calls always took place in the early morning hours because the transmission was best at that time. Once, as I was changing the frequency, the boat suddenly broached. I jumped on deck to discover that the autopilot and all instruments had failed. Guillaume crept from his berth and took over the helm while I finished the call to Graeme. He at once knew the reason for this incident "Certain frequencies interfere with your electronics. Before transmitting, you should always switch off the autopilot and instruments first."

Pirates

I was absorbed in a book when Guillaume and Luke called me on deck. A strange-looking fishing boat about 20 metres long was approaching us on a converging course. "How strange to see a boat like that so far from the coast" Guillaume said. We watched it through the binoculars and noted that it had no name or identification number and no fishing gear to speak of. After they had passed us about two miles off, black smoke came from their funnel and they changed course aiming straight at us.

"They are accelerating. They are up to something!" Luke called.

I fetched the hand-held VHF and gave it to him. "Take this and try to contact them on channel 16. Guillaume, start the engine. I am going to get our Very pistol." While Luke tried in vain to contact them, my hands were shaking with agitation as I unpacked the pistol. I then transformed it with an adapter into an emergency handgun and laid out ammunition. "They're not answering"; Luke shouted. By now, they had come to within three-quarters of a mile. A dozen men stood in their bows and looked as if they were ready to board us. Had they been in a potential emergency situation themselves they would have been acting rather differently, making some kind of distress signal. The three of us just posed on the stern and looked at them for a moment. I then took over the helm, changed our course and gave full throttle ahead. The cold engine whined in pain.

"Luke, we have to hide the hand-held VHF, so that we can call for help later if necessary!" Luke disappeared below and thrust the VHF into the oven, while Guillaume fetched our machete which we normally use for coconuts. We then switched on the autopilot and resumed our offensive pose on the aft deck. Despite the engine running flat out and a breeze of 18 knots, the motor ship was drawing closer and closer. Then our engine died.

"That's the last thing we need!" I cried in despair. I managed to start it again, but as soon as I piled on the revs, the beast stuttered and threatened to die again. Helpless, we stared at the oncoming ship. It was now so close that we could distinguish the faces of the men in her bows. A moment later, they turned away and continued on their previous course. They had either closed in for sheer curiosity, or they had realized that we would have been no easy victims. Even so, the shock went deep, as this region was known for piracy.

Flying octopus

As the sun neared the horizon, it was again time to prepare the sundowner. Luke was at the wheel and I was about to pass him a plate with a few snacks when he exclaimed angrily "Hey, Ralph, what are you doing?"

"What? I'm not doing anything" I replied in surprise.

"I thought you'd thrown something at me."

He then had a look around and found something soft and squidgy in the cockpit. Out of curiosity, Guillaume joined us in our inspection of the strange thing. Our master chef was quick to identify the unknown object "That could be a tiny octopus" he declared, and it turned out he was right. Astonished, we found that the entire deck was covered in them, as if we had been bombarded with black ink. As we were gathering them in, our fishing line jumped, but before we could haul it in, the fish had torn itself loose again. The large plastic bait showed deep teeth marks. We continued to harvest the tiny octopus and ended up with 62 of them in our bucket.

"Can anyone guess what we are having for dinner tonight?" Guillaume grinned. It seemed as if the octopus had been chased by the fish which had also tasted our bait. Panicking, the school of octopus must have jumped out of the water just as a wave was level with our decks. So, they ended up on board and in our pot.

After all the excitement of the day, we had a big party that night. The aperitif was followed by a festive menu of garlic bread, salad, octopus fried in lemon butter, and wine. To this, we fantasized about bloodthirsty pirates and a huge monster octopus of the deep.

The eighth day

The wind was E, 15–20 knots and the sun was shining. The wind and weather had calmed down enough for us to have set the full main and the cruising chute on the previous day. We had by now become used to the routine and monotony; time was slipping by largely unnoticed. The autopilot did most of the work, and we spent the days and nights on watch, sleeping, reading and eating. During the daytime it was now so hot in the cockpit that we rigged up a large sheet as an additional sun awning. At last I could attack the books that I had brought along. By day I read literature and at night it was thrillers. On night watch it was sufficient to glance around the horizon once every five minutes or so. This luxury was the privilege of being far out at sea. It was like being in the desert. Islands, the oases of the oceans, were more than a thousand miles away in every direction, and this part of the Indian

Ocean had very little commercial shipping. Even so, woe to the sailor who collides with a big ship; a tanker or freighter would probably not even notice if it ran down a yacht. Even in these remote parts of the ocean, it would have been foolhardy to sail without any night watches. During the day, we were all on deck anyway, so we only had to stick to a watch-keeping routine at night.

We had so much time that we could read a book per day on average. I particularly enjoyed the fitting title 'Three men in a boat', which describes a jolly boating trip on the Thames, undertaken by three friends around the beginning of the last century. All three of them were suffering from day-to-day stress. They were ill-tempered and depressed. As an antidote they decided on the boat trip, accompanied by a dog. They seemed to have as much fun as we were having now.

This story also showed that the potential for conflict is lower in a small crew. We, too, would have accepted the dog, if it were not for the strict quarantine laws in so many countries.

Despite the lack of space, every one of us managed to find some privacy. Guillaume could retreat to the large fore-cabin, Luke had the saloon and I the quarter berth. Only at noon and in the evenings did we get together for company and conversation. The evenings, in particular, were usually spent in lively discussion, fuelled by one or, depending on weather and mood, several glasses of whisky. We often had Latin American music playing in the background. Some songs we loved so dearly that we declared them to be our hymns of the Indian Ocean. Sometimes, Guillaume also played his guitar. He was brilliant with classical Spanish melodies.

We had our happiest moments at sunset. For me, one evening is particularly memorable. The three of us sat on the fore-deck, philosophizing, while the sun sank like a blazing red ball behind our dragon spinnaker. The fact that we were sailing towards the sunset was enough to make us euphoric. Every day brought us a bit closer to the Chagos archipelago, which was still one thousand miles ahead. In an aeroplane, this distance is covered in a mere two hours. If all went well with us, we would be needing about another week. What sublime luxury in this age to be travelling so slowly! We were also spared all the media which normally shower us day and night. On that evening, we found ourselves in perfect harmony with the sun, the sea and the wind. Time was not pressing anymore. Since our departure from Singapore I had not worn a watch. Time was roughly determined by our hungry bellies and the height of the sun. We only needed the exact time for navigation and our daily radio calls.

As I have only since realized, there was one reason which threatened to disturb the harmony on board. My friends were running out of cigarettes. Luke wrote in his diary 'We have got on so well with each other so far. It is a shame, but I can sense trouble coming because of the cigarettes. Guillaume has used up his supply, and now I am sharing my last box with him. I have now decided to only share one more packet, because otherwise I will run out too.'

As a non-smoker, I had not anticipated this problem. Also, as we were carrying fuel in canisters on deck, I had put down the rule that they were only allowed to smoke behind the wheel.

On the 15th of September, the wind was blowing 15–20 knots from the east. We were sailing down-wind under a reefed main and genoa. Everyone was engrossed in their own little world when suddenly a sharp bang threw us out of our dreams. It took us a moment to realize that we had caught a fish on our trailing line and that we should co-ordinate our reactions. We changed course to slow down and hauled away at the line. A silver coloured fish was at the end, a dorado, which was fighting madly each time we got him close to the boat. Luke took a long knife and, after several tries, succeeded in harpooning him. Once on board, the Dorado showed us how much spirit and energy was left in him; with mighty lashes of his aft fin, he forced us out of the cockpit and we thought that he was going to sink the boat. Finally, we managed to calm him down somewhat with the winch handle. We estimated his weight to be around 15 pounds and, although he did not seem huge at first, we still had more than half of him left two days later after several meals. How lucky for us that we had a small freezing unit in the galley.

As we were sailing further and further away, the day came when we lost contact with Graeme. In the hope that our courses would cross again at some point in the future, each of us sailed on – he to the east, we to the west. It's a good thing the world is round. Only Raudi now remained in touch. After we had told him about our encounter with the maybe pirates, he urged us to "Keep going, boys!"

The thirteenth day
The wind was SE, 20 knots, the sky overcast, and we had the

double-reefed main and genoa up.

Time was slowing down noticeably as we came closer to Chagos. We wondered who was going to welcome us. Might there possibly be a boatload of beautiful young ladies? I now knew why seamen had such a lively imagination.

The weather had deteriorated. The last night had been spoilt by a 35 knot wind and heavy showers. The morning dawned grey and overcast and the sea had a dreary colour. To make up for that we were often accompanied by dolphins. On this day, they were particularly entertaining. They sped along just beneath the surface and used the crests of the waves as launching pads for spectacular jumps.

We had now been 13 days at sea. The waves had been rough, with the exception of only two days. *Ryusei* had rolled and pitched drunkenly because of the heavy load, her narrow beam and our course.

Sometimes we felt as if we were on a roller-coaster. Hatches, windows and deck had started to leak in places and made life below uncomfortable. It is incredible that we managed to sleep under these circumstances, but we humans are apparently highly adaptable.

Land ho

Our autopilot had broken down during the night and we were exhausted from steering by hand. At last, after 16 days at sea, land came into sight – or rather, the tops of palm trees. We could hardly believe that the GPS had brought us here with such accuracy. In days gone by, a passage like this could well result in shipwreck or in sailing past the island altogether because of navigational errors. We danced on deck, overjoyed.

Chagos

Arriving in paradise (05°18'S/72°15'E)

Chagos is made up of three groups of coral islands – Salomon, Perros Banjos and Diego Garcia, which lie in the Indian Ocean between India and Mauritius. Chagos was once administered from the former British colony of Mauritius; today it belongs to the British Indian Ocean Territory. Originally the islands were inhabited by Mauritians of African descent who traded in cocoa-products, fish and guano. Today Diego Garcia, which lies to the south, is the only inhabited group. This natural paradise is leased by the United States who have since transformed it into the largest naval base in the Indian Ocean. Referring to the horse-shoe shape of the island, the Americans dubbed it the 'footprint of freedom'. It was from here that the planes bombarding Iraq set off during the Gulf War. The military zone on Diego Garcia is out of bounds.

The Salomon islands, lying at the north of the Chagos archipelago, are a paradise for cruising yachts. They are covered in palms and form an atoll about five miles across. Inside is a sheltered lagoon which can be reached through a narrow pass in the reef.

As the sun was high, we could easily distinguish the pass. One strong current was flowing out and another was flowing past the entrance, so we decided to motor in with Guillaume and Luke keeping a look-out. Just as we had passed the outer reef, I gave more throttle but the engine stopped; Luke and Guillaume immediately set the genoa and prepared the anchor, while I tried to restart the engine. To our relief it did fire up but, as soon as I increased the revs, it spluttered and threatened to die again. Our suspicion that the fuel filter was dirty later turned out to be correct. We continued at slow ahead, which was quite adequate as we were surrounded by large coral heads which lurked just beneath the surface. Luke directed us through the shallows from the cross-trees, where he had climbed to get a better view. The shallow patches can be seen better from a higher angle than from on deck. On our way across the lagoon, several dolphins joined us and it seemed as if they too wanted to show us the way. In the afternoon we anchored off the island of Tanaka. Only a sailor knows the feeling of relief and elation, after a long ocean passage, once the anchor is down in a secure spot.

Without further ado, we launched our inflatable and went

ashore. This was indeed paradise – dazzling white sand, clear water and palm trees. Only Eve was missing. Most of the palm trees were so small that we could pick the coconuts without having to climb them. We then wandered around the island and found that the lagoon was teeming with brightly coloured fish of all sizes, only a few metres from the beach. Full of enthusiasm, Luke wrote in his diary 'I still can't quite believe that we are really here. I know that I won't be able to sleep tonight, thinking about the adventures to come tomorrow, despite having been at sea for 16 days. It feels like being a child on Christmas Eve!'

Salomon interlude

We were woken at dawn by a cock crowing. Guillaume with his musical ear was the first to hear him and called out to us "I can hear a grilled chicken calling!" Later on, while Luke and I set up our diving headquarters on the beach, Guillaume went inland in pursuit of the cock armed with the machete but his expedition was only half successful. "I found the fresh-water well we were told about" he reported. "I also came across three chickens but as soon as they saw me they disappeared in the undergrowth. I had no chance of catching them!"

We laughed and said "They probably have a built-in alarm against hungry French sailors. Anyway, they must be more intelligent than the now-extinct Dodo of Mauritius – it must be a hundred years since the last Dodo ended up in a pot"

Later, we went on a tour in the inflatable and visited the island of Boddam on the other side of the lagoon. We wanted to visit the yacht *Star Gazy* which we had seen anchored there upon our arrival, and with whom we had already had some radio contact. She was a large heavy ferrocement ketch from Britain belonging to Derek and Virginia. They only had a few basic provisions on board and lived mainly on what they found in the sea and on the island. They knew where to find clean fresh water, where the fruit trees were, how coconuts could be used to bake bread, how palm cores could be eaten in salads or as vegetables, and where and how to fish the best fish. They also told us about the monthly routine inspection by the British officials.

"We've heard that they're due to arrive next Wednesday. I'd advise you to be anchored off Boddam by then. They always throw a party for us, including a beach barbecue with fresh steaks!"

Before returning to our own island, we also met the crews of the other two boats which were anchored off Boddam. These were

Paul and John from *Rambling Rose* and Gary and Corren from *Manxman*. Happy at having met nice new 'neighbours' we motored back over the lagoon in our inflatable trailing a fishing line behind us. A large fish took our bait and the evening meal was secured – instead of chicken we were now having fried fish in a curry sauce.

Diving

The Chagos archipelago, which rises from depths of over 3000 metres, is pure bliss for divers. The untouched coral reefs inside and outside the lagoon and wealth of fish make this place really spectacular. In the areas where the yachties have not yet started to hunt for their meals with harpoons, the fish are extremely trusting. Guillaume and Luke had never dived with full gear before, so I gave them a few lessons in the shallow water off the beach.

The following day, we ventured out on our first real diving expedition. We went to the Ile de Passe, the little islet north of the passage through the reef, in the inflatable. Even in the shallower water closer to the beach we found fantastic coral formations sticking up from the sandy bottom like tiny oases. The colours of the corals and fish and the deep blue water overwhelmed us. A reef-shark sidled past, giving Guillaume a mild attack of panic.

The most spectacular dive we made was on the outside of the reef surrounding the Salomon islands. We dived along a deep near-vertical edge where the islands drop down into the depths of the surrounding ocean. Despite the very clear water, everything just vanished in ever darker shades of blue beneath us, whereas at our level we were surrounded by an incredible display of colours and forms. Added to this there was the euphoric feeling of seemingly floating in space and it became

Taking the plunge

difficult to stick to the basic safety rules of diving. How should we always keep an eye on each other while there was so much to see all around? And how could one continuously watch the depth-meter when the big blue was so inviting...

As we were hopeless anglers, we sometimes used the harpoon to get a meal. Jack fish, lipfish and groupa were our favourites. The groupa were the easiest to hunt, as they always returned to their home territory, even if one had just missed a shot at them. Only the largest and most intelligent fish survive in places that are frequented by harpoonists. We left the big ones alone anyway, because they usually don't taste good and, once they are harpooned, it is difficult to quieten them down quickly enough. It is a known fact that dying fish attract shark and when Gary and Luke were harpooning fish for our beach barbecue a school of reef-shark gave them quite a scare.

Of course we asked ourselves whether we should be harpooning in an underwater paradise like this. The answer was both 'yes' – because we had to fill our bellies, and compared to the huge scale of industrialised over-fishing on the high seas, this was a mere drop in the ocean – and 'no' – because every time a fish is harpooned, the balance of nature is disturbed.

Yachties and rats
Despite the sharks, we accumulated enough fish to organise a beach party along with the crews of all the newly arrived yachts. One morning, a small fleet of boats had arrived, so there were eight boats anchored with us in the lagoon. As well as Derek and Virginia on *Star Gazy* from Great Britain, there were Paul and John on *Rambling Rose* from Great Britain, Gary and Corren on *Manxman* from the Isle of Man, Andy and Mandy with their children Sam and Sophie on *Nina* from Australia, Roger and Jennie with their children Scott and Lance on *Freelance* from South Africa, Tony and Monica on *Double Diamond* from South Africa, Ben and Ruth on *Colorit* from Sweden and Connie, John and Jim on *Morning Sun* from Denmark.

We soon got to know each other like a big family while busying ourselves with the preparations for the forthcoming beach buffet. Soon a cheerful fire was burning from a pile of driftwood, and alcohol was starting to loosen a few tongues. Small groups sat together discussing their exploits; yachties are adventurers and love to spin a yarn, with boat problems providing a boundless source of topics for conversation.

As soon as it grew dark, hordes of rats came running out from the undergrowth and tried to storm our buffet. We chased them off with sticks, only to find them returning a few moments later. One of them was impressive in his bravado; he climbed into a palm-tree which was hanging over our table and dropped from there bang into the middle of the food. It was not until we threw some food into the undergrowth that they left us in peace for a while.

The inhabitants of Chagos had evacuated these islands some thirty years earlier. They had left their by now overgrown houses behind, along with rats and chickens and even some mules on the neighbouring Perros Banjos.

Shipwreck

This was the day that all of us had waited for. The British officials from Diego Garcia had announced their regular visit, but more to the point were the steaks which they would hopefully be bringing with them. We were going to anchor off Boddam, so I went ashore on Tanaka and began to stow our diving gear, which we had left on the beach, in the inflatable. Just as I was going to put our harpoon into the dinghy, I saw a large inflatable alongside *Ryusei*. Harpoons are strictly forbidden on Chagos, so I immediately turned around, hid the harpoon with my body and shoved it into the undergrowth. Not knowing whether the officials had seen me with the harpoon, I was rather nervous when I returned on board.

Six uniformed men were sitting in our cockpit, speaking with my friends. "Ah, here is the captain at last!" one of them called, and they looked me up and down apparently amused by my sparse clothing. "These gentlemen would like to see our papers!" Luke said. Relieved, I said "Certainly" and fetched the folder with our documents and passports from below. Our visitors turned out to be very pleasant people. They were rather young and showed a great deal of interest in the yachtie lifestyle.

"Unfortunately, some of your friends have been very unlucky" the officers told us. "This morning we rescued an elderly French couple who had been stranded on the reef south of here for two weeks. Fortunately, they had been able to reach a small island. However, as they had only been able to salvage 20 litres of water and precious little food from their boat before it broke up completely, they were very weak when we found them. They are now on the freighter which brought us here from Diego Garcia."

We later heard from Derek and Virginia that the French

couple had only left our lagoon two weeks before. The husband was apparently so aged that he had difficulties even in setting the sails. "Still, for some, the risks of a cruising life are preferable to being shut away in an old people's home" they commented and then told us about another incident which had happened half a year earlier. An American lady who was sailing alone despite her age had a medical emergency on the way from Chagos to Mauritius and was rescued by the coastguard; thereafter she was given the same name as her yacht – *Crazy Lady!*

The British officials visited each boat and left us in the belief that the expected barbecue with fresh steaks would take place as usual. However, they had come to Salomon on a freighter belonging to the US Navy, accompanied by 30 American soldiers, and had not reckoned on so many people participating. Unfortunately, rather than leave some of us hungry, the officer in charge decided to call the entire party off. This decision was only announced at the last moment, so we found ourselves hanging around the meeting point with rumbling stomachs. As a consolation, we drank all the beer which we had reserved for the party and were soon so tipsy that we could see imaginary steaks flying past through the air.

All the former inhabitants of Salomon had lived on Boddam. Today, nearly all the huts and buildings in the small village are derelict and overgrown. The ruin of the church was especially impressive, with its remaining stained glass windows. Not far away was a small hut which displayed an ancient lifebelt with the words 'Chagos Yacht Club' painted on. Yachties from all corners of the globe have left records, in the form of names, dates and even pictures of their yachts on the walls. There was also a small visitors book. As our visit to Chagos drew to a close we too marched like pilgrims to this sacred place and left our marks. We then stayed on a while and tried to imagine how life must have been here before. Why did people settle here, isolated from the rest of the world? On our boats, we had the luxury that we could move on any time we liked.

Bread
Our fresh supplies dwindled until we only had potatoes and onions left. Even our 'water of life' – the beer – had run out. We then faced another problem, having to bake bread. Our French master chef Guillaume attacked this new challenge with all the eagerness of a research chemist. The results were impressive. The

bread was so hard that we couldn't cut it without a saw, let alone eat it. Luke suggested using it for bait, but even the fish regarded it with contempt. When we told him about our mishap, John from *Rambling Rose* offered to give us a lesson in bakery. We have enjoyed perfect bread on board ever since, so I should like to publish his recipe here for the benefit of all hungry mariners.

The ingredients of John's bread are:

1 kilo flour
1 teaspoon salt
1 teaspoon instant yeast
4 tablespoonfuls of milk powder
10 teaspoons of olive oil
2 mugs of water (total about 500 ml)

The method is to mix everything together in a large bowl and then spread the dough out on a board. Wait 15 minutes, then knead until homogenous (this is the hardest part!). Leave to rise in a warm place. Then put it in the oven and bake for 20 to 30 minutes at maximum temperature. It can also be baked in a pressure-cooker placed on the gas ring.

Peros Banjos

We would have liked to stay in Chagos for months, but time was now pressing with the cyclone season approaching fast. Suddenly, as if following some herd instinct, everybody planned to sail on the same day, apart from those on *Rambling Rose* and *Star Gazy*. Like us, *Manxman* was heading for Mauritius, while all the others were setting off for Madagascar.

Before we left Chagos completely, we had a look at the larger atoll of Peros Banjos. On our way there we lost two of our trailing lines, presumably to sizeable fish as the lines had a maximum load of about 50 kilos.

Off the Ile du Coin, which also has a deserted village, we dived for the last time in the Chagos archipelago to harpoon some fish for dinner. As soon as we were in the water, Luke and I were surrounded by sharks. They might have regarded us as a special dinner, but in our optimism we continued our dive hoping that they had come purely out of curiosity. Soon, we saw many tasty looking fish of ideal sizes. As if they knew that we could not harpoon them because of the sharks around us, they came within touching distance. We had anchored in fairly shallow water so I decided to harpoon our dinner close to the boat – we could then make a hasty retreat before the sharks could attack. Again, the fish must have sensed what was going on – they had all disappeared.

We lost our sense of time over this escapade and arrived at our planned anchorage off the Ile Longue after nightfall. For the final approach, we had to revert to the radar. During the night, the weather deteriorated and we were rolling about uncomfortably. We were happy to leave the next morning; the sharks and the weather helped us to say good-bye to the paradise in which, otherwise, we could have easily spent many more months.

Luke had used his spare time on Chagos to create a poem which was greeted with much merriment:

Three Men in a Boat
There were three men in a boat,
So laden with booze that logic
Suggested it shouldn't float.
There was Rum, Whisky, Tequila galore,
but the question troubling everyone was –
Who would be sober enough to pour?

They slipped their mooring one fine day,
but only made it to the next bay.
Of course temptation was too great.
They succumbed to their worst fate.
They stopped to have a drink or three,
But it became a drinking spree.
They woke the next day with aching heads
And found it hard to leave their beds.

They knew it somehow had to be done;
They had to reach the port of Batam.
For there lay more poison that was delicious
To fuel their voyage to Mauritius.
But Whisky was not their only temptation.
There was another of God's creations.
Yes you've guessed, fair woman it is,
One temptation they'd surely not miss.
The temptresses they met on Sibu
Now these one day they surely would rue.
Despite the laughter and the fun,
They knew that damage soon would be done...

> *On the way they stopped at Chagos,*
> *A very beautiful Archipelagos.*
> *The reason they stopped was to have some fun*
> *But also dry out − in more ways than one.*

Chagos to St Brandon

A fresh easterly hurtled us along and soon the palm trees dropped below the horizon behind us. We were back in the swell and vast space of the Indian Ocean. Heading due south, we were sailing on a beam reach which for us is the easiest course: stable, fast and pleasant. Routine took over and we once more lost all feeling of time as the miles slipped away beneath our keel − the freedom of dreams! We could always change course, for any one of a number of destinations: Madagascar, the Comoros Islands, Seychelles, Mozambique or the Maldives; we had all the relevant charts on board. All that would be needed was a little change in course and an adjustment of the sails. Another luxury we had was time.

We were about 1200 miles off Mauritius, and decided to leave the rhumb line in order to visit the archipelago of Cargados Carajos first; our anchor fell in the lee of the island of Raphael six days later.

We made this passage in record time. Our best noon-to-noon run was 187 miles. The trade wind started with about 15 to 25 knots and gradually increased so that for the last few days it was up to 40 knots. We sailed on under reduced canvas, although large breakers did give us a fright from time to time. Sadly, our most important crew member, the autopilot, went on strike. We had already repaired it on Chagos, and I had noticed that the gearbox contained plastic cog wheels. Under the constant strain, they had simply worn away to nothing, so we had been forced to steer by hand for most of the way.

I commented "In the old days, everybody had to steer by hand".

"But they had much larger crews than us" replied Luke. The easy times were gone − in the strong wind, steering was so hard that we had to relieve each other at the helm every two hours; we would have given anything for a wind vane, but the former owner of *Ryusei* had not needed one. With six large solar panels on top of the bimini, there was always enough electricity to drive an autopilot, and anyway a wind vane would not really have enhanced the looks of our classic boat.

We stayed in radio contact with the other boats from the 'Chagos group'. We exchanged positions twice a day and reported any noteworthy incidents on board. With the exception of ourselves and Gary on *Manxman*, everybody was heading for Madagascar. As they had all left at the same time, their passage soon developed into a race. We heard that *Freelance* had caught a huge marlin, and that they now had the problem of stowing it away in their cool-box. We did discuss more serious affairs too. The BBC had been reporting on the troubles in northern Madagascar, so the most frequently asked question was "Will it still be safe to land there?" After a while, we all agreed that the press often exaggerates the state of affairs, so in the end they all sailed on for Madagascar.

Mutiny

A sharp bang one day shook us out of our lethargy; a large fish had been caught and was pulling the line from its fitting. We hove to and hauled away at the line, to find a magnificent tuna at the end. We cut it into manageable sized joints and stowed some away in the freezer. For our customary sundowner, we had raw tuna as sashimi and afterwards tuna curry for dinner – we felt things could not be better.

This lavish meal was followed by a clear, starry night with a perfect wind. Euphoria was induced by the tropical wind, the sound of the sea slipping by, the feeling of speed and the vast space of the ocean. Soon – far too soon – dawn broke and we were faced with the question of what to have for breakfast. We decided on a tuna salad.

Luke, who was at the helm at the time, suddenly cried out "Hey, look over there! There is a huge swarm of sea birds!"

We were surprised to see so many birds this far away from land. "They must be on to a school of fish" we reasoned. "Let's change course and see if we can't catch one!"

Hunting fever had taken over. We bore off and soon birds were in the air all around us. The water seemed to boil from the seething masses of fish. Like missiles, the birds dived down into the water only to resurface seconds later with small fish in their beaks. Once in a while, we saw large fish breaking the waves. Seconds later, our line went taut. Instantly we hove to and hauled away. It seemed as if we were fighting a monster of the deep, while the boat was pitching and rolling in the waves with flapping sails. We had again caught a large tuna. By the time we had finally killed the slippery beast, it had spilled a lot of blood over our decks.

As soon as we had jointed it and stowed it away, the question arose "Guess what we are having for dinner tonight?"

Tuna, needless to say – first as sashimi and afterwards fried with spaghetti. Tuna stayed on the menu the next day too and the day after that. As we discussed the carte du jour and tuna continued to feature high on it, my friends began to pull long faces.

"We have to eat them before they go off" I said. "We owe that to the poor creatures!"

"I'd rather see the tuna turn sour than myself!" Luke replied angrily.

"What we took from the sea will be eaten" I teased them. "That is an order! You sure are a spoiled bunch!"

By now, Guillaume's patience had run out too. "Three days of tuna, for breakfast, lunch and dinner. That's more than enough. It's time to declare mutiny!"

"I'm with you there!" Luke agreed. "One more piece of tuna and our captain follows the captain of the Bounty – we can have the dinghy ready in no time at all!"

I was outnumbered and left with no choice, so the tuna which we could not fit into our freezer was thrown back into the sea and we decided to stop fishing. Peace returned after our traditional round of sundowners, but secretly I dreamt of the good old days when the fate of mutineers was walking the plank, or perhaps keel-hauling.

Water ingress

Mutiny was soon forgotten as the wind increased and it started to rain; we had to reef once again. *Ryusei* stampeded through the rapidly growing waves at high speed. We felt that the weight of our stream-lined boat was now helping us with an easier motion – a modern yacht would have been pitching much more violently.

During my night watch, I noticed the automatic bilge pump starting up a few times. As I was tied to the helm, I called out for Luke who was sleeping in the saloon. He checked the bilges and confirmed that there was a lot of water in the boat. "I had noticed it too – that the pump was switching on more often" he said, obviously worried. "Please could you check if the sea-cocks of the toilet are closed? We will have to take a closer look at things in daylight" I called. I then spent an uneasy night, as I remembered only too well the words of the surveyor who had inspected *La Cigale* for me in Hong Kong – that the hull could open up in heavy weather due to excessive rot. Were *Ryusei*'s planks now opening up under the strain?

First thing in the morning, we shifted half a mountain of gear and luggage to be able to inspect the bilges properly. There was a lot of stuff to be moved and it was hard work with a heeling angle of 45 degrees and the constant motion of the ship. Eventually we found that the water was coming in on the port side, somewhere between the bows and the mast. There was nothing we could do about it at the moment, so we pumped more frequently and inspected the bilge at regular intervals. At least it was a consolation knowing that we had four pumps available – two electric, one manual and one mechanical one (driven from the main engine). "The best pump is a man in a panic with a bucket" is an old and true saying, but thankfully that point had not yet been reached.

St Brandon

The silhouette of the first coral island of the Cargados Carajos archipelago came into sight and we hoisted the Mauritian courtesy flag. This group of islands, also bearing the name St Brandon, belongs to Mauritius. I had already been there two years before with a sailing boat belonging to my friend Noël Maurel, and it was then that I had got the cruising bug.

We now headed for the main island, St Raphael, which had a fishing station. As soon as they were in sight, I contacted them on VHF 16.

"What do you want here?" came the unfriendly question in French.

"We are a sailing boat en route from Chagos to Mauritius and we would like to anchor in the lee shelter of your island!"

"That is not possible unless you have an official permit."

"Listen to me" I insisted. "We have been at sea in heavy weather for a week. Our autopilot is defective, our boat is leaking and the crew is exhausted. According to international maritime law we should at least be allowed to anchor and rest. We do not have to come ashore."

"All right, go ahead and anchor. But unless I receive a permit from Mauritius, you will have to stay on board."

"Do they think that we are pirates?" exclaimed Luke who, like the rest of us, was looking forward to a break. "For a bottle of whisky, they will probably roll out the red carpet for us!"

However, just as we were anchoring in a small bay, the frosty voice came over the VHF once more "It is probable that fishermen will come by and ask you for alcohol. Do not give them any. Alcohol and women are strictly forbidden here!"

"Ralph, where on earth have you dragged us to! I am happy to hear French again but, no alcohol and no women, that is definitely going too far!" complained Guillaume.

No sooner were we on deck, than the first fishing boat chugged past. "Can you please give us some beer or rum?" the black fisherman asked.

"We are sorry, but we have nothing left" Guillaume replied, despite the fact that our bilges were full of whisky bottles. We then fell into a deep sleep until our special friend came on the VHF once again.

"Welcome to the island. We have just heard from our boss in Mauritius that you are allowed to land!"

In stark contrast to our VHF contact, the welcome ashore was very friendly. About 40 men were living on the island, mostly fishermen but also the crews of a small weather station and a minute post office which also had a telephone. From here, I called my family on Mauritius and announced our imminent arrival there. My friends conquered the small store where they were at long last able to buy cigarettes. We then visited the weather station, checked in and entered our names in the island's guest-book.

As we sat down with the administrator of the fishing station, he told us of the operation. "The fishermen are Creoles from Rodrigues, which belongs to Mauritius. The crew here is exchanged every six months. They go out in the little pirogues, which are powered by an outboard, two of them in each, and fish with hand-lines. All our pirogues together catch up to five tons of fish a day. Once in a while, the ship from Mauritius comes to pick up the frozen fish!" They did not speak about their pay but we imagined that it must have been rather meagre in spite of the hardships these people endured while isolated on this island.

Mauritius

First Mauritius was made, and then heaven (Mark Twain)

An explosion of colours

In earlier times, Mauritius was a base for commercial shipping, and the island changed hands several times because of her strategic position. However, the island lost its importance with the inauguration of the Suez Canal and today its main visitors are sun-hungry tourists who come from all over the world.

For me, Mauritius is also home; members of my family had settled here 17 years ago, and I now looked forward to our arrival with great impatience. As we approached the island, the conversation on board revolved around our expectations and what we would do ashore. It soon became apparent that we were feeling and talking like people who have to spend their whole working lives at sea; most of our desires were reduced to basic needs – sex, food, drink and a hot bath! Later, the eye-catching silhouette of the island appeared over the horizon and, as we sailed along the imposing sheer rock face of the island of Coin de Mire, fishermen waved at us cheerfully from their small pirogues.

In the lee of Mauritius we reached smooth water, and it now seemed as if *Ryusei* was going to fly. The evening sun drenched the island in deep colours. The fields of sugar cane appeared an intense green, contrasting sharply with the grey, ragged mountains in the background. The glowing evening sky was reflected in the water, and Mauritius welcomed us with a firework display of beautiful natural colours.

The Island of Mauritius

Mauritius belongs to the Mascarene Islands. Her coast is rugged, featuring many natural harbours, and an off-shore coral reef surrounds the entire island. The formerly uninhabited island was first discovered by the Arabs and Portuguese (in 1510), then inhabited by Dutch settlers who gave it its name, cleared away large areas of the woods, cultivated sugar cane and imported the Java stag. It was during this period that the dodo, a turkey-like bird, was hunted to extinction. The island remained a Dutch colony from 1598 to 1710. The French followed the Dutch colonialists in 1715 and the British took over in 1810 after the French Revolution. Mauritius became independent in 1968 but remained inside the Commonwealth. Despite the British influence, it is the French culture which dominates the island to this day. The Indians, who had originally come to the island as labour for the plantations, now form the largest ethnic group. They make up 70 percent of the population, followed by people of African descent, Creoles, Chinese and Europeans. The 1.1 million Mauritians speak mainly Creole, derived from French; the other languages spoken include French, English and various Indian and Chinese dialects.

Mauritius is often referred to as 'The Pearl of the Indian Ocean'. However, anyone like me who has visited the island regularly over a long period of time must be sobered by the changes.

The sugar industry boom was followed by an explosion in tourism and a textile industry boom. There had been large-scale development, and I have seen how small roads grew into motorways, how small picturesque houses made way for large functional buildings without character, how wildly growing urban villages spread up into the green hills and how deserted beaches were now spoiled with huge hotels.

Fortunately, a positive attitude tends to filter these things from the everyday perception. As visitors we are not allowed to complain, as we are the ones who bring about these developments. Only a wise and far-seeing political control could change things, but where in the world would that come from? The people of Mauritius may eventually wake up to the negative side one day if, for example, the nature-loving tourists stay away or if the fishermen cannot fish anymore because the sea is empty.

However, the island is still a pearl; many different ethnic groups live closely and peacefully together, and nature has ways of surviving in spite of human sins.

A hard landing
We had left nearly 4000 nautical miles behind in our wake without any really dramatic events or mishaps – it was a magnificent feeling to have crossed our first ocean!

As darkness set in, we reached the harbour approach to Port Louis. On the VHF, the harbour master asked for the technical details of our boat, including draft, before he allowed us to enter. He then directed us to a berth at the far end of the harbour. We were like horses impatiently running back to their stables and approached the berth under engine. A sudden jerk brought us to a halt, several metres away from the pier – we had run aground! We complained on the VHF and the harbour master promised to send a boat to tow us off.

Our high spirits were blown away as we waited and waited and nothing happened. I called again – again we were told that someone would arrive any moment. We then made another attempt to get off under our own power. Fortunately, a fishing-boat motored past and its wake lifted us off. We sounded our way cautiously towards the pier, until we tied up alongside an American yacht whose crew welcomed us at once with cool beers.

We had just taken a first sip when a uniformed man came along and asked us to accompany him with the ship's papers. Guillaume and Luke went with him to the customs office while I looked for the passports and documents. When I joined them in the office, I was bombarded with questions. Everything went fine until the official asked "Do you have weapons or harpoons on board?"

"No" I answered innocently. As I looked around I noticed Guillaume's pained expression.

"Are you quite sure?" the official asked again. I hesitated and the penny dropped when I again saw Guillaume, now looking desperate. He had already spoken to the official in my absence and might have mentioned the harpoon. "Well" I said. "We have something like an emergency harpoon in our survival kit for the liferaft, but that is strictly for emergencies."

"No matter for what purpose, you will have to surrender all weapons and harpoons to me. You will get them back upon your departure."

After we had delivered our harpoon and filled in the

remaining forms, we left the office in relief. "Guillaume, if you hadn't sent me the right look at the right time, we would now be in deep trouble" I said.

"But I didn't know that you were not going to declare our harpoon" he protested.

"Forget about all that" Luke interrupted. "Let's eat, drink and be merry – it's time to celebrate!" We rushed off to a restaurant in the centre of Port Louis and had 'Poulet Curry à la Mauricienne'.

Welcome

I was woken up the next morning by someone calling down from the pier. A rather skinny Indian man stood there and asked "Do you have any clothes to wash?" Had the poor chap known how many we had, he would probably have fled there and then. As it was, the ship had to be cleaned thoroughly after the long trip and we threw everything that was not attached to the boat into a large sail bag. The poor fellow nearly collapsed under the load.

Later, I climbed on to the pier and thought about my family, who were due to visit us any time now. An elegant lady rushed past and I called out "Hello, mother. Are you in a hurry?"

She turned around in surprise and only then realised that the bearded man on the pier was her son. The welcome was exuberant, but then her motherly instinct surfaced and she said "Ralph, the beard does not suit you. You'll have to shave it off!"

"Aye, aye, Captain" I replied.

Then my younger brother arrived. He also loved the sea and had studied oceanography in Europe before returning to Mauritius where he now lived with his wife and children. He immediately made the same complaint "What on earth are you carrying around under your nose?"

"Is this a proper welcome for a seaman who has travelled far and wide across the oceans?" I replied indignantly, to the amusement of all. I then continued "If we want to be in Grand Baie in time for lunch, we'd better hurry!"

Grand Baie is a lovely sheltered bay in the north-west of Mauritius. An ideal place to anchor for the day. However, the harbour master informed me on the VHF that we could only enter the bay with the permission of the coastguard. The heads of state of the Francophone nations, including Mitterrand, were holding a meeting there and so highest security was demanded. The coastguard gave us permission to go there somewhat reluctantly.

With my brother and my mother as passengers, we sped off

under full sail. We hauled in the sheets and *Ryusei* was heeling over until the water surged along her lee decks. My mother seemed to enjoy this spectacle, while my brother did not hide the fact that he preferred activities under water to those in a small and unstable boat like ours.

As we were entering Grand Baie, a large coastguard vessel came dangerously close and stopped us from continuing – of all places in a spot where we only had half a metre of water beneath our keel. "This bay is closed because of the Francophone Symposium!" the commander from his bridge shouted down at us. "Do they really want us to sail back? The coastguard of Port Louis has given us permission to come here!" my mother protested. We were quite busy trying not to run aground, when she resolutely walked to the fore-deck and waved the coastguard vessel closer. She then fired off a verbal broadside which made us, and the officials, draw in our heads and cringe. They had probably never met such a petite but vigorous lady.

Miraculously, not only did they admit us to the bay, they even escorted us politely to a perfect anchorage close to the beach. In the restaurant ashore, where we met up with more members of the family, we had a good laugh about the incident.

Mar y Sol

The days slipped past easily. We went on tours of the island and were pampered by my family. One of the highlights of our stay was a dinner on the terrace of my stepfather's house. My parents live on the Saint Felix Sugar Estate in the sparsely populated southern part of the island. Their house lies on a hill in the midst of sugar cane fields and bears the name 'Mar y Sol' (Sea and Sun). The natural beauty of the surroundings and the colourful sunset were stunning as we sat in wicker chairs on the terrace. Beyond the park, fields of sugar cane, which seemed to flow in the breeze, extended down to the coast. Then came the lagoon and the endless ocean beyond. Despite the distance to the coast, the air was filled with the murmur of the surf. We could also see part of the sugar factory, where black smoke curled up from the chimney.

We felt as if we had travelled backwards in time to the colonial era as we sat round the huge table which was overflowing with food and drink. We were served from all sides and, during the extensive dinner, everyone told a different story.

"From July to December we bring in the sugar cane" my stepfather said. "This is why our factory is so busy at the moment."

His forebears had come from France several generations ago. "I have spent my entire life managing sugar factories. First in the neighbouring 'Bel Ombre' factory and now here in Saint Felix. The sugar industry started around 1750 and went straight into an unbelievable boom. Around 1860, we had 280 sugar factories on Mauritius – today there are only 17 left of which ours, Saint Felix, is the smallest. We only process around 140,000 tons of sugar cane each year. One ton of sugar cane produces around 110 kilos of sugar."

Frederic then told us anecdotes of famous seafarers. "When Captain Slocum arrived here in 1897, in a small sailing ship, my grandfather organised a dinner in his honour. However, Slocum was rather underdressed for such a grand occasion, and in his speech he gave the reason. Apparently, he always carried a fine suit on board for festivities such as these, but he also had a coconut crab with him which he regarded like a pet. As he was about to dress for my grandfather's dinner, he found to his dismay that the pet crab had eaten away half his jacket!"

Frederic then continued "I once met a very famous sailor myself – Bernard Moitessier who lived on Mauritius for a while after the loss of his boat in Chagos."

"Yes, I remember him too" exclaimed Sybille, my brother's mother-in-law. "He was a friend of my husband who at that time owned the best restaurant on Mauritius. Bernard visited us often in those days."

Amused, Guillaume, Luke and I realised that a poor cruising sailor and gourmet such as Moitessier had done well with friendships such as these.

Later, the conversation drifted on to shipwrecks, a subject close to my brother Yann's heart. He manages the largest fish farm on Mauritius, but almost all his spare time is spent diving.

"Due to the tropical storms, the coast is covered in wrecks. The most famous are those of *La Magicienne* and *Sirius*. *Sirius* was sunk in the battle of Grand Port in 1810 which, by the way, was the only battle at sea that the French were able to win against the British."

"How about treasure?" we asked.

"With the help of some sponsors, I spent nearly a year diving on *Sirius* and other wrecks, but other than a few silver coins, buttons and broken china, we found nothing valuable. However, we did manage to measure the wreck and salvage some artifacts for the museum. Most people who are out hunting for treasure are dreamers, who seldom end up with more than a few rusty nails."

Then we learned the story of the sailing ship %Travessa, which sank between Australia and Mauritius. In 1923, at the age of 10, my stepfather witnessed the landing of the survivors in the life boat after they had covered 1610 nautical miles across the Ocean. "My father, who at that time was the manager of the neighbouring sugar factory, was called to help when the lifeboat landed. The survivors where in a shocking state. I will never forget the gruesome sight of the poor men when the heavy seaboots had to be cut off their feet. The skin peeled and with some I had the impression the bones were exposed. Today a memorial reminds us of this tragedy."

Island race

We also got friendly with the crew of the American yacht *Billfish*; we had already met them in Port Louis. *Billfish* was one of the most beautiful schooners we had ever seen. A wooden yacht with a gaff rig, she was designed by the Frenchman Bombigher, and her masts had a rakish backward slant. On board were Leslie, a Texan lady, and her South African boyfriend Patrick. They told us that Gary, whom we had met in Chagos, had done an excellent job of refitting their boat in New Zealand. Gary Cairn had already arrived in Mauritius a few days before us. He had made a sensationally quick passage

Memorial to sailors

from Chagos, in spite of trouble with his Danish shipmate. "From now on, I will continue on my own" he said. Gary was a cabinet maker and had a wooden yacht named *Manxman*, so that everyone would know that he came from the Isle of Man. He had the temperament of a terrier and it was not always easy to get along with him, but as he, too, never missed a single party, he soon joined our group.

He had already declared in Chagos "Ladies are a no-no for me. I am a married man and I have sworn eternal faithfulness to my beautiful Danish wife!" They had met in New Zealand, sailed from there to Denmark and married. "My wife then began training to become a nurse. That will take her two years, so I thought this was a good opportunity to have a quick sail around the world one more time, before finally settling down in Denmark!"

Gary was heading for a secure port. His next and final stop before Europe was to be South Africa, where he wanted to earn some money. This suited me fine, as some problem areas on *Ryusei* had become painfully obvious during our passage from Singapore to Mauritius. I asked Gary to have a look; after inspecting her thoroughly, he drew up a list of necessary repairs, including the leaking deck, some bits of rot and the re-caulking of various planks near the keel, where she had been leaking whenever the going got a bit rough. To my consolation, he also added that *Ryusei* was a strongly built and basically sound vessel.

We then stumbled head-first into our next adventure – the annual island race. My friend Noël Maurel, with whom I had sailed to St Brandon two years before, persuaded me to participate with *Ryusei*. His advanced age could not stop him from sailing and he had earned his nickname 'Loup de Mer' (sea wolf) over the years. Noël had studied ship-building in Scotland, had worked all his life as an engineer in the sugar industry and built his own wooden yachts in his spare time. His last boat, which he still sails today, is a 15-metre schooner built from teak.

My response to Noël's enthusiasm was "But in a fully laden boat like ours, we will have no chance."

"Don't worry" he brushed aside my remark. "You have a fast boat, and the whole point is taking part, not winning. Besides, the race has three legs so that we will have lots of time for parties!"

This tipped the scales and we were on, but we still had to find a competent and good-humoured crew. In the end we recruited Leslie and Patrick from *Billfish*, Michel, a Mauritian Creole and Sarah, a young lady from England who was working in a hospital on the island. With seven people on board from six different nations, we were the most cosmopolitan and riotous crew of all.

On the starting line, all was chaos and disorder. The crews gesticulated, shouted and abused each other. For us sedate cruising folk this was a rather unusual situation, but Leslie knew the scene. She had once earned her living as a sailing instructor and had sailed many races. Without her, we would have been lost; the racing rules, tactics and the optimum sail trim were all completely unknown to us.

The wind was light and the modern racing boats vanished ahead. At least there were a few other heavier boats around so that we had some competition until the wind completely died. We drifted along in slow motion with the other boats and found that our race-fever had vanished along with the wind. Time was passing without us getting noticeably closer to the finishing line. This was in the bay of Mahebourg and, as we did not want to enter there in darkness, we finally gave up and motored in. Only five of the 50 or so participating boats had made it to the finish under sail. The disappointing wind conditions of the day were in stark contrast to the party at night, held in the idyllic restaurant 'Domaine de Chasseur', high up in the hills. It was very late when we finally hit our berths and dreamt about racing.

The next morning we were roused by the urgent call "Wake up! Wake up, or you will miss the start!" Hastily, we wolfed down our breakfast and still nearly missed the start. In light airs, we again made all sail. Michel, our local expert, was outraged "For ten years in a row I've been sailing this race, and we never had as little wind as this!"

On a glassy sea, we drifted along the south-east coast which is usually battered by the ocean waves. Nevertheless, we enjoyed the scenery, swam in the sea and were amused to find that the hard-boiled racing people were just as becalmed and helpless as we were.

"Let's show them what cruising is like" I suggested. "Why don't we just ignore the programme and continue on through the night to the next stop-over?" But all competitors were invited to a huge buffet that night in the yacht club and my idea found no followers. "Let's start the engine and go – to the buffet!" is what my crew decided instead. None of the boats reached the finish under sail inside the time limit that day, but they all made it to the buffet, which was slaughtered in no time. That evening, we also got to know Julia, an attractive young German girl who was studying on the neighbouring island of Réunion. As the evening wore on, she described how wonderful the island was and we soon found that we had a new destination to sail to.

The party in the Riviere Noire Yacht Club had been somewhere close to the top of the Beaufort Scale, so we started the last leg of the race appropriately under the weather. However, we were blessed with a light breeze so that at least three quarters of the fleet reached the finish in time. For us, it turned out to be a race against the time-limit, and we crossed the finish literally in the last minute. The spectators ashore and the crews of the other boats were treated with a rare spectacle. A heavy cruising yacht was finishing under spinnaker, but without anyone at her helm. Instead, the entire team was dancing on the fore-deck to a well-known song of the Blues Brothers, like an American cheerleader gang. Our Texan lady Leslie was not only our race tactician, she was our choreographer too.

During the prize giving, we won acclaim – not so much for our race results as for our dancing show.

The smuggler's problem

The last race party was overshadowed by bad news from Guillaume. As he had wanted to organize his return flight to France, he had left the boat in Riviere Noire to return to our beach house in the Baie du Tombeau. That morning, he awoke to find that all his money and his camera equipment was missing. His jeans with the empty wallet lay under the open but barred window, although he had left them over a chair on the other side of the room when he went to sleep. Our neighbour said that the thief had angled for his booty with a fishing rod, an old and well-known trick. He advised us, rather too late, to always close all windows at night.

Guillaume had come to join us for the prize-giving party but he just wasn't in the mood. It was quite a challenge trying to cheer him up at all. "Tomorrow, we'll investigate the whole affair and report it to the police. Think positive – they may even catch the thief. Let's celebrate now; we have circumnavigated the island without much wind and without shipwreck!" None of us really felt like celebrating so we retired to our bunks early, Guillaume to the beach house, the rest of us to the boat.

When we all returned to the beach house the next day, Guillaume was clearly shaken. "The burglar was here again! After I'd been all round the house closing up, I fell into bed at midnight, completely exhausted. This morning, the CD player and nearly all the CDs are missing. How he managed to get inside is a complete mystery – there are no traces of a burglary! I don't know yet if anything else is missing."

Luke and I looked at each other. We had the same thought, rushed to the kitchen and looked in the locker underneath the sink. Complete emptiness stared us in the face.

"Damn! That gangster has also taken our whisky!"

Whisky is incredibly expensive on Mauritius, due to extreme import duties. We had bought cases of whisky, for our sundowners, on the duty-free islands of Langkawi and Batam and stowed them away in difficult-to-access areas of the boat. The problem was whether we could legally bring some ashore in Mauritius, and we had been joking about this long before setting sail.

The risk of getting caught smuggling is high – but I could sink the booty in a clearly marked spot off the shore. We could then find it afterwards, on a diving excursion…"

We even thought of suitable spots in which to sink contraband before checking in. We were going to mark the exact location with bearings ashore and the GPS. Thus we hoped to find our contraband again later.

However, this romantic scheme was now struck a mortal blow. When we made an inventory of the bottles just before arriving in Mauritius, we noted an enormous loss. Searching through all corners of the bilge, we could only find about 20 bottles. We were thunderstruck and a heated discussion followed.

"Have we really drunk so much, Captain?" was the obvious question, asked by Luke.

We thought about it and calculated our whisky consumption over the days and weeks but this major disappearance of bottles still remained a mystery, one not to be solved until Brazil, where we were delighted to find even more inaccessible areas of the bilge harbouring whisky. Meanwhile, based on this unhappy discovery, we now had to decide how many bottles were to stay on board for our own use too. Luke, who was going to sail on with me to South Africa, insisted that a good supply was essential to ensure our survival. In the end, we agreed that we would keep the remaining bottles on board, except for those we could legally bring ashore.

The dream of the treasure hunt scheme crumbled into reality. The bottles we brought ashore were stowed away under the sink in our beach house. Although Guillaume had been sleeping there, the thief had got away with quite a respectable booty: about 400 dollars in cash, one expensive camera, CDs, a CD player and our whisky.

We were dismayed – the only consolation was that we still had some bottles left in *Ryusei*'s bilge.

"Let's go to the police and report the theft immediately" I said, not knowing what problems this would cause.

The snapshot

Our encounters with the Mauritian police force definitely had comical aspects. On the downside, they cost us a lot of time, and the whole affair would have ended unsuccessfully if the thief had not tried to steal from us a third time. Guillaume, who by now was sleeping lightly, suddenly woke up three nights later with a definite feeling that someone was crawling around the house. He quietly woke me and gestured that I should follow him. We lay in wait underneath his bedroom window with a camera at the ready. Suddenly a dark shadow emerged and we fired as he tried to open the window. We were blinded by the flash light and heard the man run away.

"We have him!" we thought, but the police were less enthusiastic. "A photograph is not regarded as evidence. You will have to claim that you have actually seen him."

"How can we identify a black man in utter darkness?" we replied. "That is asking too much of our eyes!" The police did not want to hear about that, so we just did as they suggested.

Next, the criminal police appeared at the scene. After investigating, they asked for a sample of the whisky which had been stolen; it did not take long for us to massacre the two bottles which we had bought to replace the stolen ones.

We had to admit that smuggling would not have paid off in Mauritius – the losses are too heavy!

A week later, the thief was caught. We identified him in the card index at the police station, not without having had a good long look at our photograph first. Luckily for us, he had a conspicuous scar.

"This man is very clever" the police complained. "Usually, we would have beaten the truth out of him, but he has hired himself a lawyer. His profession must be very profitable, as the lawyer charges about as much as the average yearly income of a Mauritian." and continued "To be able to charge him, we need you as a witness in court."

"And when will that be?"

"Oh, maybe in about four weeks time."

"Sorry, but that is impossible. In two weeks at the latest we have to sail for South Africa, otherwise we will miss the safe season for sailing. The chances of running into a tropical storm on the way increase sharply from now on!"

A few days later I was notified that the court appearance was scheduled for November 11th at ten in the morning in a place called Pamplemouse.

This was also the time of Guillaume's departure for France, where work was waiting for him. The farewell was sad, as our sailing trip had deepened our old friendship considerably. Sarah came on board to fill Guillaume's place. During the race, she had discovered her taste for sailing and she was bold enough and had the right sense of humour to get along with the 'wild men' (Luke and myself).

We held our farewell party on the evening before the court appearance in the Bounty Bar in Grand Baie. Not surprisingly, it developed into a rather wild night and Luke nearly came to grief when he crashed down from the bar during a dancing performance between the bottles and glasses on the counter. To our relief we found him to be a living example of the South African 'tough guy'.

At six in the morning, the alarm clock shrilled in my ear. We were at anchor in Grand Baie and not in the best shape after the previous night's excesses.

"Luke, Sarah, wake up!" I croaked. "We have to be in Port Louis before nine!" But my companions were still deeply comatose and I upped the anchor and motored out of the bay by myself. Around nine we entered Port Louis and my shipmates crawled out of their bunks, moaning and complaining. As soon as we had moored, I jumped ashore and grabbed a taxi to arrive just in time at the police station in Abercombie.

I was greeted heartily like an old friend. During the course of events, I had got to know and to like the police officers. Today, they were in high spirits as the case was promising to bring a successful conclusion. "The thief is already in Pamplemouse" they informed me. "Let's go now, two colleagues will drive us there."

In front of the station, the unmarked police car which we were about to use was a battered wreck on wheels. "Are you sure we are going to make it in this?" I asked before I could check myself. "Oh, don't worry" they assured me. "The car is running perfectly – it was only a small accident the other day!" Due to the small accident, one side was completely crumpled and it was only possible to get into the car on the driver's side.

The court building was surrounded by a boisterous crowd of

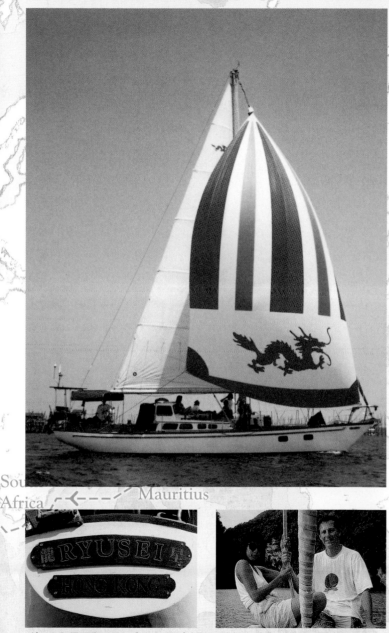

Sou...
Africa ←- - - - Mauritius

Above & Top: Ryusei, *the name of the Japanese-built yacht, means Dragon Star*

The original team: Lisa and Ralph

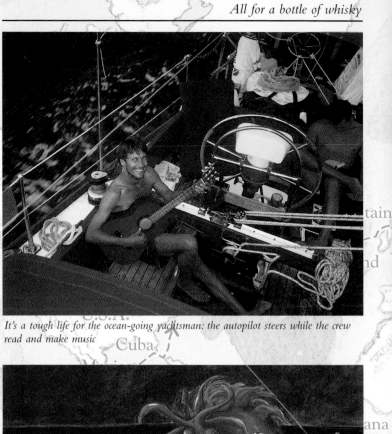

It's a tough life for the ocean-going yachtsman: the autopilot steers while the crew read and make music

The dragon

View from aloft, with the solar panels; dinghy and Luke's oil-soaked boots in tow

Singapore, a city of contrasts

A solitary anchorage in the Chagos archipelago, in the middle of the Indian Ocean, lives up to any dream

The breathtaking beauty of diving on Chagos

Reciprocal visits are a ritual amongst yachties

tain

Ireland

ana

Heler

This palm, which can give water, is known as the 'traveller's tree'

South Africa: Ryusei on the travel hoist with the high-rise Durban skyline in the background; the ice-cream vendor virtually halted the refit

French Guyana: few prisoners ever escaped Devil's Island

Mauritius: blazing colours of sunset

people. It was incredibly hot and most of them were seeking the shade of the nearby trees. The building had a grand flight of steps leading up to the entrance, and both the age and the style showed that it dated back to British colonial times.

"When are the proceedings going to start?" I inquired impatiently.

"Oh, as soon as the judge arrives!"

Much later, we were still waiting. I had a throbbing headache and retired to the shade of a tree outside. Two policemen escorted me and sat next to me. I was now sandwiched between two massive dark-skinned Indians in glittering uniforms. Instead of leaving me with my headache in peace, they were full of curiosity about my sea-travels.

"Have you sailed all the way from Singapore to here?" they asked.

"Yes" I said.

"Have you ever had huge storms at sea?"

"No."

"How long did the trip take you?"

"Two months."

"When are you leaving?"

"After the court proceedings."

"And where are you sailing to?"

"Europe."

"Which will be your next stop?"

"Réunion and South Africa."

"Who is with you?"

"My friends Luke and Sarah."

On this bit of information, their interest soared. "What – you have a woman on board? Two men and one woman?"

"Yes."

"With whom will she sleep?"

"With nobody. We sleep in separate bunks."

They did not quite believe me. "But on a long journey like that, surely the temptation is great. What then?"

I pondered a while. Then I said "Well, if you really want to know. According to ancient laws of the sea, the captain has first right. That would be me."

Roars of laughter followed. After that, the conversation was closed and we waited in silence until I demanded "When will the judge come?" Grumbling, one of the officers got up and sauntered away. We had been waiting in the unbearable heat for hours, but nobody seemed to mind. Other than myself, no one appeared to be in a hurry.

"No idea when he will arrive" the officer said upon his return. Some more time crept past until we were finally informed that the judge was ill and that he would not appear at all today.

"But what now?" I demanded. "I really cannot postpone my departure any longer!"

They were at a complete loss upon this difficult question. But all of a sudden, one of the officers a had bright idea. "We can try to carry out the proceedings in Port Louis!"

We were met by some surprised glances as we arrived before the court building in Port Louis with our battered car, especially when several policemen, a slightly shady looking foreigner and a Creole in handcuffs all climbed out. As our case had now been given priority, we managed to squeeze in between two other court cases. In the meantime, I studied the other proceedings and found that they were all about severe drug problems. At last, it was our turn. The building was crammed full with spectators and, as there was no other space, I had to share a small bench with the thief. Full of hatred he stared at me from close quarters. Tension was building, and if he had not been in handcuffs he might have jumped at me there and then. The female judge then read out the register of our man's previous convictions, which was impressive. He had already been convicted of theft and causing bodily harm five times. In the face of this and the new accusations, he was convicted to be taken to a higher court at some later stage. To my enormous relief, this would take place without me.

The harbour barber

Exhausted, I returned to the boat. In the meantime Luke and Sarah had already bought provisions for the passage to Réunion, but we still had to go through the bureaucratic rigmarole of clearance, which took a long time. In international comparisons, Mauritius ranks high on the list for the art of red tape.

We were moored in the fishing basin of Port Louis. On my way to the boat I passed a barber's shop, advertised by only a tiny sign. A gentleman with an impressive beard, reaching down to his belt, stood in the doorway and addressed me as I walked past. Judging by his clothes, he was a Muslim.

"Hello there" he said. "Would you like a hair cut?"

"No, no" I replied, startled, although I knew that my hair had grown too long and had to be sacrificed at some point soon. "I'm surprised to see a barber shop here, in the harbour area."

"I've been working here for over thirty years. My customers are seamen from all over the world. If you wish, you could have a hair cut right now!"

"No, thank you. I still have too much to do. Maybe later!"

After we had finished with all the formalities, I asked Luke. "Can you do me a favour?"

"Oh, damn, what is it this time?"

"I need you as a body-guard at the harbour barber. He looks as if he might cut his clients' throats."

Luke broke into crackling laughter. "That sounds interesting!"

So we went to the dusty salon in the cellar underneath one of the fish halls. The sole chair was occupied by a Chinese captain whose hair had already been reduced to a few millimetres length. Before he was allowed to go, he received a vigorous neck massage. I felt the urge to leave at once but, in front of Luke, I had to stay.

"And how would you like your hair cut?" the bearded barber asked when I finally sat down in the chair.

"A bit longer than my predecessor, please," but he was already upon me with flashing scissors and the next thing I knew was that I was nearly bald. He then poured some unidentifiable powder over my head, took out the sharp razor and put that to my neck. I froze in fright, but then realised with what ease this old gentleman practiced his craft. Eventually we started a conversation with him and learnt that he was a devoted Muslim who had been on a pilgrimage to Mecca twice. He also told us proudly that he had seven children and nineteen grandchildren. "My son also works as a barber and will soon take over my business here!"

We again noticed how many different religious groups coexist on Mauritius. Muslims, Hindus, Buddhists and Christians live peacefully side by side and, in some cases, there has even been intermarriage. This is why the inhabitants come in all shades of skin colour. With wars being waged between differing interests in other parts of the world, the peaceful co-existence on Mauritius is even more remarkable. We thought it might be because they live on a fairly small island. Similar to the situation on a ship, they are all in one boat and have to co-operate in order to survive. Other reasons for the peaceful co-existence are that each ethnic group has a say in the government and that the economy is quite stable, thanks to the three main industries of tourism, textiles and sugar.

Despite our bad experiences with criminals and the inefficiency of the authorities in Mauritius, we left with many good

memories of the likeable and good people we had met there. It was
with sadness in our hearts that we finally set sail.

Réunion to Africa

*Like all the oceans, the Indian Ocean seems never to end, and
ships that sail on it are small and slow. They have no speed, nor any
sense of urgency; they do not cross water, they live on it until the land
comes home. (Beryl Markham)*

Réunion

Slowly, the silhouette of Mauritius sank below the horizon. It was
a sad farewell, but I could only close my eyes and sail on. Europe
was still a long way off.

Luke and Sarah were in the highest of spirits. For Luke, the
final leg to his home in South Africa had begun, and Sarah was
enjoying an adventure which was just to her liking. In the south-
east trades, we covered the distance to Réunion quickly. Even
when we were still some 50 miles off, we could see the first lights
and, when dawn broke, we were close to the high mountains of the
island. Of volcanic origin, they reach up to more than 3000 metres.
With an area of 2500 square kilometres, Réunion is larger than
Mauritius, although it has less than half the population. Both islands
had first been visited by the Portuguese discoverer Pedro da
Mascarenas at the beginning of the 16th century. From 1642
onwards, the island was held by the French, who used it as a prison
for mutineers. Today, Réunion has the status of a French overseas

territory

We entered a different world. For the first time since leaving Singapore, we were able to use a marina which was purpose-built for pleasure yachts. The harbour master simply waved us away when we asked about the entrance formalities. "Just fill in this form and it will be all right." he said. "Because of your South African friend you would normally have to visit the immigration authority at the airport. But as you are only staying for a few days, it does not matter!" After the red-tape hassle of Mauritius, this was a welcome change. Mauritius is essentially Asian, while Réunion is European with a slight African influence.

Julia and her friend were already waiting for us with their car, and eager to drive us around the island. We stopped at a supermarket to buy some provisions for our picnic, and when we saw the wealth of different foods on the shelves, we could not believe our eyes; this was definitely Europe! However, in the end we just concentrated on the basics: cheese, wine and baguettes.

The drive up into the mountains was simply breathtaking. After incredibly steep serpentines, we reached the village of Cilaos. Réunion's central massif consists of three enormous, ancient volcano craters called Les Trois Cirques. Cilaos is located right inside one of the craters. Nature changed around us as we gained height. We had been driving through humid rain forests further down, and were now reaching alpine heights and pine trees. From Cilaos, we continued on foot through the mountains and ended up on a fantastic plateau, high above the surrounding world, where we sat down in the grass. We lay in the sun, enjoyed our picnic and talked.

Piton de la Fournaise

We also had to visit the only active volcano on the island, Piton de la Fournaise, 2500 metres high. During its last eruption, a whole village was buried. We were particularly impressed by the church, which stood like a sinking ship in the stream of lava.

The drive to the edge of the crater passed through a lunar landscape. Black and brown pebbles were strewn over the sides of the volcano and there was no sign of anything growing. From the centre of the crater, another volcano, which was the real peak, was rising towards the sky. To get there, one had to climb down into the crater, wander over a wide plain and then climb the central peak. This was a prospect that apparently held no appeal for Sarah "You march on" she said. "I shall climb the volcano in my imagination!"

As we crossed the plain, we wandered through a spectacular stony desert, full of frozen lava streams which often seemed like grotesque sculptures. The colour and the shape sometimes reminded us of a gigantic chocolate mousse, but the closer we came to the peak with its smoking furnaces, the more colourful the rock formations became – red, brown, black, bright red and yellow. Some lava rocks were so porous and light that they would have floated on water.

Finally, we reached the peak and were rewarded by the most fantastic view of the coast and the ocean. We stayed for a while, close to one of the stinking hot furnaces. It was weird to feel that, deep down underneath the earth, an enormous energy was slumbering which made us insignificant and minute in comparison. Although much larger, this volcano was, however, less dangerous than Krakatau which, due to its explosive character, sometimes spits out rocks.

The lady and the gendarme
The small marina was filled with cruising folk from all corners of the globe, some of whom we had already met in Mauritius, like the American couple who had circumnavigated on their yacht *Spellbinder*.

Another crew we dubbed 'The lady and the gendarme'. The lady was beautiful; Anne came from Paris where she was in advertising. The gendarme was her father, and had been a policeman on Réunion until his retirement. Anne had come from Paris to bring some order back into her father's life and to help him with the refit of his yacht *Askel Gwenn*. She also planned to sail with him for a while. Her near-perfect beauty next to the weathered, chain-smoking character of her father made a striking picture. In the tiny harbour bistro, we often sat together and exchanged stories. I would have taken Anne on board straight away, but Luke said "Her beauty and the storms off Africa would be our downfall!"

We were diverted from this discussion by the usual preparations for departure. We topped up our provisions, had our engine inspected and did various other jobs which we had so far successfully managed to postpone. The sea area south of Madagascar and off the South African coast is known to be very dangerous. We wanted to minimise the risk as far as possible with thorough preparation.

Chuck's Birthday

The trip to South Africa was long, but certainly not monotonous; during the 13-day passage we experienced calms, heavy weather and storm, shifting winds, wild seas and much more.

Sarah made an excellent offshore debut. Although she only brought little sailing experience with her, she quickly found her sea-legs, learnt incredibly fast, prepared wonderful meals and was always good-humoured. She fitted perfectly into our team, and I am not saying this just because we shared the forward cabin.

On our third day out we spotted a sail ahead. On the radio we found out that it was *Spellbinder* with Chuck and his wife on board. Chuck was in high spirits, as he was celebrating his birthday that day. Sarah, Luke and I decided give him a little surprise and started the engine to catch up in the light airs. They must have feared an attack when they saw us approaching with a white bow wave but instead of threatening cutlasses they only saw a basket containing some delicacies and a bottle of wine dangling from our boat-hook.

"Here's a small present for you, Chuck!" we called and also sang 'Happy Birthday' which sounded rather strange out there on the ocean. The swell made the delivery of the basket a delicate affair, but we managed it without actually running into *Spellbinder* . After this interlude, we both continued on under sail and the boats were soon separated again. Around evening, we heard Chuck on the radio. "Thank you so much, dear friends. Your present has certainly enhanced my birthday menu and now we are quite dizzy from the wonderful wine. Fair winds! See you soon in South Africa!"

An orgiastic chaos

On the evening of the fifth day out, our comfortable life was over. We were sailing down wind and failed to realise soon enough that the wind was increasing rapidly. When we finally reduced sail, reefing was very difficult in the heavy seas and near gale force winds. We continued on under a fully reefed main and the small number four working jib. During the night, vicious steep waves again and again threw our boat off her course.

These conditions revealed one of *Ryusei*'s weaknesses. She was designed for racing and speed rather than directional stability. She has a fairly short keel, cut away both forward and aft, and the rudder is close to the turning point of the boat. Going upwind, she steers perfectly, but downwind in heavy weather she is almost impossible to control. Under these downwind conditions the autopilot then failed and we had to steer by hand.

Twenty-four hours later we took down the main altogether, as the wind had reached 35 knots. Comparing the log with the distance really covered over the ground showed us that we were sailing against a current, which also explained the unusually steep seas.

The physical effort of steering manually heightened our appetites. As usual, we were taking turns at cooking but, although both Luke and Sarah were much better in the galley than I, they decided that 'in this lousy weather the captain has to cook dinner!'

"All right, but I will choose what we'll have", so I chose my speciality − pancakes. Sarah, sitting in the cockpit, eyed my preparations in the galley with interest while Luke was at the helm. The waves threw the boat about. The pancake mixture splashed back and forth, the pan slid around and the cook could only remain on station with considerable effort; when the pancakes were tossed, flying freely through the air, some of them ended up on the floorboards.

"This one will be disinfected by flaming" I decided and pulled out a bottle of rum. Just as I was pouring it out, a wave tipped us over and increased the dose dramatically with the end result that I nearly caused an explosion in the galley. However, after the first shock, the flamed pancake found great approval, and I was persuaded to continue with my fireworks in the galley.

For dinner, we had switched on the autopilot. It all went well until a particularly large wave came along and *Ryusei* broached heavily. The poled-out jib was forced aback and burst with a loud bang. Seconds later, only shreds were flapping angrily from the fore-stay. The force of the wind was by now quite terrifying. With difficulty, we took down the remains of the jib and continued under the tiny storm jib only. We then found that the autopilot was again defective, although we had just had it repaired in Mauritius, so we were again chained to the wheel.

The following day, we set the trysail for the very first time. A South African amateur radio operator, with whom we had already been in contact for some time, warned us that the weather would be deteriorating further. *Spellbinder* informed us on the radio that they had also lost a jib in the storm; it was comforting to know they were not far away. As expected, the wind increased to 40 knots and the seas were accordingly savage.

When Luke relieved me during the night, we looked at each

other and had the same thought. "Let's heave-to and wait until this sh★t weather passes!" I shouted at him and he nodded. We sheeted in the trysail, hauled the storm jib aback and lashed the rudder. We then fled below decks, closed all the hatches and disappeared into our bunks.

There is nothing nicer than crawling into a warm bunk, coming in wet and cold from the deck. Sarah comforted me and soon we had forgotten all about the orgiastic chaos outside. We were only startled once, when the ship's bell was flung loose and crashed onto the floor.

Red lights in South Africa

The gale was followed by a peaceful calm. We sighted our first whale, which was massive. We saw his huge body glisten in the sun as he blew, and the sight of this gigantic mammal filled us with awe. We would have liked to sail closer to him but the memories of Kevin, a singlehander whom we had met in Mauritius, were still fresh in our minds. He had been rammed by a whale, and the collision had carried away his rudder. It was only with a jury-rudder and a lot of luck that he managed to reach Mauritius.

When the wind came back, it blew from the south, instead of the east, as it would usually have done. As we were by now past the southern tip of Madagascar, we were able to lay a direct course for Durban. With the shout "Let's pop the dragon!" we hoisted our cruising chute. The red dragon on it seemed to give us wings and pull us along. Despite Luke's perfectly reasonable protest, I let the dragon stay up overnight.

"Ralph, I know the sea off South Africa better than you. There are sudden shifts in the wind here, and God help us if we are hit by a severe squall during the night!"

However, I did not change my mind. "The racing guys say that the chute will take up to 25 knots of wind. Also, we have a full moon, so that we can also take it down during the night if necessary."

Luke was of course right, although the squall only came during the second night. The wind shifted and blew at 30 knots from the north-east within minutes. As we were struggling to tame him and get him down, the dragon showed us his mighty strength, but luck was with us and we succeeded in the end.

I shall never forget the night before our land-fall in South Africa. Under a full moon and deeply reefed sails, we flew along towards our goal; steering was exhilarating and filled me with joy.

The sea was rough and we were sailing near full speed – it felt like riding a wild horse. The dancing reflections of the moon on the waves, the feeling of the lively boat and the knowledge that we would arrive in a few hours time put me in the highest of spirits. At five in the morning, the wind died down as suddenly as it had appeared. At the same moment, a hot breath of air passed over my face. An indescribable air, filled with the colours and scents of Africa.

On board the strange call "Land a-nose!" was heard, instead of the more conventional cry of "Land ahoy".

The night was followed by a hazy morning. Several hours passed before we could see the coast and finally the outer breakwater of Durban harbour. Luke was overjoyed and insisted on announcing our imminent arrival over the VHF. The harbour master brought him back down to earth with a jolt "*Ryusei, Ryusei*, this is Durban port control. You are not allowed to enter. A freighter is about to leave. Please remain outside until the lights on the pier-head change from red to green."

Here we were, back in the arms of civilisation. A traffic light at the entrance of our harbour! A red light was, for the moment, preventing us from entering South Africa, after we had made such a long passage to get there.

South Africa/Durban

Container cranes
The port of Durban is situated in an extensive natural lagoon.

Before going to the marina, we made a little detour. I wanted to see the container cranes because I had been involved in their construction 16 years previously. They stood on the pier like huge giraffes and as we passed underneath these monstrous structures we felt like dwarfs.

Not without pride I told my friends "I worked on the third crane from the left. Right at the top, 50 metres high, I helped to install the engine hut. The wind was whistling around our ears and the entire crane was swaying, but sometimes we even had to work without safety harnesses. I nearly wetted myself from fear. I also worked in the construction company which welded all the parts of the cranes together – that was in Johannesburg. Side by side I laboured with people from England, Boers, Blacks and Portuguese refugees from Angola and Mozambique. We toiled together but had to use separate toilets; there were toilets for white, black and coloured people. I disobeyed the regulations and went to the toilets for the Coloureds, because they were the cleanest. It was a hard time, but I preferred that to being drafted into the German army for national service and having to obey orders from crazy officers. Just like you, Luke, I preferred leaving my country to serving in the army."

I have always had this strong urge for freedom. After working in South Africa for a year, I travelled through much of Africa before returning home. It was a wild time. At the time, the country was run by president Vorster and Apartheid was a bitter reality. Nelson Mandela was locked away in prison, and the murder of the freedom fighter Biko and the riots in the black ghetto of Soweto frightened people. South Africa was under embargo and fuel had to be rationed. Many were afraid of what the future might bring. At that time I was still too young and naïve to decide upon a position in all this, but now I was curious to see how conditions were changing, shortly before the Blacks were due take over the helm.

It was good to see 'my' old cranes still functioning properly but I also had to note how few of them were actually being used. For ten cranes, there was only one ship alongside the pier for loading. In Singapore, things would have been entirely different. For ten cranes, ten ships would be lying here, with another ten waiting on the anchorage. The formerly booming economy of South Africa was apparently caught in a deep crisis.

South Africa is a land filled with contrasts; this applies to the population, as well as to the fauna and flora, the geography and the climate. It has deserts, grassland, woods, mountain ranges and a very long coast.

Many different ethnic groups live here, in this land which had been dominated by the white people from the beginnings of colonisation. The bushmen are the original inhabitants. Today, they are reduced to fringe minorities, just like the Aborigines in Australia or the Indians in America. South Africa is incredibly rich in natural reserves, which is a strong reason for the international interest in this land.

With the forthcoming elections in April 1994, the era of racial discrimination was coming to an end.

Luke piloted us through the harbour, the largest port of the continent, to the Point Yacht Club. Many helping hands appeared while we moored. Numerous yachts from all over the world were gathered here. On the pier stood Luke's father and our friend Gary, who greeted us with a "Welcome to Africa". Customs and immigration officials came on board and kept us there with the red tape for a while, before we could finally step ashore. Luke was overjoyed to be back home after all this time.

One of the paragraphs in the customs document which we found to be particularly amusing read as follows.

'The importation of books and films showing nude men and/or women or acts of sexual perversion is strictly prohibited. If such goods are in the possession of crew members or officers then they should be declared as ordinary sealable goods and they must be produced so that they can be placed under seal.'

The marina lay underneath palm trees at the edge of the town centre with its high apartment buildings. The hospitality in the Point Yacht Club was so superb that we soon felt entirely at home. Luke was a member of the club and he first led us to the showers, where we spent a long time. Afterwards, we celebrated our arrival in the club bar, where we could have spent the entire day, but Luke was getting impatient "Let's go to my old steak house. I've been dreaming of the 'Big Boys' – the famous steaks there – for over a year now!" As we were starving, we knocked back our beers and rushed off and into the restaurant like a hurricane. It was good to be back in South Africa!

The following morning, we heard a detonation which shook the entire district. Sirens were wailing and agitated people were running around. "That bang was a bit big for a firework" Luke said. We soon heard that it was an ill-fated bomb attack. The bomb had exploded on a city bus. Luckily, there had been only very few people on the bus at the time. The bomb had been carried by a black man who had been blown up with it. The official verdict was that he activated the bomb by accident.

A few days later we separated. Luke went back to his family in Johannesburg for the festive season and Sarah flew home to England. After all our shared adventures, this was a particularly difficult farewell. I remained on board to carry out the necessary repairs on *Ryusei*. In this, I had a lot of help from Gary, who was an expert with wooden boats. This was more than just welcome, in fact it was essential. On starting the refit, we had to face the fact that we had completely underestimated the amount of work needed. As soon as we attacked one problem, we found two more; this is often the way with old wooden boats.

Festivities

Originally, I had planned to spend Christmas and New Year with my family on Mauritius, but in view of the new work schedule on the boat and the short sailing season in the Cape region I cancelled this trip. *Ryusei* was transformed into a building site. Never before had I worked so hard in the festive season, but this is all part of the freedom of sailing.

I spent Christmas day with a few fellow yachties on Gary's boat *Manxman*. We decorated the boat and spent ages in the galley. The results, an enormous turkey with all the trimmings to go with it, more than justified the effort. This ended up as yet another unforgettable day.

As New Year's Eve drew closer, activities started in the yacht club. It was a tradition here that New Year is celebrated on the yachts in the middle of the harbour lagoon. I could not help thinking that many boats here actually only saw their owners on this special night. Leslie and Patrick from *Billfish* invited me on their boat. They had had a rough passage from Mauritius too. Patrick's rather heavyweight brother had sailed with them but he suffered from sea-sickness for the entire two and a half weeks. However, he had lost about 15 kilos in weight – an effective if unpleasant method of slimming.

The ship's horns sounded at midnight and the sky lit up with fireworks and flares. People were dancing, shouting, kissing and drinking heavily. It became apparent that the South Africans were great party people, and the riotous celebrations went on for many hours after midnight. It remains a mystery to this day how all the yachts with their merrily drunken crews managed to get back safely into the marina that night without sinking each other.

Both the last day of the old year and the first day of the new year were blessed with brilliant sunshine. However, I was also a bit melancholy, thinking that here, having reached the African continent, my episode in the Far East had definitely and irreversibly come to an end.

Idle Queen and Figaro V

One of the boats on the club's guest pier was a massive double-ended ketch from America, called *Idle Queen*. She was sailed single-handed by 'Old Harry', a small and wiry 80-year-old gentleman. He later earned himself an entry in the Guinness Book of Records for his solo circumnavigation at such an age.

"But why do you sail alone?" I asked him one day in the club bar.

"That's my fate" he replied. "Many years ago I sailed from America with my wife. On our way to the Bermudas she fell ill, and we returned to the States. There, they diagnosed a terminal illness, so we just sailed on together until she died. Since then, I have been on my own."

He then asked for my story. I finished by complaining how difficult it was to find a suitable female partner for this lifestyle. The old man replied "Ah, but for you that should be no problem. Just think about me, at my age! Moreover, I am looking for a rich woman who will also reef the sails in a gale."

In the end, I did not find myself a sailing companion, but a friend with her own boat. Her name was Melanie Jones, and we first met at the weekly yachtie barbecue. Originally she came from California and, after several years of traveling with her boyfriend, she ended up here in South Africa. They bought a house ashore together but afterwards, unfortunately, split up. Now they were engaged in an ongoing lawsuit over the house, which he had kept after their separation, and which she was hoping to win. She was also planning to sell the boat she was living on in order to get back home to California.

Her boat *Figaro V* was a classic racing yacht which she had bought at a modest price. A year of hard work, in which she completely renovated the boat herself, was now behind her, but she was no longer keen to actually go out sailing.

"It is funny" she said "but the older I get, the more I suffer from sea-sickness. Here in the harbour it's no problem, but once at sea, things are different!"

While the work was being done, *Ryusei* looked more like a

building site. I often escaped in my dinghy to visit Melanie on her boat in Bluff Harbour, which was at the other end of the lagoon.

She also had a cat which regularly went ashore. Just as we were settling down on deck, we heard her miaows from the nearby reeds. Normally, she jumped back on deck from the shore easily, but this time she must have slipped and fallen into the dirty harbour water. In a panic, the poor cat had paddled ashore, where Melanie now fetched her in the dinghy.

"The poor thing" she said as they both returned. "We'll have to wash her now!" With that, she dunked the creature into a bucket of water. She immediately pulled a long face and gasped "Damn! I completely forgot that the water in this bucket is full of bleach!"

The cat now stank of both harbour dirt and bleach. Melanie gave her a good scrubbing with clean water and neutralised some of the smell with some splashes of eau de Cologne. I now know why cats are so shy of water.

A man without shyness

After my arrival in South Africa, I declared half-jokingly that the time spent at sea with men was over for me. "From now on, I will only sail with women!"

This was greeted with much laughter, but my friends were confident of finding me some suitable beauties. Every time we passed it, we studied the pin-board in the yacht club. One day, Gary said "Hey Ralph, take a look! Wouldn't this be a nice shipmate for you?" He pointed to a hand-written sign saying 'French woman seeks position as crew to Madagascar.

"She's going in the wrong direction" I said, disappointed.

Then Luke spotted another advert. "Look at this big-mouthed fellow. He wants to sail to the Caribbean, but it sounds as if he was applying for a management position!"

I studied the very professionally made advert, complete with photograph, and declared "Wrong gender!"

The next day, while I was hanging around on the pier, I started talking to a beautiful looking sailing student from a boat belonging to the 'Ocean Sailing Academy'. They had just returned from a trip to Mozambique. "We have been away for two weeks" she said. "But for my certificate, I still need more sea-miles."

"Nothing could be easier" I replied. "In a few weeks we are sailing towards Cape Town and the Caribbean. You are welcome to join us!" She declined, as her university term was beginning again in a few days. "But I know a chap who would love to come along.

I'll tell him about this!"

He interrupted me at work the very next morning. "I've heard from a friend that you are sailing to the Caribbean. I'd love to come along!"

"We are really busy right now. Why don't we meet later on in the bar, and we can talk about it" said I, half hoping he might not turn up again.

How mistaken I was! Guy Hammond was the one with the professional advert which we had laughed at. Against all expectations, he fulfilled all the main criteria for our team. He had heaps of humour and was afraid neither of work nor of beer. After a stressful career, Guy had also planned a sabbatical year.

Greg kisses my green eyes

Fate often creeps up on tip-toes. As usual, I only noticed this much later on.

While searching for a suitable place to haul out *Ryusei*, I came across an impressive, big and beautiful boat. This was the schooner *Dwyn Wen*, originally built in 1908 of massive teak and around 35 metres long. I was amazed to see her here, as I had come to know her owner a couple of years before at the wedding of my brother in Mauritius. I immediately went alongside in my dinghy and a black man looked down at me from the railing.

"Are John and his family on board?" I asked.

"John will be back in a few moments, but his wife and kids flew back to Europe a few days ago."

I came on deck and met three crewmen from Mozambique and a girl. Her name was Michelle and she had the most beautiful green eyes I had ever seen. I was trying hard to flirt with her when a young, long-haired lad came sauntering up the pier, elegantly and effortlessly jumped on deck and kissed 'my' green eyes.

His name was Greg Friedrichs. In John's absence, he was responsible for the schooner and Michelle was his girlfriend. Then John came on board but he was in a great hurry, wanting to follow his family to Europe that same afternoon.

Normally, John, his wife Nanou and their three children live on board. They often charter out, but they also spend time undertaking more adventurous pastimes like archaeological diving and treasure-hunting. These interests had brought them into contact with my brother when they were in Mauritius.

After John had left, I got to know Greg better. He is a South african and lerned the trade of boat-building in America, and knew everything about wooden boats. I told him about the refit of my boat and my worries about the leaking planks. He consoled me "That is exactly my speciality. I could help you there, as we don't have much to do on *Dwyn Wen* at the moment."

Work hard, play hard

It was time to slip *Ryusei* out of the water to carry out the hull repairs. The yacht club had a trailer which was just about big enough for her. Because of her large draft, we could only slip her at spring tides. While she was being pulled ashore to the car-park by a tractor, a crowd of curious onlookers gathered round.

We faced a huge pile of jobs and time was pressing once again. However, when we resumed work in the New Year, at least the crew was complete.

Gary earned his money well and didn't waste a minute; he attacked the boat vigorously and opened up the rotting and leaking deck areas in no time. The most critical places were in the bow and at the stern. It was work which had not been carried out properly in Thailand – as with most jobs on the boat, they had only half done it. The work in Thailand had been so poor that the whole boat had to be re-painted and re-varnished again, only half a year later.

For the painting job I hired the attractive Gaynor. Together with her team of black workers she built a scaffold around the boat and started to sand her down. She was very efficient – I had not employed her for her beauty, as Greg suggested, but because of her professional reputation. 'When women are good at a job, they are not just good – they are simply unbeatable.'

When Old Harry came along and saw her at work, he whistled and said "My god, I wouldn't mind having my hull polished by her!" Gaynor was invincible in another field too – she was well known as "The South African Kick Boxing Queen". Nobody dared to provoke her and her male workers fully respected her authority.

Luke and I removed all the deck fittings in order to re-bed them with Sikaflex. We also installed a new autopilot. The old one had been repaired and was stowed away on board as a back-up. Another task high on the list of priorities was the replacement of the shrouds. As before in Singapore, the unusual way the shrouds were fastened gave us problems, and we just could not get them off the mast. In the end, we only exchanged the stays, leaving the shrouds until Cape Town.

Guy had taken over the varnishing of the deck and I had hired three black labourers to help him – Wilson, William and Robert.

In the meantime Greg examined the underwater sections, on the look-out for the leak which I had told him about. He looked inside and out, underneath the floor-boards and in every corner. At one point when he called me I was shocked to see that he had completely dismantled our toilet. In triumph, he pointed at the planks underneath and said "Here you are. This is the leak – these planks have opened up." Seeing my puzzled look, he laughed and said "You must have been so frightened in the last gale that you strained the mountings!" Thankfully, we then found a similar problem area on the starboard side, which demolished his thesis. Within a few days, Greg had spliced in thin strips of wood and re-caulked the planks.

We then had problems with our African workers. William was drunk early in the morning and refused to work. He kept saying "Gaynor wants to spray the hull today". "But they will not start before tonight" I kept replying. As I could not persuade him to get back to work, I let him go in the end. Then Robert arrived with a swollen lip and a bad eye, stinking of alcohol. After a drinking bout he had been involved in a fight during which his wages, which had just been paid to him the day before, were stolen. Against the advice of my friends I gave him another chance. Only Wilson proved to be a reliable and efficient worker. I paid him an extra bonus, kept him in our team as the only remaining Black worker and gave him a letter of reference after the work had been finished. His full name was Wilson Nkosinathi Ishentula. He was a Zulu.

We worked hard from dawn till dusk, but after our evening shower and a few beers our batteries were sufficiently recharged for some extended partying at night. We really did 'work hard, play hard'.

Dangers

During the refit, *Ryusei* was parked high and dry next to the Point Yacht Club. Inside, all was dismantled and chaos. During the day, my bed in the fore-cabin would inevitably fill up with tools and spare parts, and hundreds of other bits and pieces, so every night I had to make excavations and re-stow everything in order to reach my berth. One night there was a serious fight between some Blacks just underneath the boat so, to be on the safe side and to soothe my nerves, I took out the Very pistol and converted it into a shotgun, using the special adapter provided for this.

In the middle of the following night, a creepy noise woke me up. When I opened my eyes, I could see a shadow in the companionway. Still sleepy, I first thought it was a dream, but then the shadow started to move about in the saloon. Now wide awake, I grabbed the pistol and shouted "Who's there?" The shadow jumped and clambered hastily up the companionway, but I was also on my feet and rushed after him. The problem was that all the floor-boards had been removed so I stumbled along rather slowly. By the time I reached the cockpit, he was already four metres below on the ground. This could only be a thief, so I fired into the air and shouted "Next time, I'm going to kill you!"

The man shot away like a frightened rabbit, and then I saw more shadows disappear between the boats, so I thought twice about going after him. With my heart in my throat and thumping heavily, I went back below decks and closed all the hatches and the companionway, in spite of the humid heat. Later, I found that he had taken quite a few things, among them my laundry bag with most of my clothes; also the Hong Kong flag, my camera

Ryusei's *route around South Africa*

equipment, my deck-shoes and three bottles of whisky, reducing the rapidly dwindling stock of contraband even further.

The shot and the shouting had woken quite a few other yachties during the night and the episode was soon being discussed all along the pier. "Why didn't you kill the bastard?" was a comment which I heard more than once.

However, I was used to weapons for hunting, and the first and foremost rule – never under any circumstance point a gun at a fellow human being – was etched deep into my brain. I knew that I could have taken the law into my own hands here, and killed the thief, but for what? A short burst of satisfaction maybe, but his death on my conscience for evermore. With one shot I could have completely ruined a family which was, very probably, already pushed hard to survive.

The white South Africans saw things from a different angle: unemployment and criminality were rising at an alarming rate because of the uncertain future, and the police were not doing anything for fear of future repression under a black government. However, if criminality were allowed to flourish, the country would go under."

The serious situation in South Africa was again evident a few nights later. Machine-gun fire suddenly flared up somewhere in the town centre of Durban. Shocked, I again closed all hatches as if I was in a storm at sea, pulled my blanket over my ears and hoped that the sun would shine again tomorrow. I later heard that a group of Blacks had attacked a police-station, and that several people had been killed in the process. I came to the conclusion that life on land bears more dangers than the one at sea.

In the club bar, I met a sympathetic gentleman who was, as it turned out, responsible for the club's newsletter. He wanted to know all about the burglary on my boat, and also where I was ultimately heading. I pointed through the window to my boat and said "Can you see the flag underneath the South African courtesy flag?"

"Yes" he said. "That is the code flag for the letter M."

"Quite, but it is also the St Andrew's Cross, the flag of Scotland which is where we are heading." I then told him of my bonds with Arran and the bottle of whisky which was hopefully still waiting there.

The next issue of the newsletter had two headlines, 'Thieves in industrial area' and 'A long way for a whisky'.

Dr Thomas

In January, my friend Thomas Lingenfelser arrived from Germany. I had tried to postpone his arrival by two weeks, because of our refit, but he could not change his schedule. "As a doctor, I can't change my holidays as I wish. Never mind, as soon as I arrive the work will go ahead twice as fast and we will soon be able to set sail for Cape Town!"

But he came, saw − and was ill. The long journey and the considerable pressures in his job had apparently been too much, even for a hardened medicine-man. He spent the first two days in bed, but then attacked the work on board with breathtaking energy. Not always with the desired result, as certain things could not be speeded up, such as the periods in which the varnish had to dry. Rain showers also interrupted our work from time to time.

When she was finally launched again, *Ryusei* gleamed and shone as new. Gaynor had done a superb job on her topsides, but we were still far from ready. The wooden parts on deck needed seven layers of varnish, and we also needed time to refit the deck hardware and the pushpit and pulpit. It was not until the end of January that the boat was more or less ready again. Guy's father had visited us regularly and helped where he could, and I now had the feeling that he would have loved to sail with us. In high spirits, we sat down in the warm evening sun enjoying a barbecue and celebrating the end of the refit.

Wild coast

The coast of South Africa is notoriously dangerous. The contrast of the continental and ocean climates create unstable weather patterns. Depressions often move in along the coast between the Cape of Good Hope and Mozambique. These alone would not be a problem, but combined with the Aghulas current, which runs along the coast towards the Cape can result in dramatic situations. The depressions create strong to gale force winds from the south-west, and the current then runs against them. Especially on the edge of the continental shelf, where the current runs at up to four knots, this creates enormous seas. They can reach a height of 25 metres and can be catastrophic even for large freighters.

Anyone who is caught out by a depression on the way to Cape Town can run for the shallower water near the coast, where the seas are smaller as the current is weaker and, sometimes, even reversed. There are no problems with this tactic where the continental shelf is wide enough. Along the Transkai, this is not the case – this part of the coast is especially dangerous and is justifiably known as the 'Wild Coast'.

Planning a passage from Durban to Cape Town one should depart as soon as one depression has passed overhead and the wind swings round from south-west to north-east. Even so it is difficult to determine the right weather window, as the next possible harbour of refuge south of Durban is more than 200 miles away.

We were now preparing our departure under much pressure, as a suitable weather window seemed to be approaching. We bought stores and provisioned the ship, but had not reckoned with the usual obstacles. The electrician had problems connecting the new autopilot and the clearance formalities mutated into a never-ending nightmare. We had to travel to and fro across the town to satisfy every authority. First, the harbour master had to see our passage plan. The we went to the tax office to pay the harbour dues. The immigration authority held a special surprise for us – we had to go there twice, as they insisted on the entire crew being present in person. This took so much time that, as we arrived, the customs office closed for the day literally in front of our noses. We had to postpone our departure for a day and finally, to cap it all, return to the harbour master to prove to him that we had been through all these formalities.

Just before sailing, we had another look at the forecast. A small low was forming, but nobody could say if it would radically influence the weather. Gary, who knew the coast well, told me "Better wait here, this coast is so unpredictable. Don't forget how far it is to the next harbour. Besides, it is Friday today. Everyone knows that sailing on a Friday spells bad luck!"

Brusquely, I answered "This Friday business is pure superstition, and the weather might not be so bad, after all. I have no intention of going through all this red tape again and Thomas has come to specially South Africa to sail to Cape Town. If we don't leave now, he will never sail out of Durban. We'll just have to chance it!"

The current and the fair wind made for fast sailing. I was happy to be back at sea at last, but Guy and Thomas less so, as they suffered from sea-sickness. During the night the wind died, so that we motored a bit.

Just before dawn, Guy woke me up. "Look at that sky! Those dark clouds ahead are a weather front. As soon as they pass overhead, the wind will blow from the south-west and we'll be in hell!"

"Don't be so pessimistic" I replied. "The low which was forecast was very small. Let's wait and see." I settled down on deck with him.

The band of clouds then obscured the moon and was soon over us. We just had time to reef before the wind abruptly swung from north-east to south-west. We changed tack towards the coast to reach shallower water, as advised. The wind piped up in no time at all and transformed the calm sea to a boiling hell. Very quickly, short, steep waves were breaking all around us. We took in the sheets and tacked along the coast, but even here, we were thrown about like a toy ship.

Guy and, even more so, Thomas were now seriously sea-sick. As no tablet would stay in their stomachs long enough, we had to revert to other methods. Luckily, our doctor was well prepared. We were sitting in the cockpit, secured by safety harnesses, when Thomas handed Guy a suppository. Guy stared in shock at the huge thing in his hands, as he thought this was another pill to swallow. With unmistakable gestures, Thomas showed how it was to be used. We cringed with laughter and even forgot our grim situation for a moment.

On and on we struggled, beating into the wind, hoping that the weather would soon change again. The green, uninhabited coast indicated that we had reached the Transkai. Every time we went out into deep water, the seas became steeper and broke across our decks. On the radio, I spoke to Alistair, who is in daily radio contact from his farm near Durban with all yachties along the coast. Asking him for a forecast, he replied "I'm sorry, but I can't say how long this low will last. Just keep close to the coast – good luck!"

As time went on, we lost our nerve and thought about turning back but were still hesitant to do so. Then, nature decided for us. The wind screamed even stronger through the rigging. The anemometer now showed more than 45 knots. We had to bear off and try to reef the roller genoa further. The seas were now so incredibly huge that every manoeuvre required full concentration and all our energy reserves. Guy and Thomas were still drowsy from their medication, though they at least had the advantage of being more zonked than frightened.

Despite all our efforts, we could not roll in the genoa further. "Something's wrong, the furler is jammed!" I shouted.

Guy took the helm while I crawled to the fore-deck. What I saw filled me with horror. The new fore-stay had slipped from the brand-new Norseman terminal and was now dangling, wrapped up in the half-furled genoa. The fore-stay was held loosely in place by the few remaining strands which had not slipped out of the terminal and the mast was only being held up by the cutter-stay. "Guy, bear off down wind, quick, or we'll lose the mast!" I shouted as loud as I could and fought my way back to the cockpit. "We can't reef the genoa further, we'll have to try and take it down. Thomas, help me with the sheets!"

In all the confusion, the sheet blocked on the winch as I was paying it out. The sail now flapped around wildly, like a half-filled balloon, which made both the ship and the rig shake with the brutal force of it all. I pulled the large knife from its place in the companionway and once again made my way forward, where I managed to cut the sheets. The free sail now blew out ahead and thundered in the wind. Despite the risk of losing the mast we rounded the boat up into the wind under the engine in an attempt to take down the madly flapping sail. As he tried to come to my aid on the fore-deck, Thomas got knocked on the head and sank back into the cockpit. Thanks to a huge wave breaking into the cockpit and over him, he regained his senses quickly, but even the two of us could not tame the huge sail. Then, Guy switched on the autopilot and came to help us. I stood in the pulpit and tore down the mighty, flapping sail with all my strength, while Thomas and Guy lay on deck, trying to pin down the billowing cloth. Every second or so we were showered by breaking waves and I was thrown up and down as if in a crazy elevator – one moment hanging in the air as the bows fell down into a trough beneath my feet, the next instant up to my waist in swirling water. Guy and Thomas were frequently completely submerged but fortunately the water temperature was bearable. In the end, we somehow managed to take the genoa down. Trembling with excitement and exhaustion, we shoved the sail below deck, yanked on the storm-jib and set the spinnaker halyard up as a temporary fore-stay. During all this, there was no time for fear.

Early in the morning, two days out of Durban, we returned to the Yacht Club there. Completely exhausted, we fell into our bunks and slept until someone outside shouted "Welcome back!"

Our return was duly celebrated. Greg, Luke, Mike, Frederic, Anne from the boat *Aisa* and Melanie, as well as the crew of another yacht which had been forced to turn back, all joined us. As we told our story of the 'Wild Coast' Gary said "You should have believed me. Never sail on a Friday! Especially so, when the weather situation is iffy!"

He was right. It had been my fault. I had left the harbour under a lot of time pressure and thereby risked our lives.

The 'small' low had in fact developed into the most severe storm of the season. We were slightly consoled by the fact that we were not the first to have turned back. An American yacht attempting to sail south returned twice to Durban, the second time without its mast.

We ignored all self-made mistakes and blamed it all on the date. I vowed there and then never to sail again on a Friday.

An inseparable pair

One thing was clear: Weather and ship both had to be right before we could continue. The specialist who had supplied our new stays, Steve Maddins, came and carefully examined the damage. We could not understand why a Norseman terminal had failed. The answer was finally found in a short note in the handbook of our Furlex roller gear. In our system, the fore-stay rotates when the sail is furled. Later furlers have a fixed fore-stay, where only the profile rotates around the stay. The crucial thing, however, was that our furler needed a stay whose wire strands ran clockwise. Without knowing this, we had used the only stay available, with strands which were wound anti-clockwise. When furling the sail, the strands had been partly unwound and thus slipped out of the terminal. We were incredibly lucky not to have lost the mast.

Gary, who was on his second circumnavigation, promptly noted "I have told you time and time again that you need a new furler, for example a Profurl, for your boat. Don't try to save money on the standing rigging; any failure there could lose you the mast which would be far more expensive in the end!"

After this experience, I needed no further encouragement. Although Steve was the best rigger around, he knew neither my ancient furling gear nor the system in which the shrouds were attached to the mast. The shrouds were anchored inside the massive aluminium profile. In Durban harbour there were about 500 sailing yachts – none of them had a system which was even remotely similar and, when I tried to take the shrouds off the mast, I was just as unsuccessful as I had been in Singapore.

It was not until much later that I found out that this was an old English way of attaching the shrouds. It is usually very easy to undo, as long as it is not corroded – which in our case, of course, it was.

"The mast has to come out" Steve said, during a crisis meeting. He then added "Don't worry. I've lowered more than 300 masts and I will also cope with yours! I'll order the mobile crane for tomorrow."

The next day we brought *Ryusei* alongside the pier, where the crane was waiting. We had already disconnected all antenna cables and all electrical wiring, and now Steve climbed the mast and fastened a thick rope around the spar, which was then hooked into the crane's cable. We then undid all shrouds and stays and Steve gave the sign to the crane to start lifting. Gary, Greg, Guy, Steve and I stood around on deck and waited. The crane pulled, and nothing happened. After a while, we could feel that the entire boat was being lifted out of the water. "Stop!" Steve shouted and the boat settled back in the water. We went below and examined the mast step, which was on a huge piece of timber. Steve explained to us "The mast has a protruding piece of aluminium at the foot, which is inside the timber. But the wood may have expanded in the damp, and the whole set-up is probably corroded too. Sometimes the mast can be freed if we shake it. If not, we'll hammer wedges between the mast and the timber."

We started to work on the mast-step. We shook and hammered, but nothing budged. After a while, we tried the crane again, and again the boat was lifted up. Timber and mast made dreadful, groaning noises, and I was nearly sick with anxiety. Steve was also suffering. In a grave voice, he asked us to stay clear of the mast.

"Why?" I asked innocently.

"I was once badly injured" he explained. "When the mast comes loose suddenly under the strain of the crane, it can shoot up like a rocket. Once, I was too near and was hit between the legs. I lost one of my balls!"

We stared at him, shocked beyond speech. With a weak smile, he added "It's not as bad as you fellows think. I can still do it; my wife is now pregnant for the third time! But please be careful, anyway."

Our enthusiasm was somewhat stifled by this piece of information. As all our efforts to free the mast remained fruitless, we let the crane pull one last time. Again, the boat groaned. "Enough!" I shouted. "The mast stays in!"

The others agreed. "Mast and boat are an inseparable pair. Otherwise, we would already have lost the mast off the Wild Coast" we reckoned. All this was on a Friday, so it was no wonder that we began to grow superstitious.

The snake

After another crisis meeting we decided to change the system which attached the shrouds to the mast. We wanted to use wires with hooked terminals at the top end. To fit them, we had to drill holes for the plates where the hooks would slide into the mast. Guy and I organised a few old wooden boards, which we used to build a working platform which was then hoisted up into the mast using the halyards. We then sat on this wobbly platform and began drilling and filing the holes. For days on end we were kept busy with this work, and the glaring sun did not help. One brilliant Saturday noon, as most people were enjoying their well-earned siesta, Guy suddenly stopped working and came up with a suggestion. "How about if we went off for a trip to the mountains?" he asked.

"What do you mean?"

What he meant was – drop the tools, pack the cool-box, buy some steaks and charcoal and head off to spend the weekend in a mountain cabin belonging to some relatives of his. No sooner said than done. An hour later, we headed off with Gary, whom we had torn from his midday slumber, into the mountains.

We were going to the Karkloof Mountains near Pietermaritzburg. After an adventurous drive along rough tracks we arrived at a straw-thatched cottage. The place was phenomenal. The air was filled with the scent of the pine trees and meadows. In stark contrast to the hot and humid climate in Durban, the air was cool and fresh. From the hut, we enjoyed a grandiose view over the African scenery, with mountains, valleys and a wide plain under the soft glow of the setting sun. Soon the fire was alight and there was a delicious smell of grilled steaks and sweet corn.

The following morning, we wandered over a high plain. In some of the valleys were lakes, their crystal clear water glittering in the sun. We could have finished our journey in this wonderful place.

It very nearly did come to an end – as we were passing through a forest, we were hunted by a swarm of aggressive horse flies. Wearing only shorts, we raced on and tried to escape from them. Guy was first, but he suddenly gave a sharp cry and jumped high into the air. Gary stopped dead in his tracks and I, following, bumped into him. In the middle of the path, one of the most poisonous snakes of Africa was basking in the sun. In the rush, Guy had not seen it and his last-minute jump probably saved his life. I had almost shoved Gary right onto it, so the sleeping snake went into attack mode like lightning. We retreated carefully and then chased it back into the bushes with long sticks.

We spent two nights in this glorious place which was called Mbona. As souvenirs, I picked a few exotic flowers which afterwards decorated our saloon.

Departure

Guy and I worked for several more days up in the mast to change the shrouds. The story of the wilful mast and the brave labourers on the swinging platform was one of the hottest topics in the club bar.

Dr Thomas had returned home soon after our ill-fated trip. His view that yachties were on a never-ending holiday had been completely shattered but, in spite all hardships, he would have loved to stay on if only his job had allowed him to.

For the trip to Cape Town, Greg would replace him. "For six months now, *Dwyn Wen* has been lying in harbour. I'm longing to go sailing again!" With Greg, I recruited a very experienced sailor and someone who knew the coast to Cape Town intimately.

Just before we sailed, he introduced me to a young Danish girl whom he had met at a party. Her name was Vibeke. She was an adventurous student of architecture and after some work experience in South Africa she now wanted to sail a bit, so I interviewed her. Gary later summed up what had happened during the interview. "First, Ralph asked her if she could sail. She said no. Then he asked if she had ever been on a boat before, and she said, yes, once. On this, Ralph demanded if she was prone to sea-sickness, and she replied, no, not that she knew of. He then looked the poor girl up and down and probably realised that someone as athletic as her was fit enough to pull the sheets." My final verdict, according to Gary, had been "With us, one does not have to be a sailor. More important are humour and an appetite for adventure."

Then Paula, Guy's sister, came and saw us for lunch in the yacht club. She was a stunning beauty and worked as a model in her spare time. The old sea-dogs in the club nearly popped their eyes, and we asked Guy "How on earth can such an ugly chap like you have such a beautiful sister?" I also suggested "Why don't you stay at home and we sail with her, instead?"

Guy laughed as he replied "Sorry to shatter your dreams, boys! Paula is already spoken for and none of you guys would stand a chance against 'Mr Beachcomber' of Durban!" But for us, the story was not so easily forgotten. Whenever Guy made the slightest mistake in the days to come, we would groan and say "If we only had brought Paula along!"

A window in the weather gave the signal for departure. This time, we would not miss the chance, and most cruising boats were already underway for Cape Town. The boat was ready, the crew complete, and there was nothing to stop us now. Only one thing – it was Friday. So we had to wait until after midnight before we finally sailed. Despite the late hour, our friends and Guy's family came to wish us farewell. Gary and the crew of another boat promised to follow as soon as possible.

I was sad about saying good-bye to Melanie, who had become a good friend. "Sailing has brought us together, and sailing tears us apart now" I lamented "but the earth is round and one day we will meet again."

We stayed in contact, writing many letters until she sailed with a Swan 57 from Borneo in November, 1994. The boat, *Aphandra*, and her four-man crew then vanished without trace.

Cape of Storms

Be like me and drink to the sea, but don't untie your boat! (from a song by Lin and Larry Pardy)

Bartholomeus Diaz

As we sailed along the Wild Coast, the wind was 30–35 knots until it died down over the last few miles to East London, but the forecast again spoke of a small depression with more winds from the south-west. However, the skipper of a South African cruising catamaran which we had encountered in the harbour entrance to East London assured us over the radio that it would still be possible to sail the next 170 miles as far as Port Elizabeth. We had never spent such a short time in harbour before. We went ashore, had a shower, wolfed down a big meal and sailed on only two hours later.

The new team with Greg, Guy and Vibeke was working out well. Greg and Guy were both experienced sailors familiar with the gales along this coast, and Vibeke, after initial sea-sickness which we cured with Dr Thomas' magic medicine, was very enthusiastic. The new autopilot never really came into its own, as everyone wanted to steer the boat – especially Vibeke who was learning fast and keen to helm. Moreover, she showed great talents in the galley and pampered us with Danish delicacies. Greg was a good cook, too, although he had problems with the volume of food he produced – his first rice dinner lasted us a good two days. "On *Dwyn Wen*, I always have to cook for at least ten" he explained.

As I had secretly feared, the weather punished us before we reached Port Elizabeth. At six in the morning we had strong headwinds, rain and fog. It was as gloomy as the end of the world. To find shelter from the worst of the breaking seas, we again went inshore but had to use the radar because of the appalling visibility. We still had about 50 miles to go – upwind.

"What an idiot I am" I confessed as we discussed our situation. "Here I am, making the same mistake again!"

Greg was more encouraging "Don't worry. As long as the wind doesn't increase too much, we'll soon reach Algoa Bay which will give us a bit of shelter, and Port Elizabeth lies at the southern end of the bay."

Then, the grey curtain of fog lifted and revealed a view of the coast. Beaches and dunes stretched on as far as we could see. A single rock on the beach dominated the landscape and seemed familiar to me. I then remembered "What a coincidence! Look at the rocky hill – it is the exact spot where the Portuguese discoverer Bartholomeus Diaz marked the turning point of his voyage in 1488 with a cross." With the binoculars, we could indeed see the cross on the rock.

The crew were impressed. "How did you know about that?" they asked. "Many years ago" I answered, "I once stayed at the foot of that rock to celebrate my 20th birthday. I was looking for solitude on the deserted beach but, as I climbed the rock, I met a group of South Africans. They somehow got wind of my birthday and it all turned into a beach party when they joined me in the evening and brought a case of wine along as well!"

For the remainder of that day, we beat upwind and were glad to reach Port Elizabeth just before dusk. Again, we enjoyed the South African hospitality in the local yacht club. We were allowed to shower free of charge and were then invited to a welcome drink in the club bar, which we repaid by telling them about our adventures.

Knysna

'If you want to stay put, just talk about the weather' people would say, not without reason.

Although the forecast was bad, we were able to set sail again the following evening. As we left Algoa Bay in the dusk, a humpback whale surfaced next to us, blowing out his fountain. Clearly, we were now leaving the warmer climate. It was getting colder and shorts and T-shirts just wouldn't do anymore, especially at night. The cooler water was rich in plankton, which lit up the sea with phosphorescence throughout the night.

With the current and wind behind us, we soon reached our next destination. As we approached the rugged rocky shore it reminded me of the Breton coast – the only difference was the high mountain range rising in the background.

"Somewhere around here must be the entrance to the Knysna lagoon" I said, but we could not see anything even with the binoculars and again checked and verified our position on the chart. It was only when we were already dangerously close to the shore that we finally spotted a small gap in the rocks. This was it, but without our GPS I am sure that we would have missed it. Fortunately we had arrived at just the right time – around slack water. When the tide sets in and starts to flow, the entrance becomes untenable – according to the pilot, the seas would then be breaking on the bar.

We contacted the local radio station in Knysna and asked for assistance. The answer was "Stay where you are. In ten minutes I will be near the rocks and pilot you in from there by radio." A little bit later, the helpful soul was on the radio again, acknowledging that he could see us. He then gave his instructions "Take down the sails and approach the entrance using the motor.

Stay as close as possible to the side with the sheer cliff. Don't be fooled by the look of the other side of the passage. It looks safer, but it is full of shoals over there, and don't be afraid of the breakers. It is probably a good idea to close all hatches and the companionway and stay in the cockpit!"

These last words and the wreck of a shattered sailing yacht on the rocks made us distinctly nervous.

While I helmed, Greg stayed in contact with our pilot. As we passed through the narrow gap, with cliffs towering about 200 metres above us, I had a very uneasy feeling. The thunder of the surf was echoed back and forth by the high rock faces and the waves held us in their angry grip, but there was no turning back now. Suddenly, or so it seemed, we were in a different world, floating peacefully on completely calm water. Who would have thought that such a romantic place lay hidden behind the rugged rocks? The lagoon was vast and surrounded by wooded mountains. As we anchored in front of the yacht club, we had already made our decision to stay for a few days.

Lily Maid

On the same anchorage we found the yacht *Lily Maid*; she was an old wooden sloop whose crew we had already met in Durban –the Irish boat-builder Mike Jerret and his family. The Jerret clan were much in evidence in whichever harbour their boat lay and the red-faced chief of the clan had at least as much character as his boat. Mike and his wife lived on board with their three children, the youngest of whom was just two at the time. Then there was Mike's son by his first wife and his girlfriend and a lively little dog called Poppy.

The Knysna Yacht Club was built on poles out over the water, surrounded by a beautiful woodland. The club was transformed into our living-room, which we shared with Mike and his wild family. We spent many entertaining hours with them. Mike's stories were fantastic – he talked enthusiastically about the various boats he had sailed or renovated and about his voyages in the Indian Ocean. He was particularly fond of Madagascar.

"If I only had enough boat-building projects there, I would settle down on that island" he said. He was also fond of the native women, and told us "On my son's fifteenth birthday, I organised a local girl for him. She spent some time with him and afterwards he knew everything about the facts of life!" he said, roaring with laughter.

He then told his tales of smugglers.

"Every time we sailed from South Africa to Madagascar, we had the boat filled to the gunwales with goods that were either expensive or impossible to get in Madagascar. It wasn't really smuggling —often we bribed the customs people and we were able import the goods officially. On one of these trips, we had a boatload of Champagne on board. Bang in the middle of the Mozambique channel, we were hit by a severe gale which caused us a lot of trouble. Luckily for us, the 80-year-old ship survived, but the cargo was having problems with the heat and the violent motion – suddenly, corks were popping all around us. Of course, we couldn't let the champagne go to waste, so we spent the rest of that trip completely pissed!"

Mike, who was also called 'Short Fuse' because of his explosive temperament, was an old salt in the finest tradition, and his adventures could fill many books. Like us, he was bound for the Caribbean, where he was going to give the 1905-built yacht *Iolaire*, which belonged to his friend Donald Street, a complete refit in Venezuela.

Relaxing times

Knysna is one of the prettiest places in South Africa. We spent a really relaxing holiday there —reading a lot, hiking through the beautiful landscape and amusing ourselves wherever we could. Thanks to Guy and his brother Peter, who was living there with his family, we also met some of the local people. Peter's wife owned a restaurant, where we hungry seafarers were often treated to a great meal. Peter was a carpenter and, considering the extensive woodland around Knysna, we thought that he had chosen the right profession.

Apart from tourism and the timber industry, the region was also living off oyster farming. One oyster farm was right next to our anchorage, so it was a good place to try them. I have never been an enthusiast for oysters but with a lot of lemon and, more importantly, white wine I eventually got used to them.

We also made an excursion to Jubilee Valley, a former centre for gold mining. Although the mining had stopped centuries ago, we could still see traces of it. On the sides of the mountains, the entrances to the mines had been hewn into the rocks. Full of curiosity, we crawled into one of these gaping holes but did not venture too far, as we only had a single lighter for illumination. In the damp mouldering darkness of the old mine, we could feel the hardships that the miners must have endured on their search for gold. South Africa has the richest reserves of gold world-wide, but the miners of today have to go as deep as 4000 metres to find the expensive metal.

When we returned to the yacht club in the afternoon, we were overjoyed. Our *Manxman*, whom we had nearly given up on, had finally arrived. We immediately visited him on board. Knocking on the hull, we were greeted with grunts from below, then his head emerged from the companionway. He yawned and showered us with foul words. We laughed, as we were by now used to this.

"Gary, we thought that you were going to catch us up, and now you are four days late!" we teased him.

"You just can't imagine what it was like outside. I had two days in thick fog, in constant fear of being run down, and then I had to wait for hours on end in front of the lagoon for slack water. I am totally exhausted!" he replied and yawned again.

We could imagine how he felt. At least there were four of us on board, but Gary preferred to sail alone – he was not prepared to 'mess about with some idiot' as he had once put it. To my mind, singlehanders are strange people. They want to be completely free in their decisions so they sail alone even though they are risk their lives in so doing. Gary once told me that despite all the drawbacks, this was the way he liked it best. I countered by asking "And what do you do if, just by chance, a freighter is heading straight for you and no-one is on watch?" but he just shrugged his shoulders and said "Ralph, sailing alone can't really be described in words. You'll just have to try it one day."

An ancient steam train, which rumbled past every day, had attracted our attention ever since our arrival in Knysna. On the morning after our reunion with Gary, we wanted to take this train from Knysna to George. The only problem was that we could not get ashore, as Gary had gone home late in the night with our dinghy, and it now lay peacefully behind *Manxman* anchored a few hundred metres away. It was impossible to wake Gary over that distance – neither shouting nor the radio had any effect on his sound sleep.

"Why don't we just swim across and fetch the dinghy?" Vibeke suggested.

"Are you mad? The water is far too cold and, besides, we would have to swim against the ebb tide."

But Vibeke stayed firm. "With the flippers, it should be no

problem" she said confidently.

As I did not want to look like a coward in her eyes, I put on my flippers too and jumped in behind her. While she had slipped elegantly into the water, I gave a sharp cry of surprise as the icy cold water closed in around me. Vibeke then swam on ahead with strong strokes, leaving me to struggle on behind. "How can this girl swim like that?" I thought, frustrated, as I had always regarded myself as a good swimmer. After about three hundred metres, I had trouble breathing. Vibeke noticed this, turned back to me and suggested that I should return to the boat. Again, I did not want to admit to my weakness and carried on. Gary was making fun of me as I struggled up his boarding ladder with my last ounce of energy.

"Vibeke, where on earth did you learn to swim like that?" I gasped.

"Oh, I belonged to the Danish national swimming team for many years!" she said. From then on we called her Vibeke the Viking.

The train nearly left without us, but we just made it. Hissing, the old steam engine came to life and crept forward with the whole train rattling and squeaking. The windows were wide open and the black smoke drifted through the compartments. As the train gathered speed, we were able to enjoy the clean, fresh morning air. The trip over the mountains, through valleys and along the coast was a sensational experience. Once in a while, black clouds of smoke would burst from the engine as the chap in front shovelled more coal onto the fire. On the small station in George we had a lavish meal before returning by the same route. On the way back we drifted off to sleep from time to time – the long night before and the early morning exercise were taking their toll.

A few days later, after a farewell barbecue organised by Peter, we sailed on with *Manxman*, leaving the beautiful lagoon behind. For various reasons we were late and by the time we reached the narrow entrance and the bar, the tide had already started to ebb and the waves were starting to break over the bar. The tide was flowing too fast for us to turn back, so I gave full throttle ahead. "Hold on!" I shouted as a mountain of water rose in front of our bows. *Ryusei* was lifted high into the air and came through the breaking crest. We then hung in mid-air for a split second before crashing down into the following trough. My knuckles turned white on the helm and my eyes were glued to the echo-sounder.

A second before, it had shown ten metres of water beneath our keel, now it was reading only two metres. It was an incredibly close shave, and *Manxman* experienced the same treatment. After we had both reached deep water, Gary's trembling voice came over the radio "My god, that was close! I really thought it was the end. It was even worse than the infamous 'Hole in the wall' in Australia!"

The Capes

Good sailing conditions soon put our hair-raising departure behind us. New adventures lay ahead – we were going to round the southern tip of Africa on our way to Cape Town. Bartholomeus Diaz had named this cape the 'Cape of Storms' 500 years ago. Had it not been changed to 'Cape of Good Hope' ships might have avoided the cape, and the trade with the Far East might never have flourished as it did.

Anyway, we carried on with 'good hope' and reached Cape Agulhas (34°53'S/20°00'E), the rather unspectacular cape which is actually the southernmost point of Africa. For us the highlight came 70 miles further on, as we sailed past the Cape of Good Hope at three in the morning under a full moon. The sea was rough, it was very cold and the wind was blowing up to 35 knots. Despite the protests of my friends, I relished the loud accompaniment of Wagner's opera 'The Flying Dutchman' from the speakers below.

According to the ancient tale, an arrogant and blasphemous captain had once dared to round a stormy cape in unfavourable winds. As a punishment, he was condemned to beat against the winds for all eternity. It is bad luck for any sailor who catches sight of the flying Dutchman, and only the love of a woman can free him of his curse. As we sailed along, we had strong winds and rough seas, but we could hardly be regarded as blasphemous. We rounded the cape at speed without seeing the infamous ghost ship.

The Cape was good to us. As soon as we were past, the wind moderated and the sunrise behind the mountains of the Cape was indescribably beautiful. A thin haze was drifting over the sea. The change in colour and drop in water temperature showed us that we had now reached the Atlantic Ocean. The grandiose Table Mountain then came into view.

Cape Town

Sailing into the wide sheltered bay of Cape Town we could easily understand why this place at the boundary of two oceans has been so strategically important. Cape Town is easily the most beautiful city in South Africa and, after venturing ashore, we felt the international and cosmopolitan atmosphere which stems from the varied ethnicities of her inhabitants.

The Dutch founded a supply station here in 1652 to improve living conditions for the seafarers. In those times, more people died at sea from malnourishment than from storms or shipwreck or even wars. Later, Germans and Huguenots followed. The latter were the ones who laid the foundations for the wine industry. In 1806, the British conquered the Cape and pressurised the Dutch settlers. When slavery was abolished in 1833, an open conflict flared between the Dutch settlers, called Boers, and the British. The Boers left the Cape province in great convoys, and settled in other areas. The British followed, as they wanted to control the entire country. They waged a brutal war against the Boers, while both groups also fought against the Black tribes whose land they were taking. Conflicts of power and race determine life in South Africa to this day. Apart from the Whites of various nationalities, there are Blacks, Asians and all colours in between. Up to the time of our arrival the country had been governed by a White dictatorship, but this was about to change.

While we were in Cape Town, we witnessed a historical moment in South Africa. President De Klerk had introduced equality of rights for all races and announced new elections. There was no doubt at all that the black majority would win the elections and form the next government. In spite of all the injustices of the past, the average population in South Africa seemed to be much better off than that in most other countries of Black Africa.

Of course, the situation was neither easy nor straightforward. Anyone who feels that the Whites should leave South Africa must also agree that they should leave America and Australia. South Africans, of whatever skin colour, are very down to earth and stubborn, and are always prepared to fight for their land. It was clear to everybody that the new president would have to be a very resolute personality, accepted by all sides, if he was going to lead this country into a safe and better future. Nelson Mandela, the most obvious candidate for presidency, would carry a huge responsibility.

Three hours are enough!

We immediately sensed on our arrival in Cape Town that life ticked differently here. Sailing boats were free to move about as they wished and, in contrast to Durban, we were hindered by neither the authorities nor traffic lights on the pier. The sympathetic customs man, Fritz, whose formalities took place in the bar of the yacht club, was typical.

We quickly felt at home in the Royal Cape Yacht Club, where we attributed the distinction 'Royal' mainly to the excellent showers. We were in good company with the crews of other boats such as *Aisa, Lily Maid* and of course *Manxman*, but the separation from Greg and Vibeke did hurt – they both had to return to Durban.

Guy and I were faced with the problem of who to take on board for the Atlantic crossing, but Greg appeared to have too much on his plate with his two girlfriends, Vibeke and Michelle. The solution came sooner than we expected – a fax from Greg in Durban read 'It felt good to be back – for about 3 hours! I don't think I can stay. The past month on *Ryusei* has been great and if it is possible I would really like to carry on and sail with you across the Atlantic.'

I immediately faxed back "Dear Greg ... *Ryusei* wouldn't mind, Guy wouldn't mind, I wouldn't mind, but maybe all the virgins on the other side of the Atlantic would mind if you sailed with us ° Jump on the next steam train to Cape Town and let us know when you arrive."

After all our adventures together we were a good team and now, once again, we had 'Three men in a Boat'.

The wine excursion

In Cape Town we met Guy's father. He had come for a meeting of the South African Lifeboat Association, of which he was a board member. He gave us valuable tips regarding the best wine producers, as I wanted to fill up our by now empty bilges with wine bottles, 'To make sure that my South African crew get proper nourishment.'

One sunny morning, we took off in a minibus with a local driver. First, we visited the well known wineries of 'Klein Constantia' and 'Buitenverwachting'. As one's critical taste vanishes after the first few glasses, I did not hesitate but bought the entire stock for our voyage there. Already quite merry, we were then driven to the wine centre at Stellenbosch. Our stomachs were growling by now and so Guy, Kevin and I went off to find some solid food in the supermarket.

"Where are the others?" we asked the driver on our return.

"They went off to have few beers somewhere" he answered.

We soon found them in a beer garden. Their first beer had long been followed by more and Mike, Guy's friend, was already flirting heavily with the waitress.

"Have you completely forgotten that we are supposed to be on a wine tour?" we complained.

"Bah, who cares about wine. A real Manxman only drinks beer!" Gary bellowed back. Our trip then continued with us singing in the van. En route, cheese, sausages and bread gave the necessary foundation for the tasting at the next, and the next, and the next vineyard. I have forgotten how many we visited in the end. When we finally set a course for home, the shadows were already growing long. At some point, someone suggested "Isn't there a good place somewhere to watch the sunset?"

"Of course!" the driver said in good humour. He appeared to be enjoying the drive with such a merry and crazy crowd of tourists. He took us to Bloubergstrand. From there, we had a fantastic view of Table Mountain and the setting sun.

"Youth is drunkenness without alcohol" is what some wise guy once said, but this did not hold true for us. Several beers later, the sun had vanished below the horizon and we could go home at last. We were dropped off with our cases of wine in front of the club. As we staggered past the bar, we saw Greg and Guy's father standing there, claiming to be worried about our late return. They had drunk a few whiskies and now insisted that we should join them for one last glass.

"I just can't!" I said, but the will was, once more, too weak°

Racing in fog

The Royal Cape Yacht Club organised a race every Wednesday evening. This was usually followed by a party, which motivated us to sign up. The enthusiasm for racing was great around here – never before had I seen so many yachts leave the harbour in such a short span of time. It was like rush-hour in a major city. Just as we were reaching the starting line, the gun boomed and off went the fleet. The sun was low and drenched Table Mountain in a soft glow, while a warm wind was helping us along. We had covered about three quarters of the course when a fog bank rolled in. One moment we were sailing along in clear visibility, the next moment everything was wiped out and we could just about make out the blurred silhouette of the sun and one yacht sailing along very close to us. The cold and damp hit us like a wet towel in the face. On the radio we heard that the race had been abandoned and that we should return to the harbour as quickly as possible. Without radar, we would not have found our way back. Many other boats did in fact lose their way and had to anchor outside in the bay, while we were celebrating in the club.

That same evening, the largest yacht in the harbour had a cocktail party with a buffet on board, and the owner was imprudent enough to invite us along with the words "And bring all your friends!" Of course, the poor chap had no way of knowing who my friends were. Like pirates we boarded the elegant yacht, together with the large and lively family from *Lily Maid*. The dressed-up guests on board looked us up and down as if we were some weird creatures from outer space, but we were just hungry and thirsty yachties without too many scruples. Quickly and effectively, we mowed a clearing through the buffet and drank gallons of champagne. I could not help feeling that the owner soon regretted having invited us.

The Classic Boat Festival

Upon our arrival in Cape Town, we were informed about the forthcoming Classic Boat Festival with the words 'If you participate, you can moor free in the yacht club.' Free – the magic word, and so we signed up to participate in the festival, which would take place over two weekends.

Thankfully, the first part took place without me. Guy and Greg, and Dave from *Lily Maid*, sailed *Ryusei* in the first race for classic yachts and all went well until they approached the berth that had been allocated to them by the organisers. Just before reaching it, they ran aground, so *Ryusei* was stuck there until the incoming tide lifted her off again. In the meantime, the crews of the other yachts had quickly slaughtered the barbecue ashore and my friends were left without anything.

The second weekend culminated in the highlight of the event, when all classic yachts were moored along the waterfront in the heart of Cape Town's tourist quarter. Bars, restaurants and shops lined the quayside and we were lying in the middle of it all, with *Lily Maid* alongside us.

One American yacht was particularly interesting – *Seraffyn* with Lin and Larry Pardy. They entered the harbour basin with

Larry sculling their boat along with a long oar from the stern. We asked them what was wrong with their engine and they answered "We have no engine and no trouble. An engine would just take up too much space on board!" We then heard that they had built their beautiful boat themselves and had been cruising around the globe for many years. We remembered their entry in the guest book of the Knysna Yacht Club and were deeply impressed by the fact that they had made that entrance under sail alone.

Time for departure was drawing near. Our reputation demanded it. Even back in Durban our group had behaved so boisterously that after a while there were a number of pubs where we were no longer welcome. Moreover, many other yachts were preparing for an Atlantic crossing. The reason behind this was the uncertainty of what the future might hold for South Africa. Many South Africans, who had long dreamt about a long ocean voyage, now found the time fit for departure, and the phenomenon was duly called the 'Mandela Regatta'. "We have locked him away in prison for more than 30 years. Whatever will happen when he seizes power?" was the question uppermost in everybody's mind. Many young people, too, went abroad. They embarked on what was dubbed the 'LSD Trip' – look, see and decide.

The red tide
During the last race, we noticed that the sea had a tint of red in it. There is, unfortunately, a lot of garbage floating around in the bay of Cape Town, so at first I thought that this was some kind of pollution. But on the following day, a headline 'The red tide' in the local paper attracted our attention. In the article, it said that a warm stream of water had come through the colder water of the Cape province, which is rich in plankton. When the sea warms up, even by only a few degrees, the plankton die and the water is tinted red. At the same time, the oxygen content of the water is reduced, with the dramatic effect that not only the plankton, but many other marine species die as well. This phenomenon is usually limited to only a few patches along the coast and happens every few years.

This time around, the entire coast right up to Namibia was affected. As this region is rich in fish, a natural catastrophe of unprecedented dimensions was the result. Millions of dead fish were swept ashore and the fishermen of the entire region were suddenly out of work. For my South African friends, this was the worst 'red tide' they had ever witnessed.

Love at last sight

It seemed a strange coincidence that we always managed to get our boat ready for sea on a Friday. We discussed this important problem hotly, but could not decide whether the superstition regarding the Friday was foolish or not. On this occasion, the answer was made easy for us, as we were invited to a party by Guy's friends. We decided to leave after the party.

At exactly midnight, we cast off. Apart from the regular crew, consisting of Greg, Guy and myself, we had two guests on board. Guy's friends, Lauren and Mike, wanted to come along with us to the next harbour, which was sixty miles north of Cape Town in Saldana Bay. This trip turned out to be anything but pleasant. We had to motor as there was no wind and, because of the red tide, there was an awful stench of foul fish in the air. We spent the last night in a newly built marina, which was part of a modern holiday development in the Mediterranean style. We were sad to say farewell.

Greg was leaving his home country without knowing when or if he would ever return. For me, things were different. It had only been in South Africa that I had finally managed to distance myself from Asia. I felt free again and had experienced some of the happiest moments of my life here. For Guy, the farewell was even more dramatic. In the weeks prior to our departure, he had fallen in love with Lauren. They had already known each other for a long time, but only now did they realise that they loved each other. This was a clear case of 'love at last sight'. There were many tears and it appeared that they had sworn eternal faithfulness to each other, regardless of how long our voyage would be.

Namibia

Dolphins and diamonds

The red flood had really taken its toll. The foul smell of dead fish was with us for nearly all the 400 miles to Lüderitz. The sea was as flat as a mirror and there was not a breath of wind. Now and again we saw seals drifting along on the surface.

At night we were fascinated by the millions of bright stars and the phosphorescence of the water. In our wake we drew a long trail of greenish glitter, dancing stars, and from time to time we saw explosions of luminescence. These were caused by schools of little fish suddenly speeding away from *Ryusei*'s approaching hull. One day, we came past a patch of water which seemed to boil. We had a look with the binoculars and saw dolphins. Instantly, we changed course towards them and were surrounded by an incredible number of these fascinating animals. Never before had we seen so many dolphins in one place – they seemed to be going crazy, jumping high out of the water and performing acrobatic loops in mid-air. We stopped the engine and jumped overboard in our diving gear. Dozens of dolphins shot towards us at a frightening speed, only to turn away sharply just before actually hitting us. We were reminded that here we were visitors in an alien world, a world of which we could only catch the slightest fleeting glimpse.

Off the mouth of the River Oranje, which marks the border between South Africa and Namibia, we saw large ships with massive superstructures. These were diamond mining ships of the De Beers Mining Company and reminded us of the rich natural treasures in this region. South Africa and Namibia have the largest reserves of diamonds on earth. We passed one of these floating factories at close quarters – the booming noise of the mining equipment filled the air and some of the workers gathered along the rails to watch us and wave to us as we passed. We thought that many of them would probably have loved to swap ships.

Lüderitz

Namibia has 1.5 million inhabitants over an area which is one-and-a-half times as big as France and is thus among the most sparsely populated countries in Africa. The former German colony of Deutsch Südwestafrika was effectively controlled by South

Africa until their independence in 1990. Today, Black tribes, Whites and Coloureds share the land with each other. However, most of Namibia is desert or bush, and only around one percent can be used agriculturally.

Namibia was not new to us. My shipmates had served part of their military service here – Greg in the harbour town of Walvis Bay which was controlled by South Africa, and Guy at the furthest end of the Caprivi Strip in the far north-east of the country. I had been here before, too.

At last, we could make sail again and move on in blessed silence, without the noise of the engine. The coast was entirely made up of sand dunes, which stretched to either horizon as far as the eye could see. This was the Namib, a desert which extends as far as Angola.

When a few scattered houses appeared in this otherwise desolate area, we knew that we were approaching Lüderitz. The small harbour lies in a sheltered bay, and once it was the diamonds which helped to build the town. Today, it is the fishing industry. We beat into the bay and anchored; shortly afterwards we were being welcomed by local sailors in the bar of the yacht club. As we later walked around the town, we felt that time had come to a standstill here. The German heritage was apparent everywhere. I was surprised to see German street names and German shops. In a bakery, a black gentleman kindly greeted us in perfect German and asked how he could help us. I explained that we needed fresh bread for a long voyage across the Atlantic and, as I spoke, an elderly lady came up to us and said "It has become very quiet here in recent years. Three generations of my family have lived here, but all the young people are moving away now, so the two of us have to run the shop on our own, although we should have retired by now." We learned that most people speak German there, and even the church sermons are in German.

We then visited another shop which specialised in smoked fish and meat. Again, we were engaged in conversation by the owner, who also was of German descent. "Everybody thought that with independence and equality for all races, this country would go under. Far from the truth! We now live in peace and harmony and the economy, after some initial hiccups, is doing well. We invested when many other whites packed their cases and left, and today we are better off than ever before."

Down by the shore, we found an abandoned ship yard. The slipway and the old building shed were still intact and we could see that they used to build traditional fishing boats there. Greg, our boat-builder, immediately gave us an interesting lecture about traditional ship building and he became so enthusiastic that we suggested that he should stay. "You build the boats, and Guy and I will start up a brewery!" But Greg replied "Knowing us, we'd be the best customers for your brewery and you would then go bankrupt. I think we should sail on."

In the fishing harbour we met the harbour master. A Spanish freighter was lying alongside, taking on a load of frozen fish, and we asked him about the state of the fishing industry. "This coast rates among the best fishing grounds in the world. Most of the catch is exported to Spain. But fishing is very poor, as the area has been over-fished for so long. Take, for example, the lobster. In just one year, the catch went down from 15,000 to a bare 500 tons!"

Sand, sun and solitude

Fully provisioned, we left Lüderitz at the crack of dawn. Fifty miles further, we anchored in a wide bay called Hottentot Bay. We wanted to spend our last day on the African continent in solitude there.

A desolate landscape of sand dunes, rocks and pebbles surrounded us. We landed ashore with the dinghy although, strictly speaking, this was forbidden. The southern part of the Namib desert, including Hottentot Bay, are part of the diamond zone and thus a prohibited area. Rumour has it that, around here, diamonds would be lying about on the beach. Full of expectations, we took a sample of the rough quartz sand. Ruins and a derelict wharf, with cormorants nesting on it, indicated that diamonds had been prospected here not so very long ago. Close to the beach was a small rusty Nissen hut with a sign over it saying 'Pinguin Mining Company'. Possibly, these were the sad remains of a project in which investors had lost a fortune.

We panicked when we wanted to return and saw our dinghy drift away. A slightly larger than usual wave must have lifted it off the beach. Without thinking twice, I dashed down the dune, tearing my clothes off as I ran, and jumped into the icy cold water. By the time I had finally caught up with the dinghy, I was so weakened by the cold that I could hardly pull myself on board.

Later we realised just how lucky we had been. Lacking a detailed chart, we had anchored well out from the beach. In a water temperature of only 12 degrees Celsius, none of us would have reached the boat swimming. Even if we had made it, it would have been quite impossible to get on board from the water without the bathing ladder. There was no driftwood along the shore or any other material to build a raft, and without fresh water we would not have survived the walk to Lüderitz. Once again, we had been very lucky indeed.

In Lüderitz, we had heard that the bottom here would be crawling with lobsters. I was a bit sceptical about this, similar things having been said about the Chagos archipelago; there, we only saw one single lobster in two weeks, even though we dived every day.

With the dinghy, we found a promising spot close to a rocky bit of shore and slid into the water with our snorkelling gear. The cold shock was indescribable; our clothes, which we donned for lack of wetsuits, seemed to offer no protection whatsoever. In these temperatures, everything had to be done very fast. I swallowed my fear and dived down. The water was clear but visibility was initially impeded by sea grass. When I finally saw the rocks at the bottom, I could not believe my eyes. Everything was covered in small lobsters. After only about five minutes, we had filled our inflatable with 20 small lobsters. We couldn't have stayed in the water a second longer so, shivering with cold, we made our way back to *Ryusei*.

We were defrosted by the magical atmosphere of the evening. The sea was as flat as a mirror, the sky was clear and the setting sun created the most amazing shadows in the sea of dunes ashore. At the same time, the full moon climbed higher and higher above the Namib desert. These intense moments were accompanied by our booty of lobsters and an excellent white wine from the Cape region. We could not have had a more fitting farewell to Africa, and the last impression we had of this continent is summarised in the three words sand, sun and solitude.

Water desert
There was a fresh breeze from the south-west, and dolphins and an albatross escorted us out to sea. The sand desert sank below the horizon aft and we were now entering an even larger desert, the Atlantic Ocean.

Even on the first day, we recorded slight but notable changes. Within a few hours the water temperature had risen from 12 degrees Celsius inshore to 20 degrees out here at sea. We were getting back into the tracks of the 'bare-foot routes' –zones with Trade winds and kind temperatures. Once again, we could sail barefoot and in T-shirts. We quickly fell back into our routine. Being on watch, sleeping, reading and eating were our main activities. The sails were adjusted only occasionally and the rest was the task of the autopilot. "Doesn't this get boring after a while?" is something I am often asked ashore. Not at all is all I can say. There are a multitude of small tasks which make this routine, marked by the ever-returning sun and moon-sets, anything but monotonous.

On one of my early morning watches, I was preparing a cup of tea in the galley when a sudden squall hit us. At the time, we were sailing along under reefed main and our old cruising chute. *Ryusei* heeled over so far that the chute touched the water, and seconds later we only had a few torn shreds flapping from the halyard. The peace of the early hour was gone and my friends were wide awake.

"This is nothing compared to what I once experienced on *Dwyn Wen*" Greg said at breakfast time. "We were sailing in the Channel of Mozambique once when we were surprised by a storm. Despite our strong crew of six, we could not reef or take down the huge gaff sails. We ended up surfing down the waves with this huge 35-metre schooner. It took two of us on the helm to hold her, and the massive, long boom of the mainsail kept hitting the water. We thought we were going to lose the rigging, and when I called the three deck-hands from Mozambique on deck to help us, I found them below, praying. They thought I had come to tell them that we were sinking, but on that occasion we made it and came through without a major catastrophe."

The day we crossed the Greenwich meridian we celebrated with Mauritian rum, freshly squeezed orange juice and an apple strudel, made from some of the apples that Guy's girlfriend had gives us as a farewell present. These 'apples of seduction', as we called them, featured high on our daily menu. Some days later, Easter Sunday again gave us a good reason for a lavish feast, during which we were further entertained by the antics of a few dolphins. From time to time, the outside world caught up with us when we heard the news bulletins on the BBC. Sad and anxious, we heard about the troubles in South Africa.

Instead of boredom, we were struck by yearning – a strange longing for the new land or the lover with whom one would share this adventure. We had more than enough time to reflect upon the past, present and future. Our feeling for time completely vanished, and so we were actually surprised when one night we sighted the lights of land looming ahead. These were the lights of the island of

St Helena, located in the middle of the ocean desert as far away from the rest of the world as was Lüderitz in the middle of its sand desert.

St Helena

Escape from St Helena

Without exact methods of navigation, this island would be as hard to find as the proverbial needle in a haystack. Even so, the Portuguese came across it in the year 1502. The island has been under British sovereignty since 1659. Just like Réunion and Mauritius, St Helena is of volcanic origin.

In the diffuse light of early morning, the rugged coastline had something definitely hostile about it. We rounded the northern tip of the island and anchored off the capital, Jamestown. This place is relatively unspectacular and lies in a wide valley surrounded by bare hills. Reaching our destination filled us with a deep sense of achievement. As the sun rose higher, we sat on deck and soaked up the impressions of our new environment. Apart from us, about ten other cruising yachts were anchored there. Then, all of a sudden, hectic activities ashore disturbed the peace of this morning. "What are they doing at this time of the day?" Greg asked. "Is that our welcome committee?"

Using the binoculars, we could see uniformed men, apparently looking for something along the shore. Another group launched the rescue boat and raced off with it in a westerly direction. "How odd, they're fully armed!" said Guy, who had the binoculars at the time.

Soon afterwards, a customs man came aboard and we heard about the reason for this commotion. "A prisoner has escaped" he told us. "Hopefully it is not Napoleon" we joked, but the official was not in the mood to appreciate our sense of humour. We went through the usual formalities and then had to surrender all our diving gear. "We have a large number of wrecks along our coast" he explained. "And we just like to make sure that our visitors do not embark on any treasure-hunting expeditions." Before he left, he asked us to lock our boat carefully when we went ashore. "The prisoner is probably still on the island!"

We did as he asked and used a ferry service to take us ashore for a very modest fee. Despite the escape, Jamestown had an extremely laid back and sleepy atmosphere. It turned out to be a pretty little village in the British old colonial style. As we sauntered along the main street, we passed the fort of the governor, the botanical garden, the main square with the church and the market hall. We were especially interested in the prison, which was a small building adjacent to the church. Only a small sign saying 'Prison' made it clear that it was not the chapel.

As the evening approached, we settled down in an outdoor café near the botanical garden. This was the meeting place for seafarers. Here, we could eat well, drink and chat. Guest books showed us how many and which yachts had passed by over the last decades. The proprietress, Anne, was also known as the 'Mother of Yachties'. She very kindly fussed over us and helped with the laundry. It was a good place for catching up with the latest news, as the officials were among her regular guests. We asked them about the prisoner, and they filled us in.

"Because of him, the entire island has been turned upside down today. A South African who arrived here in a small yellow boat tried to steal a seventy-foot yacht which was also anchored here. For this, he was locked away for three months. Upon his release, he sailed away last night. At the same time, the only other prisoner vanished. His disappearance was discovered this morning and it appears that the South African has taken him on board. We chased after them with the rescue boat but, when we reached the yacht, they were already outside our territorial waters. Despite the threat of using violence, there was no stopping the yacht. The South African denied having anybody else on board with him and continued on his course under sail and power. He is so big and strong that nobody dared to board the yacht. He once belonged to a South African elite regiment which was specially trained to fight terrorism. The other one is a Dutchman who was convicted of drug trafficking and who should be serving another six years in jail. He was the captain of the rusty old fishing vessel which is still out there on the anchorage." Anne added "I think it's disgraceful. The prisoners really have no cause for complaint or escape – after all, they are allowed out into a restricted area of Jamestown each day and also to use the local library!"

The escape was a sensation. There had never been an escape from St Helena before, not even by the most famous prisoner of all, Napoleon.

Close to Anne's place is a commemorative plate for Joshua Slocum, who was here in 1898. In his diary, he wrote "When I visited St Helena, the court officials gave the governor a pair of white gloves as a present, as there had been no criminal case for the court to deal with for the entire year." After the latest turn of events, the white gloves definitely seemed to be a thing of the past.

We were taken back on board late in the evening by the merry ferryman, whom we found in the White Horse pub.

Island tour

For our tour of the island, we and a few fellow yachties hired an antique open bus. The road from Jamestown winds up into the

Tourist bus on St Helena

mountains and the bus only just coped with the ascent – it was swaying from side to side like a ship without sails at sea. My hair stood on end as the driver scraped alongside a deep abyss. Knowing that his passengers were stiff with fear, he turned around laughing and said "Don't worry, my father and my grandfather used to drive this bus – it has been coming up here since 1929 and knows the way by itself!"

The views en route were superb and on reaching the summit of the mountain we found we were in a completely different world. In contrast to the dry, leeward side of the island near Jamestown, this part was covered in lush green vegetation and the air was cool and fresh.

One of the most impressive places was Longwood, where Napoleon spent his last years of exile (1815 to 1821). We visited his house, which now is a museum, and noted how small this otherwise great man must have been, judging by the size of the bathtub and the bed. A pretty garden surrounded the house and we all agreed that he was very fortunate to end his life here, instead of being beheaded by a hostile court. Allegedly he died of a stomach ulcer, aged 52, but there are also those who say that he was poisoned. We also had a look at his original grave, which lies at a beautiful vantage point.

Standing there, one could not help but think about him – he was one of the statesmen who, in his hunger for power, had thrown the whole of Europe into war and misery. Today, his deeds are glorified, and his body was moved from St Helena to Paris where it now lies in a marble tomb under a huge golden vault. For St Helena this is no great loss – the island is far too small for his black soul.

These thoughts were soon forgotten as we carried on with our tour. Isolated farms reminded us that this island, with its 5000 inhabitants, is only sparsely populated. In stark contrast to South Africa, the population has freely intermarried and is now thoroughly mixed, though with the three main influences of Black, White and Asian still evident. They now live off fishing and agriculture. In former times they also grew hemp for making sacks and ropes, but that came to an end when cheaper substitutes were found. The distant location and the fact that there is no airport on St Helena has so far saved the island from a tourist invasion with all its inherent disadvantages, so we were able to enjoy a rich variety of unspoilt landscapes including steep bare mountain rocks and fertile highland plains.

The treasure hunt

St Helena is surrounded by crystal-clear water. We could not the resist the opportunity to join some locals on a diving excursion, and even our high expectations were not disappointed. The sea was full of tropical fish which were hunted by the locals with a kind of spear, the so-called 'Hawaiian Sling'.

Afterwards, they generously gave us some of their fish, so in the evening we set up a barbecue on the pebbly beach close to the anchorage, collecting driftwood and building a fire-place with the large round stones off the beach. We were sitting around the fire with the fish sizzling away on the grill when we were startled by a loud bang.

"What on earth was that?" I called but, before we could find an answer, there were more explosions and little chips of stone were flying past our ears. It was only then that we realised that the stones around the fire were bursting like grenades. Perhaps they contained water which, when heated up, burst the stones open. Anyway, we seemed to loose our appetites.

Word got around the yachties that a wreck was lying very close to the anchorage. We immediately donned our snorkelling gear and went on a treasure-hunt. It wasn't easy, because we were not allowed to use our diving equipment and had to take very deep breaths instead. Greg was able to stay under water for the longest time and promptly found a bottle of rum at a depth of around ten metres. In triumph, we boasted about our successful treasure hunt and invited a few neighbours along for the rum tasting. In high anticipation we drew the slightly mouldy cork from the bottle, which bore the promising name of 'Gaelic Old Smuggler' and poured a small measure into a glass. "Your health" we toasted as Greg took the first sip. "Bah, that's not rum, it's salt water!" he exclaimed. In the end, we had to go for another treasure hunt underneath *Ryusei*'s floor-boards – that proved to be much more successful.

Mango

One of the most unusual boats in St Helena at the time was the yacht *Mango*. Strictly speaking, she was not really a yacht but a converted steel fishing boat. An extraordinary and very humorous couple resided on this heavyweight of a ship, which was equipped with all the latest electronic gadgets. They were Ed from Britain and Roswita from Spain who had, like so many others, left South Africa. They were now bound for Spain and were travelling in comfort and style. In the former refrigeration room Ed, who was a talented pianist, had installed his piano. The wheel-house had been transformed into a huge multipurpose room – apart from the ship's controls and electronics this housed the kitchen, the bar and – best of all – a huge double bed which was surrounded by windows. Ed assured us that for most of the time they were driving their ship from the bed.

Anyway, lying down seemed to be one of Ed's favourite pastimes. Although the boats were rolling in the swell on the rather exposed anchorage, he rigged up his hammock and climbed in. However, this peaceful image did not last long – the hammock got into such a violent motion through the rolling of the ship that it eventually crashed onto the deck, with Ed landing painfully on his backside. Highly amused, Roswita delighted in telling everyone how she had to tend to his aching bum.

Another evening, we invited them on board for supper. After the meal, we put on Spanish music in their honour, and they jumped up to perform a fiery piece of Flamenco dancing. In the restricted space of our cockpit, glasses and plates went crashing to the floor and we all enjoyed the sudden, passionate burst of life on board. Olé!

Fire

One morning, a tiny yacht with blue sails arrived at the anchorage. We soon recognised the boat of our friend Anthony Stuart from Durban. Anthony's departure from South Africa had been accompanied by quite a wide media coverage. He was going to try and sail non-stop around the world, westbound, in the smallest boat. Something was obviously wrong, and as he came nearer it looked as if there had been a fire on board.

Later, we met him at Anne's place. We immediately knew that we had been right – he was covered in burns and had already been to the island hospital, where they treated the wounds and shaved off his burnt hair. Seldom before had I met someone as downcast as Anthony was on St Helena. All our efforts to cheer him up failed, and even Anne could not help – she already knew him from his first circumnavigation in an open boat.

After a while, Anthony told us what had happened. "Coming from Africa, I was heading directly for Brazil. The accident happened about 500 miles south of St Helena. The sky had been overcast for days and the solar panels were not delivering enough energy to send off my daily radio call, so I started the petrol generator. Stupidly, I had not topped up the tank, so it stopped after a while. The sea was rough and, while I was refilling the tank, I must have spilt some petrol. I then made the fatal mistake of restarting the generator while it was still hot. There were huge flames and before I could control the fire all my electronics had been burnt. I suppose I am lucky to be here at all, but my record attempt and voyage are now ruined. I suppose life goes on, and that's the main thing, isn't it?"

One of his main sponsors was a big insurance company. At least they could demonstrate their services in a practical way. We later heard that they were arranging to ship the boat back to South Africa on a freighter.

Normally, St Helena is more than just quiet, but this changes dramatically at the weekends, and we dived into the local nightlife with the natives. Dancing and flirting were the main activities and we had plenty of experience, especially in the latter. The result was that the voyage nearly ended there for me too. Not, as in Anthony's case, because of a fire on board, but more because of a fire in the heart. On this desolate island, I met the second Lisa of my life. She helped to heal the wounds that I still carried around with me from the first Lisa, my great love of Singapore. Both Lisas had black hair and an aesthetic figure fit for a model. While the black hair of my Singapore Lisa had been short and straight, my island Lisa had a more European look with long, black curls. We fell for each other and the nights never ended. She also gave me a much more intimate perspective of this remarkable island. Her parents had a small hotel in a place called Little Scotland. This was up in the 'highlands' amidst truly romantic scenery. I very nearly stayed there.

However, Scotland was my destination. So what was driving me on? The thirst for freedom, the lure of adventure or just the buried bottle of whisky?

The milk run
The route from South Africa to Latin America is called the 'milk run' because of the easy and reliable trade winds. Allegedly, all we had to do was to set the sails, switch on the autopilot and wait until we arrived at our destination.

Naturally, reality proved otherwise. For three days we drifted in such light airs that the sails flapped about listlessly and the sun burnt down on us without mercy. In an attempt to create more shade, we rigged bedclothes over the cockpit, but the heat still affected us and we became nervous and quarrelsome – even minor incidents were enough to let tempers flare. During this period, we all retreated into what private space we could find but, despite all this, we sternly kept our traditional round of sundowners going, gathering in the cockpit for a glass of whisky or wine at sunset. Conversation drifted around our voyage, nature and the problems of life in general. We also listened to music and discussed whichever books we were reading at the time. After that, harmony was always restored.

On the third day out, a Friday, we noticed a large amount of water in the bilge. Before we pumped it out, I tasted it and found my suspicions confirmed. Thanks to a defective valve, the entire contents of our main fresh water tank had found its way into the bilges. Fortunately, we had a second tank with about 150 litres of water plus two canisters with 40 litres between them on deck. I suppose we could have survived without water, as we had so many bottles of wine under the floor-boards.

At last the trade wind set in again and it delighted us for the rest of the passage with a constant 10 to 12 knot breeze from the south-east. We now had heaps of time and more or less continuously listened to music. The repertoire on board was large; we had pop, classical, jazz and folk music of every description with us but, as we were heading for South America and the Caribbean, Latin American music and reggae dominated our on board 'charts'. We also chose our literature appropriately – James Mitchener, for example, and none of his books had fewer than 1000 pages. We found him especially good at describing different countries and presenting their history in an entertaining and easy-to-read manner. Moreover, his novels had the spice which I suppose no seafarer wants to miss – romance. Thus, we read all his books about South Africa, the Caribbean and Mexico, and also one about Hippie times called, appropriately for us, 'The Drifters', in which he had written 'every human being should, at least once in his life, realise his dream.' It was still not clear whether this voyage would fulfil whatever I had originally dreamt of, but we had certainly achieved a lot so far. Another book had been given to me by my father – Homer's 'Odyssey'. The hero of this book took ten years for his voyage home. He had to overcome many obstacles and temptations on his travels, even though he only sailed in the Mediterranean and not, like us, on the world's true oceans. "Why should my voyage only take one year, if he took so long?" is what I started to ask myself at the time.

Originally, I had intended to visit relatives in Argentina en route but, as time was getting short, I cancelled this detour. I began to think about alternatives, studying the charts and pilot books of South America, and came up with a daring plan involving an even longer voyage! This route would take me through the Panama Canal into the Pacific. From there via the Galapagos Islands to Patagonia in Chile and around Cape Horn to Argentina. From there, I could reach Europe one year later than originally planned. I calculated all the distances and sailed the route many times in my mind's eye. However, when I realised how long our comparatively short passage to Brazil was taking us, I got cold feet.

I had also read some interesting facts about the Atlantic Ocean. Together with the fringe seas, it covers 20 percent of the earth's surface. Its length from north to south is 21,300 kilometres and its width 5500 kilometres on average. Only the Pacific Ocean is larger, and this was another good reason to postpone the Pacific to a later stage in my life.

In the meantime, Guy studied the pilot books for the Caribbean. I suspect that he had been reading too much as one morning he complained about having had the nightmare that we had run aground on one of the many coral reefs he had been reading about. He also had to put up with the fact that Greg and I occasionally made fun of him because of the endless letters he wrote to his girlfriend. Every time we raved about the wonderful life in Brazil, we used to say "Guy, this is not for your ears. You are on ice until you see your girlfriend again." I would then continue to talk about my former working colleagues who had spent some time in Brazil. As soon as anybody mentioned this country, their eyes would cloud over dreamily and they would smile. Asking them why the mere mention of Brazil had such an astonishing effect on them, they would say how amazing the women of Brazil were. "They dance like goddesses, they are amazingly natural and beautiful, and always on the lookout for adventures. In comparison, our women in Europe are prudish." Greg and I had our fantasies and, further fired up by the spectacular sunsets, we were drunk in anticipation. Guy tried to get us back down to earth "You'll look very stupid as soon as you have to speak Portuguese with them!"

"Who wants to speak?" we replied, and went on dreaming.

The radio was our only contact with the rest of the world. The BBC reported the result of the election in South Africa and, as everybody had anticipated, Nelson Mandela had become president.

The rest of the passage went by without any notable events, but we always found ways of amusing ourselves. Once, I fell victim to a prank. As always on a long passage, we were trailing two lines for fishing behind us. Greg and Guy swore by one sort of bait, I by the other, but our efforts all led to nothing as the lines either got entangled or we simply lost the bait. However, one day I was woken from my siesta by my shipmates shouting "Ralph, Ralph, quick! There's a fish on your line!"

I was instantly wide awake and rushed to the line, gripping it firmly. "He's not fighting anymore, but he must be a big one!" I said, excitedly.

Greg and Guy encouraged me as I was hauling away. "Don't be a wimp. Pull harder! Harder!"

"Idiots! Better fetch the gaff" I countered. Unfortunately, as soon as hunting fever has me in its grip I tend to lose my sense of humour. "But what is this?" I exclaimed angrily, as I brought the catch on board and my friends roared with laughter. The fish turned out to be a big old sock which they had fastened to the end of my line.

The boat had its revenge. The autopilot went on strike once again. We were already envisaging steering manually for the remainder of the voyage, but only a few screws on the steering pedestal had come loose and they were easily put right.

There was more drama when it was once again my turn to prepare dinner. My infamous pancakes were on the menu that evening, and my friends fetched the fire extinguishers just to be on the safe side. I proceeded to flame the pancakes in so much alcohol that they have since been called 'Ralph's burning pancakes'. Another galley sensation was our own baked bread. For this, we used ingredients which originated from all sorts of different places – flour from Australia, milk powder from South Africa, dried yeast from Turkey, honey from St Helena, salt from Singapore and oil from Mauritius. The result was a truly international bread.

On both of our Atlantic crossings, we sighted no other ships at sea, but we still kept to our flexible watch schedule. This worked out to three hours on and six hours off. Each day we advanced the changeover by three hours so that everyone had the same share of the pleasant and not so pleasant shifts.

On one occasion we were entertained for the whole night by two sea birds. We christened them Kamikaze 1 and Kamikaze 2, as they repeatedly tried to land on our solar panels. There, they only stayed for short moments, until the motion of the boat swept them off back into the air. They would return again immediately, only to be wiped off again – the show culminated in a loud quarrel, when K1 pulled K2 off with him during a crash landing.

We grew impatient as last remaining miles shrank away. For the arrival, we trimmed our beards and on the 25th of April we thought that we sighted a sail ahead. The sail soon turned out to be the peak of a mountain on the Brazilian island of Fernando de Noronha.

Brazil

Fernando de Noronha

Fernando de Noronha is a small archipelago off north-east Brazil. The main island is a popular stopover for yachts bound for the Caribbean and as usual there were quite a few yachts anchored when we arrived. Nearly all of them came from South Africa as part of the 'Mandela Regatta'.

However, we were in for a disappointment. The regulations had changed and nobody was allowed to land unless they had first had clearance from mainland Brazil. However, I insisted and begged and argued until, in the end, I was allowed ashore at least to buy basic provisions. Apart from some fresh vegetables, these basics mainly consisted of a large case of 'Antarctica' beer. This was really essential, as the weather was unbelievably hot and oppressive. We could not even cool off anymore by jumping over the side –

the water temperature was nearly 30 degrees Celsius!

Luckily enough, we also obtained special permission for a barbecue on the beach. This was organised with the crews of the South African yachts *Ghostdancer, Domani, Caitlin* and the Swedish yacht *Kulla*. We roasted potatoes and grilled fresh fish on the open fire. While the others tended the fire, Greg and I climbed onto the deck of a wreck which stood on the beach. This was a wooden sailing yacht with the lines and general appearance of a Colin Archer design – it must have foundered there many years before. Inside, the boat was completely empty with only the bare hull left, but this made a surprisingly sound impression. If it had not been in such a desolate place, this wreck could easily have become Greg's first restoration project.

Police on strike

The short 220 mile hop to the port of Natal, on the mainland, held its surprises too. The weather had changed and massive cumulus clouds towered above. From time to time they would shed their load of rain on us, and we enjoyed fresh-water showers on deck. The drawback was that these showers were often accompanied by severe gusts, so that we were more or less constantly working the sails.

Natal is the easternmost harbour of Brazil and is located in the estuary of the Rio Potengi. We had a critical moment when we were passing the shallow bar in the river mouth, as we did not have a large-scale chart of the area. With one eye glued to the echo sounder, we carefully negotiated our way up-river until we reached the yacht club.

As soon as our anchor had found the bottom, we were greeted by a young chap in an inflatable. He introduced himself as Henry and it was immediately obvious from his strong accent that he came from South Africa. He gave us a few valuable bits of advice, as he had been here for a while already. "Don't change too much money at one time" he said, "otherwise inflation will just eat it away!" And just before leaving, he added "Oh, I nearly forgot. Both the police and the customs people are on strike at the moment."

As Brazil is notorious for its criminality, we carefully closed and locked the companionway before going ashore. We then went as far as rigging an electric fence from the hatch to the companionway. Touching the wire is painful enough to deter any potential burglar.

Guy and I then went in search of the police station, which also dealt with immigration. Greg stayed behind in the yacht club with Henry – he had no valid visa for Brazil, as he had jumped on board for this voyage literally in the last minute. "Don't worry" we told him, "if there are any problems, we'll just hide you on board."

On our way to the police station, we passed through the old quarter of the town. Sewage ran along the streets and there were piles of garbage around, but we forgot about all this as soon as we reached the market. Life was boiling here and a stream of people shoved each other through the narrow lanes between the colourful stalls. Fruit, vegetables and seafood of every description were being offered with much shouting and gesticulating. Once again, for newly arrived travellers the first impressions of any country are always the strongest.

Our search ended in front of a building bearing the sign Policia Federal. Our way inside was barred by grim-looking officers, many of them in plain clothes. I approached the pickets and held our passports under their noses. But as I tried to explain what we wanted, I found that all my language skills had deserted me.

In the end, I tried a pantomime. Using body language, I imitated our voyage across the water, the stamping of the passports and the departure by plane. When I reached the point where I became an aeroplane with wide spread arms, they must have thought that I was completely mad. Laughing, they let us go inside at last. In the building we found a secretary who was doing some kind of emergency duty. She immediately understood and went off in search of the stamp. This search appeared endless, as she went through every single drawer in the entire police station. Eventually she found what she needed but then she had to look for an instruction leaflet on how exactly to stamp the passports. Patience is the one vital virtue when it comes to dealing with any official body, so we waited and waited. Things were especially slow due to the strike, but this turned out to be an advantage for us; we might well have been in real trouble because of Greg's lack of visa.

Later, we celebrated our arrival with Henry in the yacht club. A toast which was frequently heard was "Long live the strike!"

Henry

Henry also had his reasons to be happy about the strike. In fact, for him it was more like a gift from the gods, as we found out in the course of one evening when his tongue had been loosened by a couple of strong Caipirinhas. When we asked him about his trip, he said "Just like you, I came on a sailing boat from South Africa via St Helena. Haven't you noticed my small yellow boat, a 26-footer?"

We were astonished – he was built like Arnold Schwarzenegger and we could not believe that he had sailed all that way in such a tiny boat. "Well, crossing the Atlantic in that boat was not too comfortable" Henry admitted. "But it was still far better than my stay on St Helena!"

"Why?" I protested. "We really liked it there!"

"Well, you wouldn't if you had been unjustly jailed like me" he replied.

Slowly it dawned on us. Quite by chance, in one of the countless harbours of South America, we had run into the very man who had caused such excitement on St Helena.

Henry continued with his story. He had been with a South African elite regiment for years. He came from a wealthy family but had fallen out seriously with his father. This, as well as his military history and the forthcoming change in power, made him leave the country. A friend showed him briefly how to use a sextant and off he went, only equipped with one large pilot chart of the entire Atlantic. "I had not intended to steal the big yacht in St Helena" he said, but did not say whether he had helped to smuggle the Dutch drugs dealer away from the island.

Despite the devastating effect of the Caipirinhas and a strong tide we managed to get back to the boat in our dinghy. As usual, I grabbed the toe rail, but cried out with pain as I was hit briefly by an electric shock and nearly fell headlong into the water, to the laughter of my friends. We then found out that the night's dew was leaking the electrical charge from the wire over the entire deck.

We later found out what we had long suspected – Henry had indeed taken the Dutchman with him, and he was now to receive a reward of 5000 dollars for this service. Before arriving in Natal, Henry's passenger jumped overboard and swam ashore. The Dutchman was now trying to get a new passport from his embassy and also gain access to his funds. I wondered how Henry could be so sure of getting his reward, but Guy said "I know the elite regiment to which he belonged. They were trained to fight terrorists under the most extreme circumstances, and killing was their daily routine. Upon resigning from the troop, every single person has to go into psychiatric supervision, just to get over it."

"Well, as long as we have him as a friend and not as an enemy, I don't mind".

"But not too close a friend" Guy said, laughing. "Haven't you noticed that our Tarzan is as queer as a coot?"

Postillion d'Amour

My friends were over the moon with their nightly escapades and experiences ashore. Greg had researched the night scene in great depth and it transpired that it was not flu (as in Guy's case) which got him horizontal.

"Guy insists on remaining steadfast and faithful to his girl" Greg complained, "although I keep introducing him to the most beautiful women!"

I had had enough. "You seem to have all the fun ashore. Now it's my turn!"

That same evening, we visited a dancing bar with the Swedish yachtie Niels and his Brazilian girlfriend. The bar, which was mostly open air and under the stars, was bursting with people, and not without cause – once a year, they organised a 'Postillion d'Amour' evening. There was a pile of paper on every table, with Amor, god of all lovers, and his bow and arrows printed on it. These were to be used to dispatch letters, which would be delivered by the waiters, to other people in the bar.

This promised to be fun, and four foreign-looking men on one table did not go unnoticed. Soon, notes with Amor on came fluttering to our table from various directions. It was all very confusing as we could neither read the messages nor find out who the senders were. We were fortunate that Niels' girlfriend could translate most of them, but some messages made her blush and she said that she would certainly not translate those for us. Then the music started and things livened up. Encouraged by all the mail which had been addressed to us, we started to send out a few too. I noticed one enchanting girl who was sitting next to a palm tree a bit away from the general hubbub . Niels' girlfriend translated my little letter into Portuguese and I asked the waiter to deliver my note, but as my flame was sitting at the other end of the crowded bar, my letter was delivered to the wrong woman. As luck would have it, she was one of the most ugly ones in the bar and, as she looked around to find out who the sender was, I was tempted to crawl under the table, much to the amusement of my companions. Things then really went downhill when my next note went to the wrong address too.

"If this continues, I will deliver my letters personally!" I said bravely. In the end it worked out and contact was finally made.

The band was building up the atmosphere. I then gathered up all my courage and asked the girl next to the palm tree to dance. The music really got under the skin and I felt as if I was seeing stars. The dance seemed to go on for ever and my friends were beginning to wonder if we would ever sail on.

We agreed to meet for lunch the next day in the yacht club. Karen Christina Pinherio de Santos was her name, and she was a teacher. As she only spoke Portuguese, Guy's warning became a reality. We managed communication of sorts, using pantomime and drawings. The friendship grew and a single kiss threatened to end the voyage. Immediately, I was hit with a bad conscience and I asked myself how far I could go when I was about to sail on. As soon as I was in a condition to think clearly again I told my friends "Let's sail now. Quickly, before I change my mind!"

Guy's diary account of this episode runs as follows. ' ° Our captain hit hunting mode, set his sights on a little girl and shot off like a horse out of the starting gates ° We thought we were doomed to stay in Natal but now, thank God, we are leaving on schedule ° On the way to Trinidad we hope to take on provisions in Cayenne (French Guyana), then stop off at Devil's Island and from there we can only guess, as Ralph's plans change like the wind.'

Record run

When we went to organise clearance formalities for departure, we were barred entry to the building again. The official gestured towards our legs and made us understand that something was wrong there. Quite by chance, Niels and his girlfriend were passing by and we learned that men are not allowed to enter any public building wearing shorts. In complete contrast to us men, Niels' girlfriend was very elegantly dressed, so she took all our documents and vanished inside to complete the formalities. We then left Natal together. Niels' boat *Vision* was a former racing yacht with a huge rig but, as he had only sailed on his own so far, he had never set more than the genoa and occasionally a double-reefed main. He said he was in no hurry and did not want to run any unnecessary risks. We soon lost both Natal and *Vision* from view.

As soon as we left the continental shelf, we found a friendly current which helped to speed us along on our way. We were running downwind but frequently had rain showers which were sometimes accompanied by severe gusts. We often had to reduce sail in great haste.

One night, a squall hit us before we were able to reduce sail. We were running the main and a poled-out genoa goose-winged. As the wind hit us, we went off on a wild ride and had to steer manually. The boat became very difficult to control, and we were now rolling and yawing so much that the end of the boom repeatedly hit the water. Then a wave pushed the stern around and caused a Chinese gybe, in the course of which we very nearly lost the mast. Fortunately these squalls died down again as suddenly they had appeared. To find some peace for the rest of the night, we reduced sail anyway.

I have heard that on an Atlantic passage in the trades the boat is rolled from side to side up to a million times. The rolling and the oppressive heat was now wearing us down. The mood on board was somewhat subdued. Greg was nursing the after-effects of his excessive life in Natal and Guy suffered both from love- and sea-sickness. He was planning to fly to Europe to meet his girl there, and was already counting the days, hours and minutes left. Naturally, Greg and I made fun of the wretched chap.

"We have had enough of your long face" Greg told him, and I added "As soon as we reach the Caribbean, we will fly your woman out here and I will marry you, as the captain of this ship! After that, we will dump you both on a deserted island where you can flirt for the rest of your lives. With some luck, you may feel a bit better then!"

On the question of whether the ship had to have a minimum length in order for the captain to perform marriages, I replied "Yes. The minimum length is the width of a double bed."

On the early morning of May the 18th we crossed the Equator, accompanied by the sound of Pavarotti. The occasion was further honoured with a fruit salad spiced up with Brazilian liqueur. For my friends, it was the first crossing of the line and the gods gave us good weather for the christening. But later in the day, dark clouds gathered overhead and eventually soaked us in torrential rain.

We were now off the mouth of the Amazon, the largest estuary in the world. Over 6500 kilometres from the Andes to the Atlantic, the Amazon is fed by roughly 200 minor rivers, of which at least 100 are navigable. The humidity of the sea air, which is pushed east towards the Andes, regularly rains off over the region and this gives the Amazon enough water throughout the year to be navigable as far as Peru. The region of the estuary takes up about a third of the entire country and is simply vast. One island in the mouth of the river is the size of Switzerland.

We found all this out, and more, from the books we had been reading. Why shouldn't we visit a few of the harbours like São Luis, Belem or Manaus and explore at least a part of the estuary? In my mind's eye I could already see us visiting remote parts of the jungle in a dugout canoe, but this jungle, the desert of woods, could swallow us up for years without us reaching our main goal, Europe, which was now a bit closer.

The cumulus clouds not only produced showers, but also one of the most brilliant sunrises that I have ever seen. The transformation from night to day began with a minor shimmer of light in the east. The dark grey of the sky gradually lightened and then the first rays of sun fell on the mountainous clouds and gave them a fiery appearance. Like the final crescendo of a concert, a rainbow spanned the horizon, looming up in all colours. The drama of this moment was enhanced by the motion of the boat and the sounds of wind and water.

It was probably the rich marine life which prevented us from finding real peace. A familiar bang announced that a fish taken our trailing line. And what a fish! The shock cord in the line was stretched to its limits, and then a massive fish jumped high out of the water and performed a perfect somersault in the air. The line was attached to the frame of our bimini and I was afraid we were going to loose it, then there was another bang and the line flipped back like a shock cord. Luckily the fish, a huge marlin, won back his freedom – he would have been far too large for our galley, anyway. Inspired by this incident, we rigged up a second line. As always, the discussion was who would choose the best bait. In this case, both seemed to be good enough. A pair of dorades went to the hooks simultaneously but, after a short and wild fight, they broke loose again and vanished with our bait. We repaired the lines and it did not take long before the next dorade was there. Although we had slowed the boat down, we had an enormous fight to get her alongside. Just as Greg was about to spear her with our hook, a second dorade appeared and the first one chose this moment to fight one last time and jump off the hook. "Let's hope that the fish will survive" Greg said. "These fish live as pairs. If you catch one, the other stays around until the first one is pulled from the water. That's probably why the second one appeared – it may have encouraged the first one to try one more time to break loose."

As if this had not been enough, our spinnaker halyard broke shortly afterwards. The dragon fell to the water and we could only save the sail by instantly rounding up. After getting it back on board and drying it, Greg stowed the sail away in his cabin. "He now shares his cabin with a dragon" we teased. Our friend was not in the mood for jokes though. Stowing away the sail, one of his fingers had been caught in the ventilator above his berth. He now had an injured finger and also had to repair the ventilator which was an essential piece of kit in this tropical climate.

We then prepared thoroughly for the next fish. The Very pistol was loaded with shot and a harpoon laid in the cockpit. "What on earth is your plan?" Guy asked in view of this arms race.

"You can pull the fish alongside, and Greg and I will shoot him as soon as he is within range. Then we'll harpoon him and pull him on board!"

"Knowing your talent, we will probably kill each other while the fish escapes" Guy laughed. It was perhaps fortunate that we were spared the bloodthirsty plan – the next fish was small enough to be pulled on board easily.

My ambitions as an amateur radio operator foundered quickly. Firstly, the Caribbean network is strictly controlled by its regular users. Secondly, my imaginary license number was not accepted anymore. The users wanted to, or had to, stick to the official rules which meant in effect that a radio pirate like myself with an imaginary Panamanian license was simply not spoken to. To make up for this, we stayed in daily radio contact with all the South African yachts which we had met in Fernando de Noronha. Under the call sign 'False Bay', their home port near Cape Town, they operated their own pirate network, sharing all sorts of adventures and experiences. I somehow felt more at home amongst pirates. On the day of our equatorial celebrations, a new boat joined the daily round. This was *Cooee*, captained by Jill Knight. She said that she was on her way from São Luis to Devil's Island.

Again, what an amazing coincidence! I was immediately reminded of my friend Graeme and the times when he had helped me with my first steps into this adventure back in Singapore. Jill and Graeme knew each other well. Back in Singapore, he had told me of her while she was sailing around the world in a wooden boat. Judging by the entries in various yacht club's guest books, she had always been one step ahead of us. On the radio, I gave Graeme's call sign and asked Jill if this meant anything to her.

"But of course" she replied. "That's the call sign of my friend Graeme Ireland. Where is he?" We then agreed to meet and, instead of heading for Cayenne, we now changed course for Devil's Island.

On our entire passage to French Guyana we had ideal winds between 15 and 25 knots. At first, we were running downwind before a south-easterly but as we came further north the wind gradually changed around to east-north-east until we were sailing along on a beam reach. At the same time, a current of two to three knots helped us along. It was little wonder that we broke all our previous records under these favourable circumstances. Our best noon-to-noon run was 216 miles.

The last remaining miles turned out to become a race against darkness and with the last of the fading light we reached the sheltered anchorage in the lee of the Isle Royal.

French Guyana

Cooee

The yacht *Cooee* arrived that same evening. Jill joined us in what became an unforgettable evening. In a totally relaxed atmosphere, we exchanged our yarns and cherished the fact that after the sailing of the past days we were now anchored in complete peace.

The Australian Jill Knight, a psychologist by profession, is a special person in the big family of yachties. As a mother of several children, she tired of being a housewife one day. With a friend she renovated the 47-foot gaff cutter *Cooee*, and they sailed off together. But as sadly happens so often, they eventually split up. Since then, Jill sails alone with just her cat for company. Off the Cape of Good Hope, her boat was damaged during a storm but Jill managed to scrape through. In Cape Town, she repaired her boat and met a new friend. But neither she nor he wanted to give up their freedom, so they continued to sail on two different boats. Having met her, I could well understand why Graeme had so often talked about her. She is not only a true character, but also a very attractive and fit lady.

When we passed her on our way ashore the following morning, she was in the middle of repairing her outboard.

She also had reason to be proud of her ship. *Cooee* is the oldest yacht which I have ever seen. She was built in 1893 by Charles Bailey and Sons in New Zealand, of Kauri pine, and Jill had given her a new lease of life with her own two hands. The interior showed her sense of aesthetics and had a feminine touch which is entirely missing on our boat.

The weird islands
Both the architect and the official who have worked together on this are terrible monsters, criminal psychiatrists, filled with sadistic hatred for the prisoners. – Henry Charrière

The archipelago is called the Isles du Salut and encompasses the islands Ile du Diable, Ile Royale and Ile Saint Joseph. It is about 15 miles from the coast of French Guyana. The anchorage is in the lee of Ile Royale. During the night, a tropical rainstorm came down, lasting without pause until the late morning. When it finally stopped raining, our inflatable was three-quarters full of water. The rainy season, lasting from November to July, was now at its peak.

On Ile Royale we met a French gendarme who sat on the pier, fishing. He was also responsible for the entrance formalities and did not like the South African passports at all, but he calmed down when he noted that the captain, despite speaking with a German accent, was actually French. Anyway, he was more interested in fishing, wine and diving than in the formalities.

We then explored the islands with Jill. What we saw were the remains of a sad and tragic past. As the French saw nothing but dense jungle in their colony of Guyana, they used it to get rid of those people they did not want to have around at home. From 1795 to 1953, criminals and political opponents were banished here. On these islands were the most infamous prisons of all. On Ile Royale were the prison administration and those prisoners who had been convicted to hard labour. Ile St Joseph had those prisoners who were in solitary isolation, and Ile du Diable was reserved for the political prisoners. This tragic place eventually gained world fame through one of the convicts, Henry Charrière, with his book 'Papillon'.

Without speaking, we walked past the death cells in which people were executed by guillotine. We then went across to Devil's Island, which used to be connected to Ile Royale by a small cable car for transporting provisions. Only an evil mind is able to dub such a beautiful place 'Devil's Island', but maybe the name only referred to the diabolical deeds which were once commonplace here. Most impressive of all, however, were the blocks for the isolation cells on Ile St Joseph. Where the convicts used to vegetate, all is now dominated by nature. The roots of the trees had burst open even the thickest walls and, of the roofs, only steel frames remained. As we all had read 'Papillon', we could vividly imagine how reality had once been here. Inhuman labour, under-nourishment and the harsh tropical climate let the convicts die like flies. The dead bodies were then simply thrown into the sea, a macabre feast for the sharks. The island was criss-crossed by paths made from massive stone squares and the contrast between the black stone and the fresh, lush green of the vegetation somehow managed to lend the place a friendly atmosphere. Close to an idyllic beach we stumbled on an old cemetery, which was used for the prison's personnel. The inscriptions on the weathered tombstones showed us how shockingly young most of the people died here.

Just to make quite sure that none of the convicts would ever again return to France, a prisoner had to stay in Guyana the same length of time as his prison sentence after being released. The statistics show the immense tragedy which took place here. Of 70,000 convicts, only a bare 7000 survived this terrible exile.

To the devil with the taxes
The former living quarters for the prison officials stand on a hill on Ile Royale and are now used as a restaurant and hotel. From here I telephoned my family and was able to receive faxes. One letter was from the tax authority in Singapore which imperatively

demanded a still-outstanding tax payment from the past year, threatening prosecution otherwise. The other letter came from my bank in Singapore. They informed me that the tax authority had simply seized my remaining funds and that the account had since been closed.

Shocked about this twist of fate I sat down on the terrace. Irony had it that the reality caught up with me here, of all places, in one of the remotest corners on earth. My voyage had partly been made possible by the low taxes. As I had mainly worked abroad, my tax payments were on an acceptable level of about 25 percent of my income. If I had worked as an unmarried man in one of my two mother countries, France or Germany, I would have been liable for about 50 percent of my income and, accordingly, would have had to work twice as long to be able to afford this adventure. The tax bill from Singapore was valid for a time which I had partly spent at sea and the authorities had demanded about twice as much as would have been fair. In this respect I was lucky that I had not left too much money in my Singapore account. I drafted a letter each to the bank and the tax people in which I put my view of the situation. My letterhead bore the address: Yacht *Ryusei*, Devil's Island, French Guyana.

"What on earth happened to you?", my friends asked when they joined me on the terrace and saw my face.

"There are two things that no man or woman can ever escape from", I said, "death and taxes. One of them has just caught up with me!" From our place on the terrace, we enjoyed a wonderful view of the devilish islands. I ordered a round of beer, toasted my friends and said: "To hell and the devil with all taxes!"

My problem faded to insignificance when we spotted a note, pinned up by the coastguard, in the entrance of the hotel. It said: "*IDLE QUEEN*, an American sailing yacht, is overdue. She left South Africa bound for the Caribbean. The single sailor on board is handicapped in one arm. Anybody who hears any news about this yacht is asked to inform the coastguard."

The skipper of *Idle Queen* was of course our friend Harry, with whom we had spent many happy hours in Durban. To miss a friend or even just an acquaintance who is overdue at sea is always a bitter experience. We speculated long about the reasons for his delay or disappearance. In the end we intensely hoped that 'Old Harry' had once again, for safety reasons, only set his foresail and was just very, very slow.

Kourou

One early afternoon, after a warm good-bye from Jill, we set sail in order to reach the river mouth at Kourou with the incoming tide. We had intended to leave the anchorage under power but the overcast skies and our refrigerator nearly brought disaster upon us. The clouds reduced the energy which our solar panels were delivering and, as we had forgotten to switch off the refrigerator, the batteries were now too low to start the engine. "No problem", we said, "after all, this is a sailing boat." But we had not reckoned with the tricky currents and shifting winds in the anchorage, and at one point we drifted dangerously close to the rocky shore. At literally the last minute, a little gust of wind saved us from running aground and helped us out to sea.

Three hours later, we anchored in the river Kourou off the town bearing the same name. This place was overgrown with jungle. Only a few scattered houses along the shores indicated that this was actually one of the largest settlements in French Guyana.

The three bordering countries of The Guyanas, Guyana (formerly British Guyana), Surinam (formerly Dutch Guyana) and French Guyana are in one significant way different from the rest of the continent. This coast, which Columbus discovered in 1498, was deemed uninteresting by the Spaniards and Portuguese due to the absence of natural resources and the dense jungle. They were on the hunt for their Eldorado. I felt that, without recognising it, they had come fairly close here. It was here that they spotted the first hammocks, though they failed to see the value of this cultural heritage which we yachties hold in high esteem.

For strategic reasons, only France held on to her colony. In 1946, French Guyana gained the status of a French overseas department. Today, about 150,000 people live in this small country, which extends along the coast for 320 kilometres.

We sailed to Kourou to stock up with provisions and also to visit the European Space Centre which is located here.

The area close to the river made a desolate impression on us. As we walked along the dusty main road, a truck passed and sprayed insecticide over us. Coughing and gasping for air, we ran away. Later, we went into an obscure bar. As soon as we had ordered a drink, the doorman, an ex-legionnaire, picked a brutal fight with one of the other guests. He knocked the guest out cold and chucked his body out into the street, in imitation of a cheap western movie. As quickly as we could, we knocked back our drinks, paid and fled back to the boat.

The river adventure

During the night, it felt as if we had anchored in a mountain torrent. Rain drummed on the coachroof and a strong tide rushed past the hull at up to three knots. In the early morning, we boarded our dinghy and went up the river with the incoming tide under us. Minutes later, we were completely surrounded by mangroves and dense jungle, but we sped on and hardly noticed how the kilometres flew by. Judging by the sun, the river wound its way inland in great loops. Again and again we passed minor streams which branched off the main river. Driven by curiosity, we finally entered one of them. We immediately disappeared in dense vegetation. We continued as if we were in a green tunnel, but the stream became so small that we finally had to turn back. But before leaving, we stopped the outboard to let the atmosphere of the place sink in. It was a ghostly world around us, in complete stillness which was now and again shattered by the cries of exotic birds. Then, an army of mosquitoes descended upon us.

"If the outboard doesn't start now, we'll be eaten alive!", Greg said. "Now I know why the jungle is so often referred to as the green hell!"

As quickly as we could, we left this sinister place and the mosquitoes behind. A little bit further along, we went into another branch of the river. This one seemed more adventurous than the main stream. Startled by our appearance, colourful birds rose from the trees and changed from one shore to the other. Tree stumps which only just broke through the surface were a hazard which we had to keep a sharp look out for. Suddenly, a sign ashore surprised us. It read "Military zone – entrance forbidden!" We were, however, sure that this only referred to the land and not the river, and continued on our way. At one point, we did go in to the shore. We had by now covered an estimated 30 kilometres and the water level was slowly sinking. The ebb had begun and this was the time for us to turn back home. Just as we were leaving the shore, loud bangs tore through the stillness. We at once recognised machine-gun fire, and either there was a firing range hereabouts or we had stumbled into the middle of a manoeuvre. "Let's get out of here", I shouted and we sped downriver at full throttle. We squatted down in the boat and drove as if the devil was on our heels. It helped that we roughly knew the hazards along the way, like low branches, tree stumps and sharp corners of this river. We only calmed down once the warning sign had been left far behind and we reached our home without further incident.

Ariane
We booked an organised official tour to visit France's space centre. We found it hard to comprehend that here, in this godforsaken corner of the earth, the most sophisticated technology was in use to fire satellites up into orbit. These were mainly used for telecommunications, a technology which has changed our lives so deeply. The world, formerly incredibly big, was now reduced to the size of telephone dials using this technology and its satellites. We visited a museum, then the construction hall, the starting ramp for the carrier rockets and finally the big testing area. The rockets reach orbit in less than thirty minutes after lift-off and to achieve this costs incredible amounts of money.

To the frustration of my friends, the guided tour was conducted in French – although the fact that our guide was a lovely young woman pacified them a bit.

We asked an engineer, with whom we chatted for a while, how life was here. "Slow", he replied. "Time is measured in GMT." We looked puzzled and he laughed. "But GMT over here stands for Guyana Maybe Time!" He then continued to tell us that they were currently working under extreme pressure. "The last rocket, for the start of which even President Mitterand was flown out here, had to be destroyed in mid-flight due to a technical problem. But in a few days, a new rocket is due to lift off as part of the prestigious Ariane programme. Let us hope that it all works well this time around!"

We hoped with him, in view of the fact that a large part of this extremely costly fireworks programme is funded by the taxpayers. But in case of problems, the entire sea area north of Kourou was going to be closed for all shipping during lift-off. We had no desire to be delayed here and left the same day.

A good omen
We left Kourou at high water. We were glad to be leaving the muddy river water, the rain and the mosquitoes behind and joyfully observed how the water became bluer and bluer. During the night, the trade wind started to blow from the north-east and we flew along towards Trinidad on a perfect beam reach in 15 to 20 knots of wind for three days and nights. Nowhere else have I ever found such beautiful sailing conditions at sea as these on this last passage into the Caribbean. One day before our estimated arrival in Trinidad, I spoke on the radio with the crew of the yacht *Caitlin* whom we knew from Fernando de Noronha. They had

recently reached the harbour of Scarborough on Tobago.

"This is a harbour to my taste. Why don't you join us? I promise that you won't regret it", came the oracle from the radio. On the spot we changed course for Tobago. Until now, sun and wind had been very kind to us but, on the evening before our landfall, huge cumulus clouds towered above. The wind increased and became squally. We reduced sail as we did not want to reach the island before dawn. But the more sail we reduced, the more the wind increased. After midnight, during Guy's watch, all hell broke loose. A brutal thunderstorm chose to unleash itself around us. Accentuated by thunder and lightning, torrential rain drummed down as if we were parked beneath a waterfall. Visibility went down to zero. Huge cross seas and gusts to 40 knots made it extremely difficult to control the boat. We had reduced the foresail to a tiny triangle, but we were still sailing much too fast. Greg and I were standing by in the companionway while Guy was fighting at the wheel. We heard him swear even above the din of the storm when one huge wave crashed across the deck. In malicious delight, we shouted at him: "Guy, every time you are on watch, the weather starts to freak. How do you manage to arrange that?" His answer was mercifully drowned in a clap of thunder. And then the thunderstorm ended as quickly as it had arrived. The wind however continued to blow and the sea remained very rough. But as the rain ceased, we could see the lights of Tobago ahead. This blow had brought us to the island far too quickly. Exhausted, Guy retired to his bunk, but as Greg and I came on deck we could not resist remarking: "You see, as soon as we come on deck, the weather calms down again." But he was too exhausted even to respond and, to make matters worse, a flying fish had just slapped him right across the face.

Our behaviour towards Guy was duly revenged. At four in the morning, we were already off the entrance to Scarborough. We now had to decide whether to attempt an entry at night or wait until dawn. But the chart showed that there were bearing lights which were supposed to guide one through the gap in the outlying reef.

"As long as we can identify those lights, we should be all right", I said. Greg agreed, although he, too, had a bad gut feeling. Scarborough was brilliantly illuminated, and in that sea of lights we now had to find the bearing.

"Damn, there are too many lights ashore. I can even see some red lights, but that might be just the red light district!" exclaimed

Greg, staring through the binoculars.

At one point we thought that we had seen the correct lights and sailed towards land. As a precautionary measure, I also started the engine, as the current was flowing swiftly. Nervously, Greg eyed the echo sounder. Suddenly he screamed: "Tack! Tack as quickly as you can!" I pulled the helm hard over and gave full throttle on the reverse course. The headsail was madly flapping in the wind, but the only thing that counted now was to gain deep water.

The echo-sounder had suddenly jumped from 40 to only 4 metres depth. We had missed running bang on to the reef by a hair's breadth.

"That's enough. Never again will we attempt to enter an unknown port at night", we decided and sailed out towards the sea. There, we hung about until we could see the navigation lights of an approaching motor vessel. On channel 16, the captain tried to contact the harbour master, like us before, and just like us without success. In the end, I contacted him on the radio and said: "Motor vessel *Futura*, this is sailing yacht *Ryusei* on your starboard side. We've also tried in vain to contact the harbour master."

"Well, I suppose he's asleep", came the answer. "But we can just as well enter without his permission." I then explained to him that we had been unable to find the entrance.

"No problem", came the reassuring reply. "We are a supply vessel and know our way. Just come in behind us!"

Thus, a ship called *Futura* piloted us into our first Caribbean harbour, and after the alarms of the night we took this as a good omen.

Tobago & The Grenadines

The land of calypso

In the eastern Caribbean the islands are like a string of pearls. This region, situated between latitudes 10 and 20 North, also guarantees tropical temperatures and steady trade winds. This makes it one of the most popular destinations for sailors.

The European influence is apparent everywhere in the Caribbean. Ever since Columbus first sighted the islands, they have been fought over by the European powers. Not only the Spaniards and the Portuguese, but also the English, French, Dutch and Danes defended their interests here. Sugar was the gold of the Caribbean, and was cultivated from 1640 with the labour and sweat of the black slaves from Africa. After slavery was abolished around 1850, cheap labour was imported from India. This is why Africans and Indians dominate life in Trinidad and Tobago to this day.

Tobago changed hands more often than any other Caribbean island and the exact number of times escaped the history books. Bitter battles were fought here; names like Man of War Bay and Bloody Bay serve as a distinct reminder. In Bloody Bay, the British fought against the combined Dutch and French fleets. Legend has it that there were so many deaths that the water turned red. Another 1700 lives were wasted in yet another battle between the French and the Dutch. We could hardly imagine these bloody scenes upon seeing this beautiful and peaceful island. Around 1800, the British finally occupied Trinidad and Tobago and stayed until their independence in 1962. Large parts of the former British administration, language and culture are still evident.

After this history of misery, slavery and war it seems that Tobago has finally found a happy ending. We met cheerful people who loved music and parties. Everywhere, we heard the sound of steel drums, calypso and reggae. As we checked in, we already got our first lesson in the local culture.

"This may looks like Africa, but it is definitely very different", my friends decided. The vast majority of people in Tobago are black. As the common language is English, we could communicate without problems. The big theme of the day was the carnival.

"Hasn't that already taken place?", I asked when the customs man told me about it.

"Yes", he confirmed, "but it was such a success this year that we decided to have a second one. You see, we know our priorities here!"

In the harbour of Scarborough, we anchored next to the South African yachts *Caitlin* and *Ghostdancer*, which we had already met in Brazil. One evening, we all sat together and exchanged our experiences. Conversation drifted to the many other boats which had left South Africa at around the same time. Most of them were embarking on a long voyage for the first time. Friends, couples and families had dared to undertake an unknown adventure and, for some, the big dream turned into a nightmare. Long-standing relationships and even entire families broke up. Some could just not cope with this way of life, whilst others on the same boat thrived on it. Seasickness or fear often were enough to let the whole thing turn sour in many cases. These are the downsides to the yachtie life which are seldom mentioned. We on *Ryusei* certainly belonged to the lucky ones.

Guests

"It will be terribly crowded anyway, so one person more or less doesn't make such a big difference. Just bring her along if you want to and you will soon find out if you can really get on with her", were the words which I shouted into the telephone in French Guyana. At the other end of this very long line was my friend Karl-Heinz, alias Kalle. I had studied with him and we had also obtained our first sailing certificate then. The plan was that Kalle should sail with us with his five-year-old son Charles, for whom he was a single parent, for four weeks. He had just asked me whether he could also bring his new girlfriend Henriette along.

"She's a really charming girl. A lovely blonde Dane with long hair and blue eyes", he said.

For us, the days before the arrival of our friends were like a holiday. We had reached our destination, the Caribbean, and new plans had to be made. But first we were determined to fully recover from the long trip and the hammocks came into use. Only sports brought us to our feet. In Scarborough, a Scottish football team was to play in a friendly match against Tobago. As I am a big fan of the Scots I persuaded my friends to come along and watch the game. We went to the sports ground and gave our best to cheer the Scots on, apparently with success. Dundee United won 4 to 2 against Tobago.

When Kalle and company, as we called them, moved in it

became crowded on board. Any private space, which was very limited under normal circumstances, now vanished completely, especially as our guest had brought along a huge amount of luggage for sailing in the tropics. For Greg, Guy and myself it was a hint of how it would be if we had to earn our way chartering the boat. With good friends it was just about possible, but otherwise: no, thank you.

Black and White

On the 7th of June, our Caribbean sailing holiday really took off. With our enlarged crew, we sailed 15 miles in sunshine and 15 to 20 knots of wind. We left at 13.00 hours and arrived three hours later in Sandy Bay, south-west Tobago. This was a relaxing pace, in contrast with our previous long ocean passages. Our new guests were feeling the beginnings of sea-sickness so they, too, found this distance just about right.

In the evening we heard our first real steel band. The people of Tobago have the rhythm in their blood and, when it comes to making music, they are quite ingenious. The steel drums originate from the left-overs of Trinidad's oil industry, and are made from discarded oil barrels.

The following day, we sailed even less: ten miles, including a stop-over at the Buccoo reef. But distance is not always what counts, and this day was to become very special for us. When we dropped our hook in the anchorage of Plymouth that evening, we were even more people on board, seven instead of "only" six.

One of the most idyllic beaches of Tobago is close to the reef. We anchored and ferried across in the dinghy, swam, sun-bathed and prepared a picnic on the beach. This peaceful scene was shattered when a day-tripper boat arrived and landed a large group of rather loud people on the beach. Amongst these people, a young black woman stood out with her beauty and freshness. It did not take long until we spoke with her. As the afternoon wore on, she joined our little group and we chatted easily and laughed and joked. Her name was Jacky and she seemed to fit in naturally with our cheerful crowd.

Kalle asked the obvious question as we were preparing to leave the beach and sail back. "Why don't we ask her along to join us for the sail? She gets on wonderfully with all of us and it will be a lot of fun!" Upon our invitation, Jacky was delighted and at once agreed. She took her small beach bag and said goodbye to her perplexed companions from the day-boat. Even Greg and Guy were slightly taken aback by this surprising turn of events, but trimmed their sails quickly and commented: "This is Ralph's way of abolishing Apartheid!" Later, after the anchor had long again found its resting place on the ground of Plymouth harbour, Jacky and Henriette posed together in the pulpit for a photograph. We were stunned and unanimously agreed that 'black and white is beautiful'.

Jacky introduced us to her country. In Plymouth, she organised fish for our evening barbecue on the beach and then stayed with us for a couple of days in which we sailed from bay to bay and visited different parts of Tobago.

One fantastic bay serves as typical of many others. With its palm trees, dazzling white sand and rocks, and surrounded by lush green hills, we thought that this place had come straight from a travel brochure, although we preferred to think about how Daniel Defoe was allegedly inspired by Tobago to write his famous 'Robinson Crusoe'. Here, we could also see how the locals caught their fish. A group of muscular men boarded several small open boats and laid a circular net in the middle of the entrance to the bay. Next, they hauled away at the net from the beach, with five men pulling each end in rhythmic movements. It looked like hard labour and we could see the sweat glistening on their black skin in the sun. Birds fluttered about excitedly over the net in never-ending attempts to gain their share of the catch. A silvery mass of fish was inside and the fishermen carefully sorted out the inedible ones and threw them back into the water. As they could not use up all of this rich harvest at once, they parked the larger part of the catch in a part of the bay which was fenced off by nets.

This episode was typical for the thing we could only see by sailing with our own boat. In *Ryusei*, we reached places normally closed to land tourists and were free to stay for as long as we wished, and to sail on whenever the mood took us.

Cockroaches of the sea

Reading the local paper, the 'Sunday Guardian', amused us hugely while we were anchored in Englishman Bay. One article, which had the rather bland headline "Pacro Tea is getting rare", actually turned out to be a piece about an aphrodisiac which is won from the pacro. Pacro are small sea-snails with flexible back armour. They live off the algae on the rocks and belong to the family of *Amphineura*. Because of their oval form, the locals usually call them cockroaches of the sea. At low water, they are scraped off the rocks with a sharp knife. The article cited an old pacro expert: "…I love pacro tea. It keeps me sexually fit and soothes my nerves."

This man really should know what he was talking about. He was 85 and had 18 children. The article then presented an in-depth instruction of how to prepare this wonderful tea but, due to high demand, the tea was getting rare and more and more expensive.

The expert also described various other aphrodisiacs. "Chip Chip water has a similar effect to pacro tea. But if both of these fail to deliver the desired results, one should try Susumber or even Bois Bande. Susumber is a plant growing in the wild whose fruits are cooked in a special way. Bois Bande is outright dangerous. If the rind is mixed with white rum and taken in high doses, a sudden erection of the penis will follow that can last up to seven days. If someone takes too much Bois Bande, he normally has to use pain killers or even go to hospital for professional treatment. Luckily, though, so far we have not had any reports of lethal dosages."

Jacky immediately jumped on to the subject. Giving us men a mischievous look, she announced: "I know how to make pacro tea. Give me a knife and a bucket, maybe I'll find some along the shoreline."

Sooner than we had expected, she returned with a bucketful of creepy crawly things. Our stomachs turned even at the sight of these little creatures. But Jacky was without mercy and demanded a pot in which she cooked the wretched things. Soon, the pantry was emitting exotic scents and no male member of the crew, save young Charles, was spared. We all had to try, and who would not like to know what *Ryusei*'s planks would have to tell of the night that followed?

Charlotteville

Sharpening knives was one of Guy's favourite pastimes. I was worried about this and took it as a clear sign that the cramped living conditions on *Ryusei* were getting at him, but he just said "It soothes my nerves!" In any case, we decided to split up for a week, and the pretty little village of Charlotteville seemed ideal for our purposes. This place is located on the truly spectacular Man of War Bay in the very north of Tobago, and here we anchored and rented a small holiday flat ashore. Our guests moved to the flat and, from now on, we mainly lived on solid land for a change. We used our inflatable to make little trips to the more remote beaches and embarked on long walks into the surrounding hills. Tobago's bird-life was every bit as spectacular as its underwater scenery.

The local dive station, called Man Friday, was run by a friendly Dane. He helped us with the maintenance of our diving gear and led us to sensational diving grounds. These were aptly named London Bridge and Rocky Mountains. Finn the Dane had left family and career to start a new life over here. The diving station and the pretty little house on the hillside in which he lived were created all by himself.

Some time later I was shocked to hear that this experienced diver had not been destined to live long. A few weeks after we had left, he vanished on one deep-sea diving excursion, together with a diving guest, never to return. It also reminded me of the comment of one extremely professional diver: "Accidents often happen to the experienced divers. These are the one who go dangerously close to their limits."

Again Jacky helped to introduce us to the local scene. Together we visited a Thanksgiving feast in a village called Roxborough. Every single household had prepared specialities and all guests were entreated to try everything. Naturally, music was everywhere and the locals were not shy to share what little they had even with us foreigners. In our curiosity, we even tried the soup which was made of iguanas.

Life ticks differently on Tobago and this could be the main reason why so many Europeans come to settle down here. We often saw European women who were now living with black locals, and their children were of a sweet chocolate colour. In one case, they even spoke fluent German as the two kids went to school in Germany. This was a blessing for young Charles who at last found playmates of his own age. Just prior to this, he had met with a young Rasta boy who had at once shown him who the stronger one was.

The Rasta culture, which has its origins on Jamaica, was quite evident on Tobago. They preach the strength of the black population and the dominance of black Africa over the white nations. Emperor Haile Selassie I of Ethiopia is regarded as a kind of messiah by them, but the most famous of all Rastas was of course Bob Marley. The biblical quote "be fertile and multiply yourselves" is taken very seriously by them and there are a lot of illegitimate children about.

We got to know one Rasta, whom we called the 'Kalabash Man' as he was usually selling Kalabash shells on the beach. One evening he invited us up to his house, on the hillside above Charlotteville. He could create hypnotising rhythms on his bongo drum and naturally also shared his smoke with us. We laughed as we recalled that even the President of the United States had publicly admitted to once having smoked a joint, and we enjoyed this very special and relaxed evening.

The worst thing about cruising is that we always have to sail on – especially when we like it most in one place. But we are inquisitive and searching voyagers and if we do not allow ourselves to drift on, our goals remain out of reach. Jacky would have loved to sail on with us, but she could not swim and neither could she leave her small daughter.

Bequia

Belonging to the Grenadines are 32 partly uninhabited islands. Distances are short in this part of the Caribbean. Originally we had intended to sail to Mustique, but we were too fast during the night and arrived off this small island while it was still in darkness. Having learnt from Tobago never again to attempt a night entrance of an unfamiliar anchorage, we changed course and sailed on for the next island, Bequia. The absence of a light which was marked on the chart gave us some moments of anxiety, but the navigational aids in this part of the world are far from reliable. Reefs and islands are so close together here that I could not relax for one minute during this short passage. The same was true for our guests, who were again suffering from sea-sickness, although in the case of Kalle and young Charles, it had the effect that they retired to their bunks and slept through it all.

One hundred and twenty-five miles out from Tobago, we rounded the western tip of Bequia. Greg and I were on deck and looked at the coastline. Then I saw something that resembled a dense wood.

"What on earth is that, over there, below the hills?" I asked, and handed the binoculars over to Greg.

After only one short glance he said: "If I am not completely mistaken, those are masts. There seem to be a lot of boats around!"

Admiralty Bay was so crowded with yachts that we had a hard time finding a vacant spot in which to anchor. It seemed that Bequia had been completely taken over by tourists, both ashore and at sea. Small boats went from one anchored yacht to the next and offered all sorts of goods and services. Along the shore was a promenade with bars and restaurants.

It has been said and written that Bequia used to be an island of seafarers, once completely dependent on ships for transportation. Now, not much remained of the traditional shipbuilding skills for which this island had once been famous. Still, we could see some of the results of this once lively profession. Small wooden fishing craft were lined up along the beach, all colourfully painted, and the famous schooner *Friendship Rose*, which had also been built here, lay at anchor in the bay. Apart from her, we spotted two other traditional wooden boats on the anchorage. One was an ancient Colin Archer, whose owner had rigged an awning in his rigging, advertising his services on yachts. The other was an Italian yacht named *Aviazola*.

We were anchored not far from her and nosily went over and looked at her from our dinghy. A gentleman on deck waved to us and we came closer and introduced ourselves.

"This is a 70-foot yacht designed by Claude Worth", Kiko, the owner, told us. Not suspecting how many we were, he invited us over for the sundowner and was quite surprised when our crowd boarded his yacht, laden down with South African wine.

Kiko is an Italian and his wife Nicole is from Guadeloupe. We immediately got on well with each other. *Aviazola* had been in Kiko's family for many decades and she was beautifully kept inside and out – but we could also sense how much work these two must be putting in to maintain her to this impeccable standard.

As we talked, Kiko said: "If you know only one little bit of the Italian tax system you will understand that anyone with an income of sorts saves a lot of money when sailing. On the other hand, this boat demands a lot of work and we cannot complain about being tranquil." Asked about the large number of yachts in the bay around us, he gave the devastating answer: "This is nothing compared to what you will find further north. That's the centre of the American charter industry and the prices are accordingly high. If you want to keep away from the crowds you only have Venezuela and the western part of the Caribbean left. We'll be sailing soon for Venezuela, where *Aviazola* will have another refit."

A sabbatical year at sea has 24 months (July 1994)

The small island of Mayreau lies about 30 miles south of Bequia. Our pilot book described a nice anchorage with space for about ten boats. As we reached Salt Whistle Bay, at least 20 yachts were already anchored there and we very nearly left again, but the manager of the holiday resort assured us that we could safely anchor off in the entrance to the bay.

This was the place where my voyage from Asia to Europe took an unexpected turn. In the cosy beach bar I met the English couple Christopher and Molly. They told me about the good times they were having here and their various diving adventures. They then asked me how I had come to be here and I pointed towards the boat and told my tale. It ended with me saying: "And now we have to sail to Europe quickly before the hurricane season arrives."

Christopher looked at me and said: "That is not a very wise decision. If someone succeeds in doing a voyage such as yours, he should not be hurried along by a few months. In Europe, you will arrive in autumn and then have the winter. After all these years in the tropics you will be so frustrated by the winter in Europe that you will probably pack your bags before spring and disappear again. In your place I would simply spend the winter in the southern Caribbean, away from the tracks of the Hurricanes."

He then continued to tell me how difficult it had been for him and his wife to free themselves from the restraints of their professions and to at last enjoy their lives. "I envy you your adventure. But if you want to hear my advice, stay a bit longer in the Caribbean, instead of freezing in Europe." His wife and my friends supported this advice.

Admittedly, the plan to extend my voyage had been at the back of my mind for quite a while already. It was only one year ago that I had left my job in Singapore, then spent months refitting the boat and then sailed 13,000 miles. Countries, harbours and anchorages slid by, but where was the easy life in the hammock that we were all dreaming about?

That night I got no sleep. At the first crack of dawn I swam ashore and climbed the peak of the island's hill. I sat there and pondered, and the wonderful sunrise finally tipped the scales.

My friends were a bit surprised when I invited them ashore for breakfast, along with Christopher and Molly. In the holiday resort I found a bottle of champagne and, as the cork popped, I announced my new plan. "I have come to the decision that we should spent the forthcoming European winter here, in the Caribbean! Let us drink to the fact that a sabbatical year at sea has 24 months!"

Everyone applauded and during the course of the breakfast the consensus was that I was coming to my senses at last.

PART II

Grand Bruit, Newfoundland, July 1995

THINGS HAD QUIETENED DOWN considerably in the Cramalott Inn. It was not only the alcohol, but probably also my endless tale which had sent even the keenest listener to sleep. One sat in the corner, his head on his chest, another one lay stretched out on the bench, and several heads had dropped to the tables. Everyone else had already left, anyway. The summer nights end early in Newfoundland and they were still exhausted from the wedding festivities the night before. Even Malley and Elizabeth had long since retired to their bunks on board. I, however, was wide awake and my voyage so far was like a film before my mind's eye. I could have continued for hours, but my voice as well as my listeners failed me.

This tale was obviously a bit too much to be told like this. If I wanted to pass my adventures and experiences on to friends, family and any other interested person, I would have to write it all down. Any reader could then take it in homeopathic doses.

I knocked back the last few drops of my long-stale beer and staggered outside. Something hissed in my ears and I remembered that we were in Grand Bruit, meaning big noise, and that the noise came from the waterfall which continuously emptied itself into the bay.

The same noise made me wonder, on waking the next morning, if we were anchored in a river stream. Coffee was already steaming on the stove; Malley and Elizabeth were up and active. Slightly befuddled, I carefully crept from my bunk and looked outside. It was the same dull picture, everything swallowed in thick fog. Breakfast brought me back to my feet and gave us the motivation for a little wander ashore. From time to time the veil of fog would be torn apart for short moments, offering a glimpse of the world beyond. The landscape was hilly and covered in grass; black rocks stuck out like giant fingers. We had to take care not to lose our bearings. Then we reached the shoreline. The mighty swell of the ocean lazily came along, then built up and rose to break with thunder on the rocky shore. While my friends wandered on, I settled down in a snug place.

And dived back into my memories of the past few months. "How had we come here?", was the question I had tried to answer the previous night in the Cramalott Inn, and now I sailed on in retrospective. The dull grey of the fog turned into colour and the wet, clammy breeze became a warm tropical wind and suddenly I thought I was there again, where I had stopped in my yarn last night.

Grenada

Curse of paradise

The Caribbean disappointed us. In the Tobago Cays, we had a milky sky and not the brilliant azure blue of the archetypal picture. The water was murky and not clear and, instead of nature, we just found a very crowded and noisy place. When we arrived in the morning, we shared the anchorage with about five other yachts. Only a short while later, the number had grown to more than fifty. Amongst these were several large catamarans who carried screaming hordes of day trippers. In the evening, we wanted to grill a fish over a fire on the beach. The problem was that we could not find one piece of firewood. It had all been used up, down to the last minute twig, by our many predecessors. In the evening

The route through the Caribbean

dusk, we made a spirited dash in the inflatable over the reefs to another, outlying and thus unpopular, island where we found what we needed for our barbecue.

"Let's just get out of here fast!" we decided, before the daily invasion of charter boats and day trippers set in the next morning. The curse of paradise: as soon as we think that we have found one, everybody rushes in with their hunger for nature and solitude and so it is quickly destroyed.

Carriacou

Allegedly, the island of Carriacou, belonging to Grenada, has 100 rum shops but only one single petrol station. It is also said that all her inhabitants make their living by smuggling alcohol and cigarettes – which is, probably, much more profitable than fishing. Anyway, this fact was common knowledge in the entire Caribbean and also drew us to this island. Our anchor had only just bitten the ground of Tyrrel Bay as the first little boat came alongside, offering cheap wine. Our stores were seriously diminished, so we eagerly seized the opportunity.

During the clearance procedure ashore, we got to know another way of securing income. As we knew that after official hours the fees were much higher, we hurried up and arrived at the harbour office half an hour before closing time. The harbour master checked us in immediately, but his colleagues from customs and immigration had a clever idea. They put our papers to one side and sat there, staring at us motionless, while the clock was ticking away. One minute after closing time, they duly picked up our papers and proceeded with the formalities. In cold blood and without even blushing they then demanded the substantially higher fees for working after hours. We were speechless, but protest would have been fruitless – officials in countries like these always have very much the upper hand.

There was also a small boatyard in Tyrrel Bay which was building and repairing wooden boats. Here, we heard that the dog of the yard owner was accused of having killed six sheep belonging to the local farmer. This affair was debated at the yard in the presence of the local chief of police, who had arrived in the company of the lamenting peasant and two of his assistants. Soon, all were engaged in a lively discussion which rather rapidly deteriorated into a shouting match. Only the chief of police remained cool and aloof, in his opulent uniform which would have been fit for the greatest of admirals. Cocksure like a proud rooster he underlined his comments by swinging his riding cane against his highly polished boots. Only the alleged culprit was entirely undisturbed by the whole thing and peacefully slept in the shadow of a big tree.

The same day, *Aviazola* arrived. Kiko and Nicole came on board and joined us for a wine tasting. The first bottle of our newly purchased wine could not be opened with the corkscrew, and, rapidly losing my patience, I finally attacked it with a drill. The wine was so utterly miserable that we poured the contents of that bottle over the side and decided to reserve the others for emergencies, such as getting rid of guests or the like. We then dived deep into our bilges and found a bottle of superb South African wine which we shared with our friends.

Grenada

Grenada is densely wooded and mountainous. As most of the Antilles, she was originally inhabited by the Indian tribes of Arawaks and Caribs. Today, the majority of the inhabitants are descendants of the African slaves which worked the plantations of British and French colonialists. The economy is now mainly about the export of nutmeg, cocoa beans and bananas.

However, Grenada did not show off her best side when we anchored in Halifax Bay. The scenery was very pretty, but millions of flies descended on us and a nauseating stench drifted across the lovely bay. The local rubbish dump was just behind the beach, so we fled and anchored instead in the equally beautiful Dragon Bay.

With our arrival in St George's, Grenada's capital, the end of the journey for our guests was drawing closer. St George's must surely rank among the most beautiful harbours in the Caribbean. As we entered the lagoon, several people from the pier waved to us. "Look how friendly they are", we said, and only realised in the last minute that they were trying to make us change course. We were heading straight for a sandbank, having missed one of the entrance buoys. Just before we touched, I was able to stop the boat with full throttle astern. This shock was followed by a pleasant surprise: we saw *Lily Maid* lying in the harbour and, in the yacht club, we celebrated our reunion with Mike and his clan.

"We saw you come in and made a bet that you'd run aground", Mike shouted from far off by way of a greeting. "Every time a new yacht comes in, we enjoy the spectacle. Sadly enough, I've lost a round this time!"

Mike was just about to leave St George's, but our arrival

changed his schedule. "Well, Donald Street and his *Iolaire* will just have to wait a few days longer in Venezuela", he said. So we immediately dived into our usual mode of celebrating and found that we had good reason to do so, having sailed the Atlantic and also more or less withstood the temptations of Brazil. Moreover, the football world cup claimed our attention and each evening we gathered with a boisterous and international crowd of yachties in front of the club's TV.

The last days with our guests were spent along Grenada's south coast. Henriette and Kalle moved ashore into a hotel, while Charles remained with us on board. He had become used to the boat and enjoyed hugely keeping us on our toes. He was quite a handful, and we unanimously agreed that the upbringing of a child is no easy job. In this respect we admired Kalle and how he managed as a single parent.

In the cramped quarters on a boat, relationships are tested to the limits. During the last few days we could not fail to notice that the vibes between Kalle and Henriette had changed. It came as no great surprise that soon after this holiday their paths diverged.

Mr Green, world traveller

One of the most fascinating characters we met on our voyage was Mr Green from Grenada. Greg found out that there was one blacksmith in St George who still knew the art of forging specialist tools for ship-building. The trail led to Mr Green, who was happy about these customers who wanted something special: a caulking iron. This tool is used to hammer the sealant between the planks of the hull. Greg had several of these chisels in his tool-box, but one special size was missing.

As I entered Mr Green's workshop a little while after my friends, I was amazed by what I saw. The inside of the ancient shack was black with soot. The most astonishing trappings dangled from the walls. Chicken were happily jumping about on scrap metal piled high in the corners. Rays of sunlight filtered through the holes in the roof and cut through the smoke-filled air. Greg stood by the fire and pumped the huge bellows, while Guy had just placed the red hot piece of iron on the anvil. The central point of the scene was a black man. He held the iron with the tongs and picked up the hammer in one shaky hand. At first I thought that the hammer would just fall from his ancient claw, but then it swished through the air and hit the iron with immense precision. This was repeated several times, until the iron was heated once more and then again worked on. In due time and after many little pauses the caulking chisel began to take on its form.

One would think there was nothing special about watching a blacksmith at his work. But Mr Green was 93 years of age and had worked in his profession much longer than many other people lived. He was deeply religious. When the work was finished, he said a little prayer of thanks and gave us his blessing for our onward voyage.

Before we left Grenada, we met him a second time and invited him for a coffee. Conversation led to where we came from and we spoke about various countries in Asia, Africa and Europe. Mr Green seemed to know all these places well, and there was no country about which he could not make at least one intelligent and up-to-date remark. He spoke so knowledgeably about foreign places that we thought he must have travelled a great deal. But when we asked him when he had been to all these places, he surprised us again by saying: "I have never left Grenada in my life. But I read a lot and travel in my mind."

Venezuela

Death in Cabo San Francisco

Close hauled and in rough seas we fought our way overnight from Grenada to Venezuela. The distance was short but the contrast sharp. Venezuela lies outside the tracks of the tropical storms, but here was a gale brewing. Due to a banking crash, this country, so rich in natural resources, was on the brink of civil war. As was usual in cases such as these, those responsible had long left for other countries. As a result, the Bolivar fell drastically in value and now the victims who had lost out on a big scale were protesting sharply. The international press had reported in depth about the crises, and we started to wonder where the bigger risk lay – further north in the zone of the hurricanes or here in Venezuela. Before leaving Grenada, I phoned relatives of mine in Caracas, and they calmed us down. "Don't worry", they assured me. "Venezuela has been through many crises like this."

So we set sail for Venezuela.

In the early morning hours we anchored in a bay called Cabo San Francisco in eastern Venezuela. We were treated to overwhelmingly beautiful scenery. High mountains with clouds clinging to their flanks and completely covered in dense jungle surrounded us. In some places, the bright colours of tropical blooms shimmered through the thick undergrowth. Streams carrying crystal-clear water ran across the beach. One American yacht, aptly named *Little Haste*, was already anchored in the bay. Following the usual practice, we spent the evening with her crew. Marty and Beth turned out to be a pensioned couple who sailed the Caribbean at their leisure. They agreed with us that neither of us had ever anchored in such a spectacular bay.

The following morning saw us diving extensively. Our booty was a big sack full of mussels, which we cooked to a French recipe (Moules Marinière: cook the cleaned mussels in a big pot with chopped carrots and onions in white wine. Add garlic to taste. Simmer with the lid on until the mussels open up, then add cream and fresh parsley).

After this meal, we went ashore and entered the jungle. In the strange cool twilight we could see endless variations of green. Any biologist or botanist would have found his Eldorado here.

"Shall we make a small expedition?", I suggested.

"What about the poisonous snakes?" The others were a bit hesitant. "There must be lots of them around here?"

"It can't be worse than South Africa. If we make enough noise, surely they'll disappear!"

So we tried to penetrate the jungle, which turned out to be extremely difficult. We had to climb uphill and fight every inch of the way through the dense scrub. We nearly lost our way, but stumbled on a small stream which led us back downhill to the beach.

Later, we proudly told the locals in Carúpano about our excursion and they were completely horrified. They informed us that an extremely nasty species of poisonous snake lives in the area around Cabo San Francisco; it is very aggressive and attacks anything which comes close, noise or no noise. Some weeks before, a woman from a French yacht had been bitten by one. Emergency calls on the radio brought no response and, by then desperate for help, her husband had sought help in a nearby fishing village. The local medicine-man, however, had been unable to do anything and the trip of seventy miles to the next hospital, which was in Carúpano, became a race against time which they tragically lost. By the time she arrived in hospital, it was far too late for help.

This lethal incident shows that cruising people in remote corners of the earth live without the security network which most of us take for granted. We discussed the obvious question of whether anything could have been done by the right initial treatment. Various ways of treating snake bites came up, but the final word came from the Survival Handbook. Here it said that a wound like the one in question should not be cut out, nor should one attempt to suck the poison from the wound. The only thing to do is to calm the victim and make him lie down, positioning the bite lower than the heart. Cool the wound with cold water or ice if possible, wash it with cold water and soap. To stop the poison from spreading, put a tight bandage (but not completely cutting off the bloodstream) on and above the wound. If, for example, someone has been bitten in the ankle, the bandage should go from the knee downwards. Treatment for shock and artificial ventilation may become necessary.

Plagues

We sailed further west along the monumental mountain ranges of this coastal region. Just before dusk we anchored in "Ensa Mejillones". I was just writing up the log when Greg called me by the name he had chosen for me: "Ralphman!"

"What's up?"

"Quick, come on deck. We have visitors and I am sure they want to see you!"

One glance was enough. I immediately fled back below decks, laughing, and said: "They're your concern. The captain is not available!"

The visitors were two extremely fat women who had paddled over from the fishing huts in a tiny boat. Their offers were unambiguous. My friends apparently had a hard time explaining to them that they were not interested.

"You bastard!", they shouted when I put my head through the companionway a bit later and innocently asked: "Have they left you?"

Soon, the sun dropped below the horizon and darkness descended. We lit candles and settled down in the cockpit for dinner. It was completely still and very romantic. Very hungry, I attacked my meal at the very instant when an insect landed on my plate. My friends displayed their malicious sense of humour, but only for a few seconds. Suddenly, the insects were upon us in their thousands. A plague of frightening dimension started, and the candles were suffocated under the onslaught of insects drawn there by the light. The crawling mass quickly built up around and underneath our paraffin lamp, which we had rigged as a riding light. This invasion reminded us of Hitchcock and even we hardened adventurers were decidedly uncomfortable with it all. The insects were flying ants, which apparently went off together in their millions. Hastily we fled below decks and closed all ports and hatches, despite the humid tropical heat. During the night, we heard the rattling of an anchor chain which meant that the only other yacht in the bay was leaving. In the morning, we found the entire boat covered in a thick layer of insects. With buckets full of water we swept them off the deck and ended this grisly episode.

Negotiations for clearance

Two days later we arrived in Carúpano, a port of entry, where our stay in Venezuela officially began. In the brooding mid-day heat we tramped along to the offices of customs and immigration, and I could not help thinking of the old Asian saying: "Only mad dogs and Englishmen go out in the mid-day sun." Anyway, we found the office and in my few words of Spanish I explained why we had come and presented our impressive array of documents, including the visa and permits which we had previously obtained in Trinidad. The whole affair of checking in was a complicated, time-consuming and expensive procedure. The official studied our paperwork with obvious boredom, sighed and leant back in his chair. We perspired in the hot, motionless air. More and more papers and documents were produced; all had to be filled in and signed. At long last, we thought that the ordeal was over and that we could now leave. We should have known that there was still the crucial question.

"Money?"

"Yes", the official replied and lazily lifted six flabby fingers into the air.

"Six dollars?" We thought this to be expensive, but the crook unashamedly demanded sixty dollars. We had already paid all fees for clearance into Venezuela, so we had been told in the Venezuelan embassy in Trinidad when we had obtained our visas and permits. Now what? Time ticked past. I did not have nearly enough money on me, just about 20 dollars. We lamented and gesticulated, then finally turned our pockets inside out and found another five dollars. The face of the official lit up.

"That will be enough", he said. "But only because it is you!"

We fled from the office quickly before he could change his mind again.

The harbour master's office was at the other end of town. When we finally arrived there, the building looked empty and deserted and a glance at my watch confirmed it: siesta time. We slumped down into the shade of a tree and waited. When the harbour master finally arrived, we had to endure a similar scene to the one with his customs colleague.

Clearing in here demands a lot of money and cunning negotiations.

Venezuela

Exhausted from the clearance procedures and the heat, we sank into our hammocks, which we had rigged between the end of the boom and the shrouds. Time to read up on this country which was still completely new to us. We learnt that the coastline is 1600 nautical miles long and has 72 outlying islands. Twenty million people live here, in an area of 912,000 square kilometres. The majority of inhabitants are of Indian and Spanish descent, with some Africans along the coast. Under the leadership of Simon Bolivar, Venezuela gained her independence from Spain in 1823 along with Colombia, Ecuador and Panama. Venezuela is made up of four very different regions: the highlands in the west and along the coast, the lowlands around Lake Maracaibo, the Llanos which is a vast plain around the Orinoco and finally the highland of Guyana, which extends for over half the country.

Basic facts about day-to-day life in this country were given to us by the owner of a classic French schooner who was anchored close to us and who invited us on board for the traditional round of sundowners. "Life for us foreigners is very cheap here after the devaluation of the Bolivar", he said. "Fuels, such as diesel, beer and rum, can be had for almost nothing!" With this he filled our glasses generously as if to prove his point.

Three cans of the local beer, 'Polar', only cost one dollar at the time, and rum was nearly as cheap, the best brands being 'Pampero' and 'Cazique'. But our French friend also warned us that criminality was extremely high. A yacht should never be left unattended and it was suicide to venture ashore in the harbour towns after midnight. During the course of the evening we also learnt that our host was recovering from a heart attack.

"Sailing is the best medicine of all", he maintained.

He had bought this 18-metre ship for only around 10,000 dollars and was planing to renovate her here in Venezuela. The schooner originated from a yard near Boulogne in the north of France, which is where I had first learnt sailing in my youth.

In Carúpano, I temporarily left *Ryusei* and my friends to visit my cousin in Caracas, while Greg and Guy sailed on alone. They jumped at the idea and apparently loved the prospect of sailing without their 'restless' skipper. I trusted them completely with the boat and had no problems whatsoever with the idea of letting them sail *Ryusei*.

However, as I later heard, they very nearly met with catastrophe on their trip. As Guy wrote in a letter to his girlfriend: 'We had a great sail from Carúpano to the island of Testigos. Under way we saw a huge whale and while looking at him we almost ran over a fishing boat anchored on a reef twenty miles offshore. The yelling of the fishermen saved us, virtually at the last second, from colliding with them.'

The entry in the log was more positive, mainly about snorkelling off Tortuga:

'The reef was vibrant with marine life. This was the best spot we have ever dived. Ralph would have gone mad, too, seeing this spectacular show with uncountable fish and coral species.'

My visit to Caracas gave me an impressive insight into the 'normal' life in Venezuela at the time. One of my two cousins picked me up at the airport and we drove along a wide highway into town. On the outskirts, we passed slums with shacks which clung to the mountainside in a most precarious fashion. The traffic reminded me of the chaos of Asian cities, only that here the South American temperament makes it even hotter to drive – stopping at a red traffic light will inevitably provoke an angry concerto of horns behind you. My cousin stayed cool about this and also the fact that the quarter in which he lived had to be guarded by armed sentries.

"There has always been a lot of criminality in this country and we have simply grown used to it", he said, "although the situation has worsened a bit lately." With this, he slapped the pistol which he was carrying in a holster slung from his belt. "But don't worry. I know how to use this!" He had been carrying a weapon ever since he had been spectacularly kidnapped to Colombia in his own plane a few years ago. He got off lightly, having managed to escape and make his own way back to Venezuela. About the current situation he said: "I don't believe that we will have a civil war. Our government is totally useless and corrupt, but we have survived worse situations. A few years ago there was a putsch with a lot of fighting and shooting. I retired to the roof of my house with my wife and kids and a few weapons."

My two cousins came to Venezuela when their parents emigrated and settled here, along with about 800,000 others, after the last World War. They had studied in the United States and had a flourishing engineering company in Caracas. They also managed a farm in Llanos which they had inherited from their parents. Both my cousins and their children all held Venezuelan passports. "In Germany, with all the legislation and restriction, we would surely suffocate", they told me. "This may sometimes be like the Wild West, but we can cope with it."

A few days later I rejoined my friends and *Ryusei*.

Golfo de Cariacu

The gulf of Cariacu is bordered by the peninsula of Araya. On our way to Cumana, we wanted to visit some anchorages in the gulf which were mentioned in the pilot book. We had a pleasant sail in steady winds – until we rounded the eastern tip of the peninsula. We sailed past a shallow lagoon in which the Spaniards used to collect salt as early as the 16th century. Salt was of course extremely valuable then, as it was used to conserve provisions. To protect their interests here, they built the most impressive fortress of Castillo de Santiago de Araya here in 1665.

All our attention was focused on the ruins of this castillo. At this moment, sudden gusts of great force howled from the land to us and before we knew what had happened *Ryusei* lay on her side and rounded up into the wind, the autopilot having had no chance to keep her on course in this onslaught. There was a great crash below decks, and the cabin was transformed into chaos. For this short distance, we had not bothered to stow away our things properly. We rolled away most of the genoa and let the main out. Now on a reach, *Ryusei* flew away, with white water foaming along her lee rails and the deck often awash. The log showed impressive speeds and then, as suddenly as it had come, the wind died again.

"That was close", Greg said. "It was probably the wind funnelling through the valley in which the salt pans lie."

But then we reached the anchorage of Laguna Chica and the beauty of this near-prefect spot quickly made us forget this unfortunate incident. Chica is a bay which is almost completely enclosed by land. From a nearby hill, we enjoyed another spectacular sunset and overlooked the Laguna Grande, which was a few miles further. Once there, we were spoilt for choice with dozens of perfect anchorages. The landscape mainly consisted of bare hills, coloured reddish-brown, with cactuses and shrub. Goats wandered about ashore and pelicans floated on the water. We anchored and brought a stern-line ashore, which we tied to the mangroves which grew in abundance along the shore. Then we used the dinghy to explore our surroundings. Soon, we found that *Little Haste* was also anchored close by, drawn here, as we were, by the exceptional natural beauty of this lagoon.

The evening was spent under a full moon around a camp fire ashore, on which we grilled a freshly caught fish. I liked this spot so much that I decided to sleep ashore and rigged my hammock between the mangroves. I also won a bet with Guy, who doubted my courage to sleep ashore in the wilderness – although I nearly died with fright when, early in the morning, goats came to the cold fire in search of food and I only noticed them when they suddenly started to bleat, only a few feet away.

Marty and Betsi from *Little Haste* visited us for breakfast. This developed into a brunch and from there it became a lunch-time beer party which went on into the afternoon. Then, quite abruptly, we decided to leave. Guy described it as follows: 'They (Marty & Betsi) said there were some pretty waitresses at the Club Maigualida across the Gulf. So Ralph alters our plans and off we go to Puntar Mariguitar with full sails and 33 knots wind as we rounded the point. Net result is, I got soaked from head to toe and was not too impressed; although later on the hot shower in the Club made up for it.'

The waitresses turned out be quite friendly but could not compete with the excellent steaks which we were served in this holiday resort. Also, the activities of the day had completely exhausted us. Back on board, Greg and I watched Guy as he was unpacking his shower bag. He put his hand inside, gave a high-pitched shriek, threw the bag away in panic and jumped into the air, all at the same time. Greg and I doubled up laughing, as we knew the reason for these antics: back ashore, we had found a crab in the showers and hid it in Guy's bag. On the downside, his promise of revenge kept us on our toes for days.

Rather less entertainingly, Greg complained about pain in his foot. A few days ago he had scratched himself, a minor injury which he had ignored, and now it was inflamed and the foot swollen.

"Well, our first-aid kit has all we need, including a knife for amputations", I joked. But then we realised that this might be serious and returned ashore, where the helpful manager of the resort drove us to a doctor, although it was by now very late at night. Here, Greg was treated with injections and antibiotics.

"In this region, even the smallest injuries can lead to blood poisoning", the young doctor told us. "You were lucky to have come here. By tomorrow, the entire leg would have been badly swollen!"

He then flatly refused to accept any form of payment.

The following afternoon, we were underway again. It was only a very short hop to Cumana, so we left the hammocks rigged and sailed only under genoa on a reach, roughly parallel to the coast. "No problem", I thought and made myself comfortable in the hammock, glancing at the horizon and checking our position with only half an eye. Sun, music and the easy motion spoilt us. While *Ryusei* sailed along under autopilot, her skipper lay in the hammock, Greg slept in his bunk and Guy dozed lazily in the cockpit. Once again I glimpsed at the horizon, checking course and position. All seemed fine – and then we grounded. First we bumped softly, then more definitely, and finally we were firmly stuck. Never before had I left my hammock at such speed, and Greg shot up on deck like lightning. Seconds later, the genoa flapped in the breeze and the engine roared, with black smoke spilling from the exhaust. Luckily, small waves sometimes lifted us ever so slightly and, agonisingly slowly, we hobbled off the shoal back into deep water. The mistake had been mine, of course. One bank extended one and a half miles offshore and, choosing the shortest route to Cumana, I had overlooked this shoal patch and had not left enough margin from the coast.

And as it this wasn't enough, we again grounded in the entrance to the marina at Cumana. "Don't worry!", the marina man said on the radio. "The entrance is a bit silted up, but it's all soft!" So we scraped across until we made fast in deeper water alongside the jetty.

Cumana

Cumana, on the Gulf of Cariacu, is one of Venezuela's largest ports. Here, we also found a well-guarded yacht marina. Even the entry formalities went quickly and smoothly. Roberto, a local who had specialised in yacht services and the management of the marina, dealt with all the relevant authorities. We spent our time working on *Ryusei*. The list was long: servicing the main engine and the outboard, repair of the sails, several layers of varnish on the wooden parts on deck, fitting of a new bilge pump, replacement of worn out sheets and halyards, a complete cleaning of the boat, and so on.

The nightlife of Cumana was not very thrilling, but this changed all of a sudden. Alongside the neighbouring pontoon was a small, deserted Spanish yacht called *Borracho*. Then her owner arrived, a very attractive Spanish-German lady from Barcelona. Anna had critically injured her knee in a parachute crash-landing and spent three years with many operations in various hospitals, after which she was only just able to walk again. With the money from the insurance she had bought herself the boat and went off sailing, which is how she came to be in Venezuela. She had just returned from a visit to Europe and was now preparing the boat. Her sister's family was going to join her for a cruise along Venezuela's coast.

At first, everyone worked by themselves on their own boats. But soon we grew together as one working team and things got positively turbulent when Anna's sister Layena arrived, together with her husband Cavio and her kids Pablo and Samaya. One evening, all of them joined us on board for drinks, as well as the Spanish couple Angel and Elli from a catamaran, whom Anna had met on her outward voyage from Europe. The evening developed into a spirited party, so to speak, but all went well until our guests started to stagger home. In the darkness, Angel missed his footing on the dock, fell, hit *Ryusei*'s hull with his head and splashed into the water between pier and boat. We quickly recovered him and inspected his wound. His head was bleeding, but luckily Roberto was around and he offered to drive us to the hospital in his jeep.

Cavio and I took our injured friend between us and carried him to the car park. Roberto's jeep was a sorry affair. The front seats stood loosely on the floor, the exhaust dangled on the ground, brakes were non-existent and the gears had to held in place by the co-driver. Still, it seemed better to drive in this vehicle than to walk and carry Angel.

Roberto drove with gusto and apparently great confidence in his personal guardian angel. But two kilometres on, the engine spluttered and died.

"Mierda!", shouted Roberto. "I have forgotten to fill up with petrol! But there's a hotel over there, we will surely find a taxi there." He took our still bleeding friend under the arms and hurried off with him to the hotel, while Cavio and I pushed the jeep from the road with what little energy we had left.

Angel survived this evening. As a reminder, he carried away an impressive scar and he was tormented by headaches the following morning. But nobody could say whether these came from his injury or the rum.

Roberto's jeep was rehabilitated when we bought our provisions at the market. Although we were buying stores for several weeks, the overall cost was very low, thanks to the devaluation of the Venezuelan currency. Sacks and crates full of fruit and vegetables were piled on top of each other in the jeep, and in the end there was only one tiny space left for Roberto in the driver's seat. We followed by taxi. After everything had been stowed away on board, we left the harbour with *Borracho* and anchored only shortly afterwards in the romantic Laguna Chica bay.

Again, we were treated to a dazzling sunset, plus our open fire and barbecue on the beach beneath a brilliant starlit night sky. From time to time, we cooled off in the water. The fluorescent water caused explosions of greenish light at each movement and it seemed as if these glowing sparks wanted to challenge the glow of the stars above. Ashore, we kept the fire going with driftwood and Anna played her guitar and started to sing.

But despite the obvious joy, I felt misery on this magical evening. That same day I had received a message that my friend, with whom I was going to sail the last leg of my voyage to Europe, had tragically died in a car crash. I was aware of the passing of life and that somewhere the end is waiting for all of us. All it took was a tiny bit of negligence or a whim of nature.

The invasion

La Blanquilla is a remote island about one hundred miles off the coast of Venezuela. We sailed there on a memorable night passage. The wind was fine and everything as usual when, just before dawn, I spotted the navigation lights of two ships that were approaching us on a converging course.

As they were very slow, I at first believed them to be fishing boats. Then I saw lightning on the horizon, followed by claps of thunder. The sky was completely clear and I thought I had imagined something when I saw and heard them again. But were those not horizontal streaks of lightning?

I woke up my shipmate: "Greg, listen. I think we are on collision course with two ships and I am imagining horizontal bolts of lightning. Maybe I'm going mad!"

A pale shimmer on the horizon preceded the break of dawn. We looked in the general direction where I had seen the lightning before. There it was again, clearer than before – horizontal flashes. A battleship firing her artillery.

"This seems to be an exercise", Greg said.

"Let's hope so! But what shall we do with the two ships to starboard? They are coming nearer and nearer."

"I'd contact them on VHF 16", Greg replied.

So I went below and sent off a call on the radio: "Motor vessel, motor vessel heading west – this is sailing vessel one mile off your port bow heading north. We are on a collision course. Please advise. Over!"

No answer came and with decreasing distance we grew more and more nervous. Then we heard a curt and distinctly American voice on the radio:

"Sailing vessel calling – This is a Navy convoy. You are requested to stand by on our port side until the whole convoy has passed – Out"

Reluctantly we reduced our genoa and tacked. As the morning grew lighter, more and more ships came into sight. We could soon distinguish deck houses and guns while they slowly carried on westwards. Suddenly they all changed course by 90 degrees and came straight towards us. This time, we neither hesitated or asked, but tacked back onto our previous course and sailed through the armada, with more and more navy ships materialising from the haze. We felt surrounded by them and this helpless feeling was increased when helicopters started to lift off from the decks of various ships. One of them buzzed around our mast and created such turbulence that our sails flapped about. In the open door we could see some Marines, laughing and waving to us.

Soon afterwards, we heard that the US Navy had landed in Haiti.

Venezuelan islands

*Nothing is more rewarding then spending
the whole day doing nothing,
and after having done so – to rest!*

In the weeks to follow, we found ample rest and idleness in the islands of Venezuela. First, we landed on Blanquilla which treated us to spectacular beaches, clear water and ideal diving grounds. The island itself was low and sparsely vegetated, mostly by thousands of cactuses all in full bloom. On one of the beaches we found a group of palm trees which could not have been better suited to support our hammocks. We sometimes asked ourselves, in the face of this perfect island, what drove us to continue sailing on and on. The evenings were spent with the crew of *Borracho* on the beach. We watched the sunsets in the hope of catching the legendary green flash. Or we lay in the sand and told stories or just studied the stars above. Anna was our expert in astrology and we listened to her in fascination, although the rhythmic swoosh of the water lapping on the beach was a powerful narcotic.

The most spectacular bay we found was on the eastern side of Blanquilla. There was just enough room inside for our two boats to anchor and a natural rock bridge extended over the water on one side.

But all this was topped by Los Roques. As we were approaching this group of islands, we saw a green shimmer in the clouds over the western horizon. The intense green of the mangroves was reflected in the clouds. We were lucky to reach the pass in the outside reef at the right time. If the sun had been in a different angle, we would not have been able to see the shallows due to the sunlight reflecting on the water. *Borracho* was not quite so lucky; they arrived during the night at had to heave-to outside until dawn.

Another boat already lay at anchor in the lagoon and a very attractive French girl came across to us to ask if we could take her to Chile. "Chile sounds very tempting", I replied, "but I'm afraid it is not on our route. I don't even know if we will ever leave here again!", I added, looking around.

Later, I took out my secret calculations, as this was exactly my old dream. Panama, Galapagos, Chile, Cape Horn, Argentina and then Scotland – why not? Together with a sweet Frenchwoman. My friends laughed at my ideas.

"Ralph, you are incurable!"

But then I finally made up my mind. "14,000 miles is too much!" Instead, I concentrated on Los Roques.

This archipelago extends over an area of 25 miles in length and 14 in width. It is a small paradise full of coral reefs, idyllic islands and mangroves. There are sheltered waters for sailing and innumerable anchorages. Depending on the depth, the colour of the water had all possible variations. In the dinghy, we embarked on long trips through the endless labyrinth of lakes and mangrove trees. The water was shallow, clear and full of fish. Once, we ran aground at high speed, but luckily we were able to start the outboard again. Otherwise, the mosquitoes would have drained us of all blood.

We also, of course, dived on the coral reefs. For this, we had to wade through the surf on the reef into deeper water. And as soon as we were in the water, a frightening barracuda stared at us from close quarters, and as if this were not enough a shark also appeared on the scene. We hoped that he was driven less by hunger than by curiosity and continued to dive. Later, we were successful at fishing and caught a barracuda – possibly the very same one which had given us a fright earlier on.

Two days later we sailed to the main island, Gran Roques. Here we intended to do our paperwork for clearing in, as the regulations dictated. As was to be expected, our documentation was once again not complete. One of the clearance documents had expired, we were told, and we had to sail back to the mainland to have it extended. Whether this was true or only down to the lack of bribe we could not establish, but promised to sail away immediately. We then set a course for the next bar. Cavio was celebrating his birthday and this was more than enough reason to throw a few bottles of Polar beer down our thirsty throats. The party then continued on Anna's boat and in the end not only the boat but all the guests could be called *Borracho*, which simply means drunk.

In the anchorage of the neighbouring island we met the Japanese boat *Yu-U*, which Anna already knew from the earlier stages of her voyage. In the evening they all came across to *Ryusei* and in their honour and to their surprise, we hoisted the flag of the rising sun. When her skipper, Yoshi, asked me how we came to have the Japanese flag on board, I told him of *Ryusei*'s history. When he heard that she had been built by the yard 'Kato Boat', he bowed, deeply impressed, and said: "That is our best yard for wooden boats in Japan. They specialise in fishing boats but whatever they build is extremely solid!"

Yoshi also unravelled a secret which had been left unsolved by the previous owner. There was an inscription in Japanese on the side of our ship's bell and he translated it for us. "It says 'Fuji' and gives a date, April 1966. This is probably your boat's original name and the date of her launching."

For us Europeans, Japanese are the one people from the East with the greatest cultural differences. Despite this, we always found very basic subjects of common interest, such as fishing, eating and drinking. We heard that Yoshi and his friends mainly sailed around the world to fish. He was an engineer by profession. But he also owned a shushi bar in Osaka, and it had been there that, in a moment of exuberance, he had decided to sail around the world. For Greg, Guy and myself it turned out to be an instructive evening, as we learnt a lot about the preparation of various fish. In their broken English, they explained how they lived: "We live off rice, fish and fruit", Yoshi said. "And beer and rum", his girlfriend Sako added, laughing.

"And as we do not want to live off rice alone, we fish as often as we can. We love the small fish. They are tastier than the big ones. For sashimi, raw fish, we only use the very best parts."

Some of Yoshi's tips I noted down in our log:

The preparation of fish:
• clean inside and out, remove all scales
• rinse in saltwater
• cut up or fillet
• important: afterwards, do not clean any more with water

For raw marinated fish:
• cut the fish into thin strips
• marinate for three to five hours in a mixture of soy sauce, sugar, garlic and spices

For air-dried fish:
• prepare as above, but only marinate for one to three hours
• dry in an airy spot
• before eating, fry the fish briefly

The days drifted by in perfect harmony. Usually, we slept long, had breakfast, then went fishing or diving, read or had siestas in our hammocks. From time to time we would move on to the next anchorage, again make dinghy or diving trips and then gather with our friends for sundowners and the evening meal.

The nature ashore and underwater was so varied that we lost all sense of time. According to our log, we anchored on the 14th of August off the island of Carenero. This magic place drew our friends here as well, and soon we were united again: *Borracho*, the catamaran *Bumero* with Angel and Elli, as well as *Yu-U*. Already in the anchorage was an ancient fishing boat, gaff rigged, by the name of *Martha*. We celebrated every single evening, on each boat in turn. We came from all corners of the globe, including the Far East, and yet were one family. Angel and Elli served their national dish on their boat, a huge paella. This went well with Spanish wine, music and, later, dancing. The following day, we were the hosts and we prepared an Indian fish curry. Finally, the Japanese showed us what they had in store. For days on end we saw them fishing feverishly. Twenty-four hours before the planned feast they started to prepare the meal.

When we asked how we could help, Yoshi replied: "We have enough small fish, but we still need a few larger ones." So off we went on a fishing trip, criss-crossing the lagoon in *Ryusei* and trailing our lines. It was a fun day, as Anna and her crew had joined us, although our success in fishing was more on the moderate side and we only caught three and a half fish. This last one was bitten in half by a cannibal fish just as we were hauling it in.

Yoshi and his team amazed us. Even during all my years in the far east have I never seen such a variety of fish – grilled, marinated and dried in many different ways, including octopus, crabs and mussels. We also had, naturally, sushi, as well as fish bones fried in oil which we ate like potato chips. After this lavish meal, we all drank from Yoshi's so-called 'friendship cup', which was one half of a watermelon filled with rum and fruit. This went round and round until we were all dizzy from the alcohol.

Another most romantic night we had on the deck of *Martha*.

Here, we enjoyed the spectacle of the setting sun. Fish herons had already settled in their sleeping trees ashore and the trees and yachts were reflected in the still water. This peaceful atmosphere was then shattered by the pelicans, which dive-bombed into the water close around us by the dozen. To the amusement of our Japanese friends, I remarked: "This looks like the attack on Pearl Harbour."

Christian, our host, explained: "They do this every morning and every evening. The water here is full of fish shoals."

Without tiring, the pelicans continued to dive. Upon surfacing, they put their heads far back and their beaks in the air, and let the water flow out to before swallowing their prey. Sometimes, an especially courageous seagull would land on one of the pelican's heads and try to steal part of their catch.

Martha was the last fishing boat under sail to have been built in Sweden, in the year 1912. The Austrian Christian had renovated her with his Swedish wife before they set off on their long voyage. But it now sounded as if their trip would come to an end here in Venezuela.

"Here we can live with very little money, and maybe also renovate our rotten boat. If only the Venezuelan authorities would not cause us so much aggravation!", Christian said. He then showed me the most astonishing engine I have ever set my eyes upon. It was a huge single-cylinder diesel. "This one has no gearbox. When going into reverse, the propeller blades are adjusted accordingly. But despite the age, this engine is still completely reliable!"

Martha's saloon was fitted out like an Alpine hut and was quite spacious, although with 17 of us sitting around the table, it soon got a bit cramped. The interior was lined with slatted wood and, on inspecting this, I found that there were some sliding doors with berths behind along the sides. After another lavish meal we went on deck, where the night air cooled us down a little. Our sailing family from seven nations lounged underneath the oil lamp on sails, ropes and boxes, and soon the sounds of guitars and singing drifted up through the ancient rigging to the brilliant stars above.

Another extract from Guy's diary:

'It was a beautiful moment this morning as I got woken up by pelicans dive bombing around the boat with the sun just beginning to poke its head over the horizon. I had breakfast and went for a snorkel on the reef next to the boat, which was really exceptional. Hundreds upon hundreds of tiny fish, which the pelicans eat, blocked the view. Beautiful coral heads covered with tiny Christmas trees of white, yellow, orange, red, purple and mixtures. Large purple and white sea anemones. Beautiful little yellow fish, yellow with black dots, grey with black dots, purple pink parrot fish, blue angel fish, brown and fluorescent green rock cod, multicoloured long thin fish, green corals and purple-yellow fish, little black ones with fluorescent blue dots, larger ones with blue dots on their heads and yellow tails and many others I have forgotten about.'

West of Los Roques are two smaller archipelagos named the Islas Las Aves. As we approached the first group, Aves de Barlovento, under spinnaker, we saw a cloud of sea-birds hover over the main island. None of us had ever seen so many birds in one flock before. They inhabit the island completely, noisily fight for their place in the trees or defend their nests. Islas de Aves, the Birds' Islands, are aptly named.

Strong wind made our first anchorage unsafe so, on the following morning, *Borracho* and we looked for a more sheltered spot behind the horse-shoe-shaped reef. We motored carefully through the water, which was full of coral heads – but then we touched. A small lapse in concentration caused us to collide with one of them. We got away with a shock and a small scratch on the keel, but the damage to nature was far greater. Our temporary grounding must have destroyed coral structures which had grown over centuries. This destruction gets even worse when anchor chains drag over the coral ground. This is why we took great care to always choose clear, sandy spots in which to anchor.

Towards evening, the usual activities for the preparation of our beach camp and barbecue began. Collecting driftwood, piling it up and setting fire to it, then ferrying drinks, food and some pots and pans across. We had run out of alcoholic drinks, but the beauty of the surrounding nature was enough to make us drunk. As the setting sun painted a kaleidoscope of colours across the sky, the full moon rose on the opposite horizon. At the same time, thousands of birds drifted across the sky, as if they belonged to this perfect picture.

That night and the following day, I had problems with my stomach, and the same complaints were heard from *Borracho*. Pablo and Samaya had even thrown up. We guessed that the cause might be the grilled barracuda we had eaten. Guy seemed to be better off, as all he wrote in his diary was: 'Today is August the 20th and I was, what you call, at the height of laziness, alternating between bunk and the hammock reading my book.'

The neighbouring archipelago of Aves de Sotavento was every bit as spectacular. Islands with white sand and palm trees, surrounded by coral reefs. On one of the islands we found a huge pile of empty conch shells. We spotted accordingly few living shells under water. We got the impression that conch shells and lobsters are becoming extinct in this part of the world, due to ruthless exploitation – and we also sometimes ate conch and lobster, so we too were culpable. While we lay at anchor, a small fishing boat came alongside. They had caught a lobster and wanted to sell it. 'If we don't take it, someone else will', we persuaded ourselves and struck the bargain. For one can of coke and two tins from our supplies, we received the lobster. Our last night in this Venezuelan island world we spent ashore in a derelict fishing hut. In the flickering, dancing light of our camp fire, we again thought about this wonderful but far too short time.

Bonaire

The island of Bonaire is only 35 miles west of Aves de Sotavento. She and her neighbours, the islands of Aruba and Curaçao, form the Dutch Antilles. These islands, under Dutch influence, are affluent due to their tax-free status and tourism industry. Bonaire also has the sea as an asset: in a shallow lagoon in the south part, salt is won from the sea-water. But she also has spectacular diving grounds with crystal-clear water that attracts tourists from all over the world. We were astonished when we saw the large new buildings along the waterfront. But when we paid

Guy with barracuda

the mooring fee in the marina, we also found that this luxury has its price. Still, we chose to stay here as we had a lot of jobs to do and also wanted the luxury of a truly hot shower. The entry formalities were quick and easy, so we entered 'Karels Bar' for our sundowner shortly after arriving. This bar on the waterfront is the meeting place for yachties and here it did not take us long to learn about the strategic points on Bonaire.

Daily, we went on diving trips. The best diving spots were marked with buoys and anchoring was forbidden here. In contrast to the neighbouring countries, this was a place where law and order were enforced so, this time around, we kept to the rules and let the boat drift with one of us on board while we took turns in diving. But this exercise was well worth it. Underwater, we found steep vertical cliffs overgrown with coral while the water had an unbelievable transparency. At the same time, we were surprised by the number of fish, small and large, who swam close to us without fear. Some of them came so close in a demanding fashion that it seemed like an attack. We later heard that the fish were fed for the attraction of the tourists.

Our onward journey threatened to be delayed. In the customs office, the key for the arms chamber could not be found. But this was the place where our harpoon was locked away.

"Where is this stupid key?" the customs inspector cursed, opening every single drawer in the office.

We watched him, amused, and finally he said: "Come back in one hour. Maybe one of my colleagues has taken the key with him by mistake." We returned, but still the key was missing. We could see that the official was highly embarrassed. That this should happen in such an organised country!

"I am sorry. The key is gone. I have phoned the locksmith. He will come any minute now and break open the door."

Any minute meant at least another hour. Finally, the door was open and the official said: "Identify your own harpoon, that is much quicker:" We went in and saw a room full of weapons: pistols, rifles and harpoons.

"Are all these weapons which have been brought here by visiting yachts?", I asked, astonished. The official grinned and said: "Yes. You sailors seem to be quite scared on your travels!"

Borracho had already sailed for Venezuela. As we were faster, we could wait until evening. We spent the remaining hours on Peter's catamaran *Halejj*. The boat was of Russian design and looked rather fragile at first glance, but on closer inspection it turned out to be a piece of quite intelligent engineering. Peter, a psychologist from Austria, had bought the catamaran for very little money in Israel.

"The speed of this thing has frightened me more than once", he told us. "Once, in a storm, I took down all sails, but the wing-mast still had so much area that we were doing ten knots anyway!"

Peter had been in the region for some time and could tell us a lot. One subject was especially interesting for us: ciguatera. In some regions, there are toxic algae which grow on dead coral. Through the normal food chain the poison gets into the fish, especially those of barracuda. The poison attacks the nervous system and can cause lasting paralysis in human bodies; in extreme cases it can even be lethal. In this context I remembered our stomach problems a few days before, after we had eaten the barracuda. For some nights afterwards I woke up, hot and sweaty, although the night air had been rather cool. I also had painfully itching feet and hands. Peter confirmed that these were symptoms of ciguatera poisoning. He recommended eating less fish in the future, and particularly not the larger ones which are caught near coral reefs.

The music from Karels Bar drifted across the anchorage when we finally set sail. A strong wind brought an uncomfortable night and this must have been the night during which Guy decided to continue his travels ashore. He was suffering from the two worst illnesses that a seafarer can have: sea-sickness and love-sickness. Guy wanted to return as quickly as possible back home, or so he had told his girlfriend on the telephone. But she answered: "You don't have to hurry, Guy. Not for me, anyway!"

The message was clear. For our friend, who had been faithful to his girl through all temptations, this was a bitter pill indeed.

Chichirivichi and Morocoy

Every Venezuelan knows these places, as these are the two most popular weekend and holiday spots of the region. We were easily able to identify Chichirivichi and the entrance to the Golfo de Cuare. The beaches along the outlying islands were covered with sunshades and people. Small motorboats zoomed around. But we were not deterred by all this hectic activity and sailed past into the gulf and anchored beneath a vertical cliff face next to *Borracho*. The humidity and the heat made breathing difficult, and even the water was not cooling, with a temperature of 31 degrees Celsius. In the deep crevices in the cliff were the remains of ancient Indian settlements.

Cavio had left Anna's team, and the 15-year-old Pablo was now alone on board with his sister, his mother and his aunt. All these women got on his nerves, so he jumped ship and joined us before we sailed on to the neighbouring Morocoy National Park. This place was again crowded with holidaymakers, but everyone seemed happy and there was music and dancing and laughter. The park was like an inland sea with some mangrove-covered islands in it, extending over an area of 60 square kilometres.

The evening light was just about sufficient to thread our way through the labyrinth of mangroves and shallows. Several times, we missed running aground by a hair's breadth. A motorboat which had just sped past us was suddenly high and dry on a shallow patch. We only briefly touched the bottom once, which came close to a miracle considering our draft. With the last light we reached the destined anchorage near a small mangrove island. *Borracho*, however, did not make it in daylight.

We saw a fascinating spectacle at dusk. Huge swarms of birds came up to us in the fading light, fluttered around us and then descended on the small island. These birds had red feathers and long beaks, and we identified them as red ibis. They were returning to their accustomed roosting trees, as they did every night.

With the first light of dawn they flew away again, bound for distant feeding grounds. Only a few feathers drifting in the water remained of them.

A local fishing boat came up to us early that morning. "Hello, are you all awake?", a familiar voice called out to us. It was Layena.

"What happened", asked Greg, who was on deck at the time. "Where are the others?"

"We ran aground last night and need you help to get her off again", she replied. We laughed and said to young Pablo: "Seems like you just changed ship at the right moment!"

As quickly as we could we then lifted our anchor and went to the place where it had happened. It was the same bank on which the motorboat had grounded that previous night. A buoy, which was shown on the chart, was missing. But Anna had tried to reach our anchorage despite the oncoming darkness. "You women always have to follow us men blindly", we joked but then set to work to get the boat off. *Borracho* had been lying on her side on the bank for the whole night, and together we put our warp anchor out far to one side of *Borracho*, then tied her spinnaker halyard to it. We then heeled her over even further with the halyard winch. Anna then started the engine and gave full throttle, but nothing happened. Only when we also used our dinghy with the 15 horsepower outboard did the boat inch forward. It took many more attempts until they were fully afloat once again.

Puerto Cabello

"Be warned. After darkness, especially in the unlit parts of town, you could easily be mugged." These were the words with which we were greeted by a heavily armed man on the pier of the yacht harbour. He was the guard of the marina off which we had just anchored. "And above all, never leave your boat unattended!"

"Welcome to Puerto Cabello", I joked. We went into a small, open restaurant and were constantly hassled by prostitutes and beggars. Puerto Cabello is Venezuela's largest natural harbour, but sadly it is nearly completely taken over by the navy. The town was, however, quite pleasant, at least during the day, and it offered all facilities for stocking up. Even the usually harassing formalities went smoothly, but this was due to Marianella, who runs the local yacht service for visiting yachts.

On the dock of the harbour master lay a very run down catamaran, and we got to know its owner later in the bar.

"Whatever happened to your boat?", we asked.

His report was rather sobering. "I arrived here a few months ago. I made the mistake of anchoring outside, rather than use the marina. I then made the even greater mistake of getting involved with a beautiful Venezuelan lady. While I spent the night with her ashore, my anchor chain was cut. When I returned, my boat lay ashore and was completely stripped out. And as if that was not enough, the authorities then got on to me. They had my boat towed to the harbour master's dock and then claimed several thousand dollars for doing so, as well as fees for the illegal import of yachting gear and equipment. They could not care less about the fact that all my equipment had been stolen from the boat. In the present state, the boat is probably worth less than 1000 dollars, so let them keep it! For me, the sailing trip is over. But I like it here; everything is so cheap that the little money that I have left keeps me going quite well."

After his conversation I was relieved to find our boat where we had left her. First thing next morning we moved to a berth inside the marina. I also gave the armed guard an extra tip, so that he would hopefully keep more than half a watchful eye on *Ryusei*.

Puerto Cabello was also the place where our courses diverged from each other again. Anna's family went back to Germany, and she had her hands full renovating her boat. I went on a journey deep inland, to visit the farm of my relatives. Greg stayed on board, while Guy packed his bags and went ashore; he now wanted to spend a few months travelling overland in South America before returning to South Africa. Sailing had brought us together. But now, it also separated us again. Would we ever see each other again? No one could tell, but one thing was sure: the memories of our shared adventure would keep us together for the rest of our lives.

Difficult excursion

When I returned from my inland expedition, I was greeted in the marina as if I was coming home. Peter and his girlfriend Coco had in the meantime arrived with their catamaran and they, Anna and Greg longed for a change from the usual marina life. Marianella had the right idea: "Why don't you go to the cascade in the mountains. That spot is a dream for bathing!"

Immediately, we packed our bags for the day and set off, a boisterous party of seven. Marianella would have loved to come along, and she would probably have saved us much hassle, but she had to teach. However, she gave Anna some detailed instructions for the route, and led us to a bus stop where we boarded a completely overcrowded bus.

"Yes, yes, this one is going into the right direction", we assured each other. After we had made a half-hour round trip of the whole of Puerto Cabello, we landed back where we had started from, at the bus station in front of the marina. At this stage, we were still laughing about this little hiccup. For the second attempt, we used a shared taxi. With about twenty people in all, we squeezed into the open back of a completely overloaded jeep. This time, the course seemed about right. But as soon as we had reached the outskirts of town, the engine spluttered and finally died. The crowd of passengers now gathered around the unfortunate vehicle, wildly gesticulating and arguing about how the ancient wreck could once again be coaxed back into life. We then tried to push it, until our tongues nearly touched the ground. There was nothing for it: we needed a new taxi.

Luck seemed on our side. A new taxi emerged and Anna persuaded the driver to take our party along. He hesitated but eagerly agreed when he heard the word "extra payment". Again, we squeezed into the crowded vehicle but, three kilometres on, the taxi stopped with smouldering tyres. The ancient American car was so overloaded that the bodywork had scraped on the tyres all the way. At least we had by now reached a cross-roads from where the actual road leading to the cascade began. Again, we were lucky and a delivery van took us along. After a long and winding drive uphill, we reached the stream and got out. From here, we had to cross a precarious looking suspension bridge on foot and then walk for another few kilometres along a rough track through the jungle. Our mood was plummeting fast when yet another miracle happened. A car came along and took us on board. This was driven by a friendly missionary who told us about his work and seized the opportunity of trying to convert us. At long last, we reached the waterfalls, where nature and the cool stream were enough rewards for the difficult journey. Admittedly we stayed in the water for a very long time, simply because we were somewhat afraid of the prospect of having to get back to the marina. But although it had taken five vehicles to get us here, we only used one for the return. Still, as Greg later remarked: "Now we know why sailors are not so keen on venturing too far inland!"

The thief

At some point the day arrived when our pockets were empty. We needed cash to pay for the marina fees and to buy provisions. I mentioned this when as we were sitting with Peter and Coco.

"We also have to get some money", Peter said.

But I groaned: "Last time, they counted out all my money in public in the bank. Thanks to all these warnings about mugging and criminality, I was really frightened on my way back to the boat!"

"Why don't we go to the bank together", Peter suggested. "I'll take my revolver along, just in case."

So the next day, Peter and I went to the bank, accompanied by Coco and Greg. Due to the devaluation, the money we got in exchange for one hundred US dollars came in a great pile. Again, this immense sum was counted out in front of everybody. Peter put the money in his shorts pocket, but they were tight to begin with and, as he also had the revolver, he was now having difficulties walking.

Greg, who had made fun of us over our safety precautions, then had a nasty surprise. We had just bought provisions and were carrying heavy bags in both hands. Greg was walking in front of me on the pavement. Suddenly, a cyclist came up from behind, overtook us very close, bumped into Greg and sped off. "Damn, my watch!", he shouted, dropped his bags and started after the cyclist. I joined in the chase, which was a mistake. On foot, we had no hope of catching up with the bike. The street was crowded with people, but nobody dared to stop the thief. When we finally returned to the place where we had dropped our bags, more than half of our shopping had also disappeared. Around us, everyone was smiling and nobody had seen anything.

The thief had stolen Greg's valuable diving watch. Angry, Greg said: "I'm sure it was the bastard who asked me what time it was just before. He probably just wanted to check if my watch was worth stealing!"

Emergency

For family reasons I had to go to Europe for a month. As I did not want to leave *Ryusei* in Venezuela during my absence, we sailed back to Bonaire. After my return, we intended to go back to Puerto Cabello to spent Christmas there and also to meet Anna, who had decided to stay in Venezuela. Because of the comparatively high prices in Bonaire we bunkered a lot of provisions and all essential fluids, which were fuel, beer and rum.

Guy's place was temporarily taken over by Greg's girlfriend Amy. They knew each other from the time when Greg had served his apprenticeship as a boat-builder in Maine. On my return from Europe I realised that their old love must have been inflamed again. One sure indication of the seriousness of the affair was Greg's insistent plea for us to sail to Maine, where Amy lived. His descriptions of this fantastic sailing area did not fail to impress me.

In the marina of Bonaire, another surprise was in store for me. Our friend Mike Johnson, with his boat *Aisa*, was in the harbour. We knew each other from South Africa. Moreover, *Yu-U* had turned up, and nothing better could have happened to us. An unforeseen event such as this clearly demands the assistance of drinking friends.

Upon my return from Europe, Greg came to me and said: "Ralph, we have a little problem."

"What's up? Are you going to be a father?"

"No, worse. Come and have a look."

He then lifted the floor-boards underneath which all our beer was stowed. A sour stench drifted up.

"It smells like a brewery. But thank god you haven't drunk

it all!"

But Greg insisted: "Take one of the six-packs!"

I grabbed one of them and found to my surprise that they were as light as a feather.

"What has happened?"

"I can only think that the cans have corroded in places and so all the beer has run into the bilge. They must be tiny cracks, invisible to the naked eye!" We then checked our stock and found that half of the beer had gone.

"The cockroaches are probably having a wild party down there. What now?"

Greg knew the answer. "Silly question. We will declare a state of emergency, gather all our friends and finish off the rest before it vanishes as well!"

Our emergency was a great success, and we could not complain about a lack of help.

Aisa's wonder-weapon

Mike told us about his adventures one night in *Aisa*'s cosy cabin. He had left Cape Town after us and sailed up the Amazon before coming here. He was now bound back for the United States, but planned to haul out his boat in Curaçao before continuing. When I told him of our plan to visit Colombia and Central America, he asked: "You don't by chance need a weapon? As far as I know those countries you are about to visit are extremely unsafe!"

"So far our Very pistol and the harpoon have been sufficient"

But Mike insisted. "I have something eminently suitable for you. It is a South African shotgun which I bought for the trip up the Amazon. But it happens to be the kind of weapon which is, under the new legislation, illegal to import into the United States."

"But a shotgun's nothing special", I replied.

"I'll show it you." With that he disappeared and returned with a harmless looking black sports bag. But what he pulled from it made us speechless. The weapon looked more like Al Capone's machine gun. It was a twelve-shot, 12-bore shotgun that worked on the revolver principle. It had an extendible stock, allowing it to either be used as a handgun or held up to the shoulder The weapon had a large ammunition drum and was semi-automatic.

"This gun falls into the category of assault weapons and these are now illegal for private use in the US. Luckily I didn't have to fire a single shot on my trip."

"Can you show me the manual?", I asked. The first few lines convinced me. I read: Shotgun-type Protector. Specially designed for use in confined spaces. Ideal family protection weapon.

After some short negotiations we were the owners of the 'Protector' and a sack full of ammunition. Gangsters and pirates beware!

That same day, we sailed with *Aisa* for Curaçao.

Imperial Poona Yacht Club

We were greeted by an unusual skyline with chimneys instead of palm trees. These belonged to Curaçao's refineries. The petrochemical industry and shipbuilding are the main activities in Curaçao, which is about twice as big as Bonaire. The population speaks a curious mixture of Dutch, Spanish and Portuguese which is called Papiamento. A floating bridge barred our entrance to the inner harbour and, while we waited for it to be opened, we drifted about in front of Willemstad's impressive waterfront.

Gesturing towards the Dutch architecture, I said: "I left Asia to sail to Europe, and now this looks just like Europe, although we're still far away!"

We then moored at the pier of the shipyard, with *Aisa*. Our boats were dwarfed by the mighty bows of a large freighter, and above all towered a huge shipyard crane which was going to lift Mike's boat from the water.

"Mike, this crane will lift your cockleshell of a boat straight into the clouds", we joked. "You'll make history as the first flying sailor!"

But he was worried about his boat and not in the mood to appreciate our banter – and this was a man who had rounded all major capes on earth in his own boat, Cape Horn twice.

This had earned him memberships in the world's oldest yacht club, the Irish Royal Cork Yacht Club, and of the Cape Horn Society. One evening, as we sat together discussing various brands of rum, he said: "I am also a member of a very special club. The Imperial Poona Yacht Club!"

"And what is so special about that?", Greg asked.

"Drink up your rum first. Then I'll tell you more", replied Mike.

After a while, he continued. "Well, first it is the most majestic club of all. It is not simply royal, but imperial!"

"Just about right for us", I remarked.

"And then, we are on a special mission." His face held the

promise of some sinister secret.

"Come on, spill the beans. What mission?"

But first we had another round of rum. Only then did Mike explain: "The Imperial Poona Yacht Club is dedicated to research about the origins of rum!" Facing me, he continued: "I've know you since Durban, and from the first moment I could not fail to notice the large collection of rum you had on board. Now, the variety of rum you carry has, if anything, increased. This and the fact that you have the right sense of humour has convinced me that I can invite you to join the exclusive circle of the club. My membership allows me to nominate special members."

"And what obligations are connected to this?", I asked, slightly suspicious.

"Oh, only one. Meetings are held for the sole purpose of tasting rum of all sorts. You just have to survive the initiation ceremony!"

This turned out to be the tasting of a large number of rum brands, and carefully writing a testimony about it. The report should include our description of the rum as well as a points system to establish the different qualities. But, unlike wine, rum has a devastating effect even if drunk in only small measures. We just about managed to finish the tasting and write the report and then slipped beneath the table one after the other. But we survived and, in another solemn ceremony, Mike handed us our membership cards and some photocopies to prove the authenticity of the club. These were mainly the reports of previous rum tasting ceremonies. The club's burgee, by the way, is yellow with three black dots in the centre.

"A fitting burgee", as Greg and I agreed.

Sensation in the bar

Before returning to Venezuela, we visited Curaçao's most popular anchorage, Spanish Waters. This sheltered lagoon has one of the nicest marinas I have seen anywhere. Sarifundi Marina is most popular among yachties, and the clubhouse, built out over the water on stakes, is the living-room of the sailors. What we had omitted in Willemstad, the entrance formalities, we now did here. The customs officer in charge was friendly and came to visit us in the "living-room". He then asked if we had to declare any weapons, and truthfully I said yes.

"We will have to take you weapons into storage for the duration of your stay here", he said. So I went to fetch our new "protector" from the boat. When I returned, we stood in the very busy and crowded bar and he asked if he could take a look at the gun.

"What – here, in public?"

"Yes", he insisted.

Greg stood next to me and watched, amused. He must have known what was coming. I opened the innocent bag and out came the beast. I placed our dreadful looking weapon on the bar and added the 130 rounds of ammunition. Conversation ceased around us as everybody stared at the thing in amazement. Nosily, they crowded around us and stared in wonder. None of them had ever seen a weapon like this before. It seemed indecent that one of us, belonging to the fraternity of peaceful yachties, should possess such a dreadful thing. The officer however revelled in being at the centre of attention and took his time inspecting the gun. He then took the boxes of ammunition and proceeded to count. I could have sunk into the earth, and Greg was by now at the other end of the bar, pretending not to belong to me.

On that day I vowed never again to declare a weapon. For one thing, the gun would be unavailable should we have to use it, and for another I just did not want to be exposed to such a humiliating scene again.

Venezuela – final curtain

Thanks to the steady trade winds of the Caribbean, we had a fast return passage to Puerto Cabello. Three ladies welcomed us warmly: Anna, Marianella and her friend Cherill. Our return to paradise could not have been better. The next day, we went to the naval port to see where *Ryusei* and *Borracho* could be slipped for maintenance. Marianella was going to organise this for us, as she had good contacts in the navy. But when we arrived, the officer in charge grimaced.

"When do you think we can slip the boats?", we asked.

"Well, there is a small problem. The space where we are going to put the boats still has to be cleared."

But Marianella insisted, and finally we were given a provisional date of the 24th of November. Not quite sure if it would really happen, we left.

But then the weekend came and this is the time when the Venezuelans excel. Marianella was extremely happy as her boyfriend Shawn was coming from America to see her. On the Saturday, they invited us on a little trip. The reason for the outing was to buy a few calves for her parents' farm. When the day ended, we had no calves, but we did have a new farm. Shawn and Anna had agreed to buy a plantation for lemons and oranges, including a house with electricity and water, for 5,000 US dollars.

"At home, we wouldn't even get a car for that price" is all that we could comment.

Sunday was the day of the apocalypse. I invited Marianella, her friends and Anna for a trip to Isla Grande. The beach here was the meeting place for half the population of Puerto Cabello. Hundreds of small motor-boats were in the water and the beach was lined with colourful sunshades. We got a convincing demonstration of the liveliness of the Latin Americans. What a contrast to life in Asia! This is what I had missed there: young and old mingled on the beach, where the sun, music and dancing made the elderly forget about their age. Alcohol was doing its bit as well, and soon we were among the fun and games ashore. But during the afternoon, the black clouds of an approaching thunderstorm loomed over the scene, and hastily we packed our things, went back on board and motored home. Soon, the rain was lashing down and the sky grew dark. Greg handled the boat while I entertained our guests. Now, there are certain occasions when the mind of a man comes to a standstill. Cherill was one such an occasion. She was a beautiful lady and came below deck as I was getting a few drinks from the refrigerator. In the darkness of the cabin, she pressed her body against mine and gave me a passionate kiss. Outside, lightning struck and thunder bellowed. But there is no real privacy on board a yacht and everyone had noticed our temporary absence. My reputation was in smithereens and the atmosphere poisoned. When the navy postponed the hauling out of our boats by another month, there was only one decision – to leave.

Colombia

Pirate scare
The winds in the Caribbean are ideal for sailing ships. We made good use of this fact when we left Venezuela. The usual routine at sea set in quickly, but it was harder as we had lost the third man on board. We decided to anchor one night in Aruba before setting off on the long leg to Cartagena.

As we arrived, we contacted the harbour master on the VHF. "Before you anchor, we will have to check your papers. Please moor at the pier first", he instructed us.

Reluctantly we obliged. People ashore helped us to belay our lines on the very high pier and, before we could do more, a customs man jumped on board. He was in a hurry, looked at our documents and demanded that we should fill out his forms at once. At this moment, a seagoing tug left the harbour at high speed. *Ryusei* lifted to his wash. Then we felt a sharp jerk and heard the noise of splintering wood. In the rush we had omitted to leave enough play in the mooring lines and in the wash *Ryusei* dropped, with the mooring line ripping the aft fair-lead and part of the stern railing from the deck.

"All this because of the stupid red tape", I cursed.

We would have loved to chuck the customs officer over board, but this would probably have meant the end of our voyage. As quickly as we could, we went through the remaining formalities, left and anchored in one corner of the harbour.

"At last we can sleep", my friend remarked as we vanished into our berths. But this was another false assumption as, not knowing better, we had anchored right next to the busy airport.

During the following night, we passed the gulf of Maracaibo. During Greg's watch, we were cornered by several freighters and tankers. Once we could only avoid collision by tacking fast and fleeing under power. But once we had left Punta de Gallinas behind, the shipping ceased. We were now in the pirate-infested waters of Colombia.

Just to be prepared for the worst, we organised a practise shooting at sea. "If we have a weapon on board, we might just as well know how to use it", I said. "Especially here, where the area is supposed to be full of pirates."

So we fired away at empty beer cans which we threw into the air. The aim was not only to hit the cans, but to sink them. The din of ten exploding shots in one round was deafening. But our artillery proved impressive and, within a very short time, we had fired away half our ammunition. As before in the South China Sea, we sailed without navigation lights at night and kept a safety distance of at least 15 miles from the coast.

Including our stop-over in Aruba, we took five days for the 555 miles from Puerto Cabello to Cartagena. On the afternoon of the third day, the easy part of the passage was over. The wind was aft of the beam but reached 30 knots. We had failed to reef early enough and *Ryusei* was rolling heavily in the quartering seas. Soon, it became very hard work at the helm to keep her on course, so we took down the main. During the night, the wind increased further. We reduced the genoa to a small triangle and surfed down the waves, which felt like being on a roller-coaster ride. The difference was that a roller-coaster ride usually only lasts about five minutes.

In the middle of the night we were caught by a very strong gust. At the same time, the quality of the air seemed to change. It was warmer and we smelt the most intensive scent of pine trees which I have ever experienced. In the near complete darkness, I could almost imagine that the night was full of colours. Imagination created an image of mountains and pine forests. At dawn, this image proved to be at least partly real. Hovering on the south-eastern horizon were the outlines of a massive mountain range. This was the Sierra Nevada de Santa Martha, which rises from the depths of the Caribbean Sea to a height of 5,800 metres.

There is nothing comparable on any other coast of this world, and the scented gusts during the night had come straight from there.

During the course of the day, the weather quietened down again. As if to make up for this, the colour of the water changed. Coming from the deep blue, we were now sailing along in a muddy brown and murky sea. Trees, bushes, weed and garbage floated on the surface and we knew that we were now in the delta of the Rio Magdalena estuary, a river which flows over a thousand kilometres from the Andes to the sea.

When we finally reached the entrance to the lagoon of Cartagena, it was already dark. Exhausted from the long passage, we looked forward to a quiet night at anchor. Bowing to the temptation, we broke our vow never to enter a strange harbour at night. We just did not want to sail up and down in front of the entrance for the rest of the night.

Greg egged me on. "Why not?", he said. "The channel is marked by lit buoys and we have all the necessary navigation instruments."

Despite this, it was a risky undertaking. The lights of the town of Cartagena and the swell made it extremely difficult to identify the buoys and, once inside the first lagoon, we found our way into slightly shallower water with the echo-sounder, dropped the anchor, switched on the riding light and sank into our berths.

The morning greeted us with an idyllic scene. The sea was as flat as a mirror and the early morning haze had a reddish tint to it. The impressive fort which had once been built to defend Cartagena was in sight. Not far from our boat, a dugout canoe floated peacefully on the water. An elderly man sat in it and curiously eyed *Ryusei*. As soon as he spotted me, he came alongside and asked in Spanish if he could have some bread, but as we had run out of bread ourselves we could only give him a packet of biscuits and some lemonade.

"Have you gone completely out of your mind?" were the first words we heard in the marina of Cartagena. Puzzled, I asked back: "Why? What's so wrong about anchoring in the lagoon for the night?"

"This is one of the most notorious places for pirates in Colombia, that's why. The inhabitants of the village usually mug every foreigner who comes anywhere near them!"

Greg and I grinned at each other. We had the same thought: whoever was contemplating attacking us must have sensed that we had a "Protector" on board. During that night, the gun was loaded and next to my pillow.

Cartagena

Nowhere else in the New World can we find a town where the architecture of the Spanish colonial times is as perfectly conserved and authentic as here. Cartagena ranks as the most beautiful, and oldest, town in South America. Hidden behind massive defensive walls is a maze of winding alleyways, palaces, churches, cloisters, public plazas and cool, shady backyards, large stone houses with towering balconies and romantic, hidden gardens. For the Spaniards, this was the central distribution place for the transport of their South American booty back home. There were many attacks by pirates as well as the British navy, so the fortifications are stunning. San Felipe is Cartagena's largest fortress, and from here we enjoyed a wonderful all-round view. A man called Blas de Lezo had won a remarkable victory here in 1741. A British fleet with 170 ships and 28,000 men attacked Cartagena, and allegedly this fleet was even larger than the ill-fated Spanish armada with whom the Spaniards had tried to invade England. Blas de Lezo was, at any rate, a hard and proven fighter: he had only one leg, one arm and one eye left. However, he was also lucky in that nature helped him. In the end, most of the attackers were not killed by Spanish action, but simply died of tropical fevers.

Today, around three-quarters of a million people of all shades live in Cartagena. The darker skins colours are in a majority and still remind us of one of the darkest chapters in history, the slave trade.

Norman, the owner of the yacht club, tried to set our minds at rest: "Here in the marina, you are completely safe. My people are here for security, especially so at night. If anyone suspicious comes near the boats, my guards will fire flares into the air and we immediately get help from the navy, which is stationed just across the bay." Indeed, the club was known as a safe haven in these rather unsure surroundings and there was quite a number of cruising boats here.

We were lucky to get a berth alongside the temporary pontoon. The authorities had not allowed the extension of the pontoons, but Norman found a solution which was typical of Latin America. He sunk an old ship so that the decks remained just above water, and this was the new jetty. We moored up to this wreck to do the repairs to our stern. What really worried me was that the wreck was half eaten away by toredo worms. They love wooden ships and even eat away teak, of which *Ryusei's* hull is made, and which is among the most worm-resistant woods.

Again, we met many fellow cruising people, among them Jack with his boat *Compadre*. He was a professor of marine biology at the university of Hawaii. In Réunion, I had been given a scientific study about whales – to deliver to him. "But how on earth can I meet up with a man I don't even know?", I'd asked.

"Don't worry, you cruising people live in a global village. You'll meet him, sooner or later, as long as you sail towards the west."

And now, one year and 10,000 miles later, we had really found him and the study was handed over. There's nothing more reliable than sending mail by sailing ship!

Mad Austrians

"Looks as if they need help", Greg remarked as we passed another yacht in our dinghy. Both the ship and the two young guys apparently fighting the anchor winch looked rather derelict.

We went closer and saw that the boat was called *Think* and flew an Austrian flag. "Can we help?", I asked in German.

"Yes", came the answer. "We'd like to move to the jetty, but our anchor winch is jammed!"

With joint forces we were able to lift the anchor and afterwards we helped them with mooring their boat. We then introduced ourselves and chatted for a while. Michael and Benjamin, from Vienna, told us the most amazing story:

Three friends from Vienna decided to change their boring lives and got hold of the building plans for a sailing yacht. They then resigned from their jobs, filled a container with their worldly goods including the tools and materials to build the boat and went to Venezuela. Here, on the tax-free island of Margarita, they had intended to build their boat and then sail away on their great voyage. Being engineers, they had thought about everything – save one: the corrupt officials of Venezuela. These turned their container upside down and invented all sorts of reasons to hassle them.

"It was clear from the very start that they just wanted to confiscate our valuable tools and equipment", Michael said. "First they claimed that our music videos contained pornography. But when this was not sufficient to confiscate our container, they also invented drugs."

Instead of now paying them off with a substantial bribe, two of the friends raised a lot of trouble and consequently ended up in jail. Weeks, or rather months, later, one of them was released again. Their project was over before it had even begun, as Michael and Benjamin were only able to salvage a few of their tools from the container.

"And where is your friend?"

"We don't know for sure, probably in jail somewhere." And with that, they sounded as if they did not want to know. For some reason, their friendship must have gone down the drain, as well as everything else.

Michael then continued: "By chance, we found an abandoned yacht in the harbour of Cumana, the 40-foot *Think*. The owner had disappeared years before. As the mooring fees were not paid, the marina now owned the boat and we got her for just 5000 dollars. But then we woke up to a nasty surprise. Inspecting her more closely, we had to admit that we had bought a heap of junk. The hull was so corroded in many places that hosing her down with a high pressure cleaner was enough to perforate her. We had to take radical measures. In the yard, nobody believed that we would ever be able to rebuild her and they called us 'los austriacos locos', the crazy Austrians. But we had no choice, and for five months we worked day and night on the boat. It was an incredibly dirty job – cutting, sanding, welding and sandblasting were our main tasks. We repaired the frames, hull and deck and modified the cockpit including the steering system. Building new would probably have cost us less effort. Towards the end we were also under serious time pressure as our visas were expiring. The authorities were threatening to confiscate *Think*. So we launched her when she was half finished and sailed for Bonaire."

After a small pause, in which we could hardly digest what we had just heard, Benjamin took up the tale. "I must also tell you that none of us had any experience of sailing. We are engineers and as such believed that we could manage anything. For navigation we relied on a GPS which was built for aeroplanes. According to our plan, we should have reached Bonaire during the day. But just before dawn in the second night, the pattern of the waves suddenly changed. Something was wrong, but I could not see anything in the darkness. The next thing I remember is a brutal crash and breaking waves all around. We had run onto the easterly reef of Aves Sotevento, which is about 35 miles off Bonaire. In the morning, a Venezuelan fishing boat arrived and offered to tow us off. But they demanded more money than we had left. As we negotiated with them, we were pushed further and further on to the reef. Then the coastguard appeared and demanded that we should give up the boat, but we flatly refused. We had fought for two years over this project and *Think* was all we had left. Time passed and we were pushed over the first reef into a small pool where she floated at high water. It was then that we realised that the hull was still intact. Again, we had no choice but to save the boat. We even have a video of the salvage, but somewhere along the way we ran out of batteries, so we can only show you the first part."

The footage was sensational. It showed *Think* in all phases of the renovation job and high on the reef. With incredible perseverance they hacked a channel through the reef at low water, using hammer and chisel. They buried several anchors which they connected with pulleys to their manual anchor winch. Luckily, they had salvaged steel cables and several blocks from the wreck of an old freighter. At high water, they pulled the boat inch by inch towards the lagoon inside the reef.

"We had days in which we could not move her one bit. Sometimes we worked up to the waist in water for the entire day. But without the help of the cruising community, we would never have survived. They provided us with food and water and we ate as much as we could to gain energy for our labour. Then we reached the sandy part, but even here we had to carry on digging, as it was still too shallow. It took two months of this murderous torture until, finally, *Think* swam in deeper water once more."

One scene of the film remains unforgettable for me. Our friend Christian had come with his ancient fishing trawler *Martha* to try and tow his compatriots off the reef. A strong cable was passed from *Martha* to *Think* and Christian gave full throttle with his impressive single-cylinder engine. But nothing moved except the circular puffs of smoke which rose from the exhaust of his boat, looking just like Indian smoke signals.

But even then, the remarkable odyssey of *Think* was not quite over. On their way to Cartagena they ran aground once more while trying to reach an anchorage in the dusk. Luckily, it was at low water so they floated off again later. Next, they collided with a freighter. "Two freighters came towards us, one from the left and one from the right. It was difficult to judge the distance, and then it banged and the sparks flew as if we were a fireworks display while we scrubbed along the hull of the freighter.

"But despite all this, she is still afloat. This is the best measure

Venezuela, Los Roques: the Spanish yacht Borracho *in front of the Danish fishing cutter* Martha

Venezuela, Islas Las Aves: the conch is a local delicacy; unfortunately they are now seldom to be found on the sea bed

Symbol of freedom

The 'Deschamps Daughters' take over command

In the shadow of the skyscrapers

Mally and Elizabeth – two top-rate crew

The legendary Bluenose II

Maine: Rockland schooners sail out of Pulpit Harbour at dawn

Cramalott Inn, local gathering-point

Petites is one of the most beautiful
fishing villages in Newfoundland

The fishing port of Grand Bruit in thick fog

Malley with a cod caught with a traditional 'jigger'

Malley and Elizabeth enjoying the first European landfall

Journey's end — Scotland; Holy Island, on which a Buddhist monastery is to be found

Ryusei's signal: Whisky Galore

of the quality of our work!"

However, it seems that Michael and Benjamin had lost their appetite for sailing. The next day, they packed their rucksacks and vanished off towards the mountains.

Cockroaches

No yachtie in the tropics lives without them: cockroaches. At first, they are rare. But then, they multiply until it gets too much. We have always tried to keep the creepy things under control, but they always find their way on board. They either fly or they walk along the mooring lines or hitch a lift on board in food packaging. On our boat, the cockroaches thrived. The countless nooks and recesses of a wooden boat are ideal nesting places for them. And not one of our counter-measures had any noteworthy success. We tried boric acid mixed with milk powder, the famous Harris' roach pills, insect spray and the good old fly-swat.

One day, I lost my temper. A cockroach had been insolent enough to nibble at my breakfast. Greg's girlfriend Amy was also on board, which made this incident even more embarrassing.

"Enough is enough!", I decided and organised a whole carton of insect spray.

"What on earth are you up to?", Greg and Amy asked, highly amused, when they saw me putting on the diving gear.

"I will destroy the cockroach pest once and for all!", I announced.

I opened every single drawer, locker and door inside the boat and closed all outside hatches. I then put on the diving mask and sprayed the inside of the boat with five cans of insect poison. The stench was so incredibly foul that we had to sleep on deck that night. But at last we were rid of this special plague – for a while at least, as we were to find out in due course.

The mountain is beckoning

Colombia is a country full of variety. There are high mountain ranges and low plains which border on the Caribbean, the Pacific, the Amazon and the Orinoco. Colombia's 35 million inhabitants mainly work in agriculture, farming and mining. We also could not fail to notice Colombia's major problems: terrorism and drugs dealing. Cartagena was full of security personnel after terrorists had blown up a bus full of people. Even in the marina, some were making a profit from the drugs scene. It had become a known fact that sailing yachts could be sold here for ridiculously high prices.

We heard of one French guy who had sold his boat here for double the market value. As we arrived, this yacht passed us under power and the crew on board positively looked like gangsters. It was clear that they were not bound for a holiday cruise.

On one of the boats, a young American lived a life full of cocaine, marihuana and girls. Once, he surprised us with a sloth and commented: "May I introduce the prototype of all cruising sailors?"

In the bar of the yacht club, we sat the lazy animal on a barstool, where it remained perfectly cool and idle, even when we photographed it with a beer and a cigarette in its claw. Later we were able to watch how swiftly it disappeared to the top of a tree, where it again settled down to lazily watch our hectic world from above.

The damage on our stern had to be repaired and Greg was looking forward to working in his chosen profession once more. First, however, we spent several days finding suitable wood. There were also other jobs to do: varnishing, painting the deck, overhauling the diesel engine and repairing our inflatable dinghy.

All this work and the heat made us think of cool, fresh mountain air. We remembered the mountains which had greeted us out at sea with their scent of clean pine trees. So we decided that the mountain, or rather the Sierra Nevada de Santa Martha, was beckoning us.

A bus took us from Cartagena to Santa Martha. From there, we made our way to the small village of San Sebastian de Rebago, where we spent the night at the foot of the mountain range. In the open back of a jeep we then drove along a rough mountain track to Nabusimake, the highest mountain community. But the incredible beauty of the mountains let us forget about the hard ascent. A wide mountain valley with wooded flanks welcomed us and the air was clear, cool and dry. It was exactly as we had dreamt of it.

We moved into a small thatched hut at the edge of a swift mountain stream. We instantly felt at home, as the murmur of the stream resembled the noise of the waves at sea. Amy, Greg and I then embarked on long hikes through the countryside; these were not without effort, given the thin air at 3000 metres. The fresh scent of meadows and woods was magical and reminded me of alpine regions back home in Europe. From time to time we met Indios who belonged to the tribe of the Arhuacos. They live in remote huts and work their sparse fields. Temptation was great to attempt the climb up to the 5800 metre high peak of the Sierra Nevada, but this was forbidden. One Indio from the administration of the reserve told us why. "According to the ancient belief of the Indios, the gods live in those upper regions, and anyone who disturbs them is asking for misfortune. The mountain has already claimed a lot of people."

Time was pressing and on the 28th of December, the day of my 38th birthday, we were ready to depart for Panama. But we had reckoned without the ship. As I had forgotten to switch off the refrigerator overnight, the batteries were so low that we were unable to start the engine on this calm morning. But the problem was easily resolved. We sat down to a leisurely breakfast and celebrated my birthday. In the meantime, the sun climbed higher and shone on our six large solar panels, after which we could start the engine.

Panama

Forgotten

We were in a hurry due to the imminent arrival of a friend from Germany. We had arranged to meet her on a remote island in the San Blas archipelago. But fate always gets in the way of those who rush around. First, the engine would not start. Once we had it going, we had to keep it going, motor-sailing along as the wind was too light.

"How lucky that we have enough wind in the engine room", we agreed.

We spoke too soon. The alarm of the diesel rang out as if in protest. One glance at the instrument panel was enough: the oil pressure was zero. We stopped the engine and soon found that the oil filter washer was defective. Again, we were lucky in having a spare filter and enough oil on board to top up the engine. We finally reached our meeting point, the island of Porvenir, three hours late.

I wondered aloud what the poor girl might do, after a 24-hour flight from Frankfurt via New York, Miami and Panama City, landing on this remote island to find we were not here. But my friends said: "Don't worry. She'll just have to wait. After all, we are just a few hours late."

As soon as the anchor was set, we went ashore in the dinghy. Porvenir was a small sandy hump with a few palm trees, some huts and a landing strip. We asked a man who was dozing in the shadow of the palms. "Yes, the plane from Panama City stopped here. But I didn't notice your friend."

Two other boats were in the anchorage and one of them was, to our great surprise, *Yu-U*. We were happy to see our Japanese friends again, and asked about our lost friend. To this, Yoshi replied: "A few hours ago a girl paddled past in a dugout canoe and inquired about you. I could only tell her that I had last seen you a few months ago in Venezuela. She then went across to the American boat over there."

"Ahoy, anybody on board?", I shouted as we came alongside the yacht *Starship* in our dinghy. A man emerged from the companionway; he turned out to be David, the owner. I introduced myself and again asked about our friend.

"Ah, so you're the guys the poor girl was searching for like mad", he replied. "Such a beauty just had to be helped. I put out a search enquiry on the ham radio and now the entire Caribbean is on the look-out for you!"

"And where can we find her now?" I demanded impatiently.

David's eyes sparkled. "I would have loved to take her on board. She looked as if she could use a hero like me. But then she asked her boatman to take her to the next island. They said there is a hostel there."

Arriving at the neighbouring island by dinghy, we were at once greeted by the now familiar words: "Ah, you are the ones belonging to the poor, lost girl!" We were relieved when we finally found Caroline, but her relief must have been even greater. She was rather upset at the thought that we had forgotten all about her.

San Blas archipelago

Panama is in a strategically important location. It is the natural bridge between North and South America as well on the border between the two great oceans. In the narrowest part of the country, the distance between the Atlantic and Pacific oceans being only 50 kilometres. The idea to build a canal here was born in 1524, but it was not until 1914 that the canal was finally finished. Life in Panama revolves around the canal.

For us, however, the central point of interest was the San Blas islands. These are about 365 islands which are scattered along the east coast of Panama, from the Golfo de San Blas to just before the Colombian border. The archipelago is inhabited by the Kuna Indians, who have allegedly maintained their traditional form of life.

On the morning after our arrival, the last day of the year, we were in for a surprise. A big cruise liner had appeared and the island of Porvenir was transformed into a fun-fair. The Indians had sailed over from many other islands in their dugout canoes to trade with the tourists, and a huge number of stalls selling various goods had been erected along the landing strip. The main item on sale here was the traditional handmade mola, which is a colourful piece of embroidery that is normally worn on the fronts and backs of the traditional clothing of the Kuna Indians. At the other end of the airstrip, the crew of the luxury liner had installed a buffet for their passengers. After the tourists had gone through the Indian stalls like a swarm of bees, they all gathered at the buffet for drinks and snacks. Yoshi (from *Yu-U*) and I watched this remarkable scene, in which the contrast between the poor Indians and the elderly, overweight tourists who were dressed as if going to a cocktail party was striking. When we wanted to buy a drink at the cruise-ship buffet, we were impolitely turned down: "This is only for our passengers. We cannot sell you anything."

Yoshi and I grinned at each other, and he said what I was thinking: "Let's go, but fast!"

The wind was favourable and so *Ryusei* and *Yu-U* sailed along side-by-side through the islands on the look-out for a quieter place. On the radio we heard that the cruising fraternity was planning a huge New Year's feast in the Hollandis Cays. This night of course was anything but quiet. After a peaceful and harmonic evening around the beach fire things got lively as midnight approached. Corks popped and old flares were fired off. We fell into each other's arms, with wishes for a happy new year and, above all, fair winds. We all could use fair winds, having come here from all points of the compass and, after the feast, sailing away towards different horizons. Yoshi, for example, was heading back for Japan to complete his circumnavigation in this new year. I was still bound for Scotland, although even now uncertain about the exact route.

The party continued on board *Starship*. On our way there, we nearly wrecked our dinghy on the coral reef, and we were all quite merry. David started to flirt heavily with Caroline and was not even deterred by the fact that his wife was on board. With the threadbare excuse of fetching more bottles of wine, he again and again tried to persuade her to come below decks with him, but our friend was too clever for this Romeo, and she held him at bay while selecting the most exquisite bottles from his stock. The rest of the party in the cockpit always applauded when she emerged with new booty from the vain assaults of the skipper.

Japanese delicacies

After we had recovered from the excesses of the new year's party, we fled with Yu-U and continued on our search for a quiet place and, above all, better fishing grounds. After we had found a suitable place among the islands, we went fishing and were once again impressed by the expertise of our Japanese friends, not only in catching but also in preparing the fish. One day, Susumu caught a large puffer fish. These fish pump themselves full of water whenever they are threatened and so increase their size radically. They also have spikes to defend themselves.

"In our country, this fish is one of the best delicacies", Yoshi said. "But we have to be careful. If the fish is prepared in the wrong way, it can be lethal!"

We watched not without apprehension as Susumu prepared the fish. In the meantime, Yoshi gave us the finer details:

Puffer fish à la *Yu-U*:

• The fish should be held with pliers for skinning and cutting off the fins. Be careful not to injure yourself, although the spines themselves are not poisonous.

• Grill the fins. Put two fins into a glass of hot rice wine and drink.

• After skinning the fish, all innards should be removed. Cut the backbone near the head. Carefully remove all skin, and blood

vessels from the spine.
   • The underside of the head contains a lot of meat.
   • All organs, especially the liver, but also the brain, eyes, stomach and eggs are very poisonous and have to be removed carefully.
   • The meat can then be grilled.

When the grilled fish was served, we said: "We hope you did a good job cleaning the fish. Otherwise, there will be two ghost ships soon."

"Never fear. We are master chefs of Japanese cuisine", Yoshi replied confidently.

As far as the taste went, the fish reminded us of chicken, but much more refined. To help with the digestion, we then had a round of hot saké with the fish's fins in it. During the course of that evening, we exchanged a lot of stories. Our friends had sailed with *Yu-U* from Japan via Thailand, the Indian Ocean, the Red Sea, the Mediterranean and the Atlantic to here. They were now bound for the Panama Canal and the Pacific. There was a lot to say and when the stories were finished Yoshi took out his guitar and we began to sing.

Baptising of an island

Our anchorage was surrounded by a multitude of tiny islands. During one of our excursions, we found a small sandy hump which had grown on top of the coral reef. This was now going to be our island for the day. Laden down with diving gear, drinks and cooking utensils, we landed there.

"Now we have to earn our meal", our Japanese friends said. Apart from a few fruits, we only had a sack of rice with us, so we had to dive and catch some fish. The remainder of the morning was spent under water, and it was fascinating to see how easily and efficiently the Japanese swam. They were true masters of underwater hunting. Fish were abundant and so we could pick and choose, although we also had to be careful. As soon as a fish was hit by the harpoon, it attracted the sharks in its death throes. It was quite frightening how suddenly the sharks came from the deep blue surrounding us, and how abruptly they also disappeared again after they had stilled their curiosity. Most of them were reef-sharks which were not dangerous to us. One of them lay sleeping in a cave, but we left him. Shark's fins were not on our menu.

It is quite disgraceful that because of delicacies such as these, sharks are nearly extinct in Asia nowadays. Sharks are much better than their reputation. Out of about 350 different species of shark, only very few are actually dangerous to humans. The statistics show that the reverse case is true. From all attacks by sharks, only about one dozen per year are lethal. On the other hand, humans kill about 700,000 tons of sharks each year. Often, the fishermen only cut off the fins and throw the still-living creatures back into the water, leaving them to a miserable death.

We only caught as much fish as we were actually going to eat. Apart from a few snappers, we also found one lobster and two crabs. The others who had remained ashore had in the meantime collected driftwood and lit a fire on which we cooked our meal. It is not easy to describe the special quality of this day in paradise with mere words. Clear water surrounded our tiny islet. The sun shone. We had enough to eat and to drink and we had, above all, good company. We came from four different continents – Asia, Africa, America and Europe – and yet we were in perfect harmony.

At one point, somebody asked: "Does anyone know what this island is called?"

"I had a look at the chart", someone else replied. "But it only shows a shallow spot and no island at all."

"It has probably grown over the last few years."

"And it looks more like a sand-bank, anyway. An island only deserves a name when there are at least a few palm trees growing on it."

"Well, we could change that by planting a few. That would also give us the right to baptise the island."

At once, activity started. A delegation went across to the neighbouring island to fetch three small palm trees which we planted at sunset. One tree was for *Yu-U*, one for *Ryusei* and one for the friendship between us. The island we then named 'Play island'.

The next day our friends set sail and headed off towards Japan, their home and the land where *Ryusei* was born.

Different ways to Scotland

We lost our feeling for time. In the tropical climate, living under the sun and the stars, we did not notice how it was passing. We just indulged. We slept whenever we felt like it, including in the hammocks during the day. Meals were prepared and eaten when we were hungry. When the sun went down it was time for our aperitif and when the moon rose it was time for romantic gatherings around our beach fires. Life in our respective 'homes' seemed further away than ever before. Even the air pressure, something like the pulse of the seafarer, remained in a steady shallow sine wave.

On Green Island, we met up again with Jack. Green Island is another sandy hump with a lot of green on it, surrounded by a coral reef pulsing with life. Jack's boat, *Compadre*, was actually more of an aqua-biological research vessel than a yacht. We also met Claire and Dick from America, who had named their boat *Runaway* for obvious reasons. They had ended their careers to live their big dream.

Claire and Dick opened up a new chapter for me: the United States. Their descriptions of the east coast were highly tempting and very similar to what Greg kept telling me. Should we sail there? One day, I noted in the log: freedom to decide causes headaches.

It was only later that I realised that I had already made the decision. The east coast of the United States could not be left out, just as we could not have sailed past Latin America or the Caribbean. After all, there are many different ways to Scotland.

Garbage and telecommunications

Whenever yachties chat to each other, they invariably also talk about the day-to-day concerns of their way of life on board. And each time, we learnt something new.

Once we asked Jack what he did with his garbage. As a seasoned sailor, he should have an answer. On our arrival in the San Blas archipelago, we had left our garbage sacks in the waste collection place of a local village. This turned out to be a grave mistake. The same day we saw an Indian who piled all the garbage into his canoe and paddled out to sea, and a little while later the whole lot floated past us.

"We cannot allow this paradise to be spoiled by our garbage", we said. "But on the other hand, we just can't sail around keeping it on board for months on end!"

Jack had the simple answer. "Biological waste can go over board. Bottles are filled with water and sunk far out at sea. The rest is burnt."

We got a practical demonstration of this after our next barbecue. After we had eaten our meal, we stirred the fire up once more and burnt our garbage sacks. They contained plastics, aluminium and tin cans. But if the heat is intense enough, the aluminium cans melt, as well as the outer, anti-corrosion layer of the tin cans. The tin rusts away to nothing after a few years. After our private rubbish dump had burnt down, we buried the last few remaining items in the sand.

Again and again we were confronted with the waste disposal problem of this world. Even hundreds and thousands of miles away from civilisation, we saw conglomerations of plastic, metal and waste of many other types, either far out at sea or on remote beaches – not to mention the oil slicks which we noted at sea again and again. Seventy percent of the entire world population lives in coastal regions, and most of the waste and garbage is still thrown into the sea. Matters are extremely bad in the underdeveloped countries who just don't have any money for professional garbage disposal. Even worse is the fact that fifty percent of the world's fish population and, above all, their breeding grounds, are in coastal waters and that, consequently, the human race is thereby threatening its own existence.

From Dick on *Runaway*, we got a lecture in telecommunications. He surprised us one day by saying: "as long as you have a ham radio on board, you can telephone anywhere in the world."

"And how does that work?"

Dick gave us the frequencies of the American land radio station and showed us how we could contact the telecommunications giant AT&T via them. AT&T would then connect the desired telephone call. The costs were charged to a credit card. I was only concerned that I had no radio license, but Dick said: "Don't worry about that. As long as they can make money out of you, they're not interested in whether you have a license or not – so long as you have a credit card!"

Diabolical Chilli

On our way to the village of Rio Diabolo we were drenched in a heavy tropical downpour, but then the clouds parted and a wonderful rainbow appeared.

The village is one of the largest in the San Blas islands. It is located on a small island in the estuary of the Rio Diabolo. We went here to buy provisions and to top up our fresh water tanks. Also, the name of the river was interesting enough to invite exploration. On our way upstream, we passed dense jungle but then came to some clearings where the Indians had built small plantations. Once in a while, we met Kuna Indians in their dugout canoes on the river. One of them, who was on his way to the village, stopped and sold us Juca roots and small chillies. As we ventured further upstream, the muddy water suddenly became clear like a fresh mountain stream. Then, falls and eddies barred our way and the river ceased to be navigable even for our inflatable. We pulled the dinghy ashore and dived into the clear water. Anyone who knows the humid heat of the tropics will also know how refreshing this can be.

Compadre and *Runaway* also had difficulties in obtaining fresh vegetables, so our Juca roots and chillies were highly welcome when we shared them out. However, the joy did not last long. Claire had used the chillies for cooking, and the result was devastating. On the radio, she complained: "Have you tried your chillies yet? They are so hot that we can't even breathe properly any more. Any ideas what we can do against them?"

In our innocence, we laughed and suggested drinking milk or eating dry bread. But as soon as we tried the chillies ourselves, we stopped laughing. They were so hot that they even burnt beneath the finger-nails as we cut them. They were truly diabolic and in the end we threw them over board. Later, I heard that the natives apparently use them to produce a sort of antifouling for their canoes.

Flying change

Our crew went through a flying change. My brother arrived and Caroline, sun-tanned and truly relaxed, went back home. Axel landed in an ancient and overloaded propeller plane. He was very pale, and this was not only due to the lack of sun in Europe – he was still terrified from the flight.

"When the pilot started the engine in Panama City I could see the rivets shaking and it was only because there were so many of them that I half trusted the plane. During the flight I had an outboard engine in my neck, and neither the engine nor myself were strapped in because all the seatbelts were broken."

But now he had made it and his arrival was like Christmas for us. He brought with him news of the family, mail and provisions from back home. "The customs people in Panama City took me apart", he said. "They wanted to confiscate the German sausages and the cheese I have brought along. As I don't speak their language, I put on my carnival captain's hat and tried to explain in sign language that these are the emergency rations for the lifeboat. They nearly fell over laughing and let me pass unscathed in the end!"

Part of the 'emergency rations' were also a row of whisky bottles and a large parcel from my father. This contained, among other items, many rolls of vitamin tablets and the urgent request to take them regularly. He must have thought that we were about to die of scurvy on board, like our ancient seafaring ancestors.

Anyway, before we could depart for Honduras, we had to stock up with fresh food. In the village of Rio Diabolo was one store with a very small selection of food. We were lucky to get enough fruits and vegetables, but meat had to be ordered from Panama City. After living exclusively off fish for weeks on end, we were craving some meat, so we ordered three chickens, which were due to arrive deep-frozen a few days later. But while our guests had arrived on time, the chickens were late. Every time one of the ancient planes fell from the sky to touch down on the landing strip we went across in the dinghy, but not until a day later could we take delivery of our chicken.

With them in the freezer, we anchored off the typical caricature island. A sandy hump, three palm trees and nothing else. However, the palm trees were the perfect distance from each other for our hammocks. Here, we thought, was nature at its most ideal. But it was, once again, more the lush world under water which really made us euphoric. There were corals and fish in excess. The San Blas islands could have held us in their spell for a long while yet, had not the wind swung round from north to north-east. Nature had given us the sign for departure, and we duly sailed, heading north.

After all this bliss, we were in for a rough time at sea, and our lee rail and parts of the deck were constantly awash. Life on board became extremely uncomfortable with violent motion, but at least we were making good speed towards our next destination, Honduras.

Honduras

High and dry

At first, it was a barely visible line on the horizon and could well have been the silhouette of a distant cloud. But as the wind drove us on, the contours of the island Guanaja became clearer and clearer. After six days at sea with two short stops near the island Providencia and near the border to Honduras we were now looking forward to our arrival. Tension mounted as we passed through a narrow channel in the coral reef to the north-east of Guanaja. But then we were in calm waters and the anchor chain rattled away. Guanaja is the easternmost of the three Bay Islands in the Gulf of Honduras. These islands, Roatan, Utila and Guanaja, lie at the world's second largest barrier reef which extends from the Mexican peninsula of Yucatan all the way to Honduras. Guanaja, about 18 kilometres long, 6 kilometres wide and with some mountains that reach up to 400 metres, is in turn enclosed by a reef on which a few small islets lie, rather like satellites.

We had anchored not far off one of these satellites. The white beach with the palm trees seemed inviting enough, but the idyllic image held a false promise. We were greeted by mosquitoes and sandflies.

"Mosquitoes are not too bad", I declared, "but if these sandflies are of the same species that I know from Singapore, then we'd better sailed on immediately. Their bites give an incredible itch and are easily inflamed!"

"Don't worry", Greg said. "We only want to stay for three days, anyway!"

Towards evening, my brother and I made a trip in the inflatable to the next village, which was Savannah Bight, in the north-east of the main island. Colourful huts on poles stood along the shore, some of them built out over the water so that their inhabitants could moor their boats directly to their verandas. Behind the village were meadows and palm trees. At the very end we came to a place which at first glance looked like a scrap metal depot, but which turned out to be a boat-yard. An elderly gentleman who had one leg in plaster and stood with a crutch waved to us and we soon struck up a conversation. He was called Fred Stone and was the owner of the yard. Gesturing towards the ancient cradle on the slipway rails, I asked: "Can you haul out boats on that?"

Indignantly, he replied: "Of course. Ships and sail boats up to a length of 40 metres! But for the next couple of weeks, we are completely booked up."

"What a shame. Our boat would have to be hauled out urgently to get a new coat of antifouling. But I suppose we can postpone it."

With that, our conversation ended.

The next morning, we wanted to move to a new anchorage. On our way there, I made a little detour to Fred's yard, as I wanted to show Greg and Amy the village and the yard. We went very slowly, as the water was full of coral heads. Just as we were passing the yard, a dark-skinned man waved to us and shouted in English: "Ahoy there. Do you still want to haul out?"

"Well, not really. Anyway, I thought you were booked up!"

"No, not at all; things have changed this morning. The ship which we were about to slip has engine trouble and Fred would not mind at all if you took her place. You'll just have to ask him!"

"Greg, what do you think? How about this huge ancient cradle – do you think it would be suitable for *Ryusei*?"

"I should think so, although the whole set-up hardly inspires confidence."

I then asked the man ashore. "Where can we find Fred?"

"He went to the main village of Bonacca. From there, he's going to take the noon ferry to the mainland. He has to go to hospital to have his broken leg examined. Just hurry up if you still want to catch him!"

Greg and Axel anchored *Ryusei*, while I dashed away in the dinghy with the man Kiki, who turned out to be Fred's assistant. Kiki gave me directions: "Bonacca is about five miles south of here. All we have to do is follow the coastline. There are no roads on Guanaja, all transport is by boat. Most of the time we use single-log boats which we call Cayucos."

The beauty of the nature was once again astonishing. The water was clear and as flat as a mirror, and reflected all colours. Behind the beaches, which were sprinkled with rocks, the green wooded hills rose high and steep. From time to time we passed huts which seemed to hover over the water. Then we reached the strange settlement of Bonacca which lies on a small island about a mile off the coast of Guanaja. Between the little huts, footpaths and canals wind their way, and life was pulsating in this 'little Venice' of the Caribbean. Kiki had to lead the way, otherwise I would have lost my bearings in the labyrinth of narrow alleyways. He knew exactly where to find Fred, who was in his usual pub. On the condition that we would be hauled out today, a Friday, and would go back into the water on Monday, we agreed on a price.

Fred declared: "This price includes the slipping of your boat and the cleaning of the underwater hull. I only agree as one other client has dropped out on short notice. There are other yachts which have been waiting to be hauled out for weeks, and they would be annoyed if they heard about you!"

"Shouldn't we clear in to Honduras first?", I enquired.

But Fred waved this idea aside. "Don't worry about it. Here, we are in the Bay Islands and we have our own rules. All you have to do is go to the police station and have your passports stamped for entry. If you tell the policeman that you are friends of mine you will have no problems at all."

In a hurry, we returned to the yard. Kiki drummed up the yard people and gave instructions. It was already Friday afternoon and we had no time to lose. The diesel engine driving the hauling winch was started up and gave a cloud of black smoke. The engine rattled as if it would burst apart any moment. The wheels of the slipping cradle, which was thirty metres long, had seized up with rust so that the cradle had to be pushed down into the sea with a bulldozer. Then we started to position *Ryusei* and stabilize her in place. The supporting poles along the sides had to be modified with a welding kit as they were made for large fishing vessels. To my surprise, the workers knew what they were doing and I dived beneath *Ryusei* with them to check that her keel was supported properly. Finally, we gave the driver at the winch the sign to haul up, and the seized wheels scraped along the rails. All went well until the cradle started to rock, probably due to the flexibility of the cable. *Ryusei* was now swaying madly and I stopped the entire procedure several times to secure her with even more warps. The motion was torturing our fragile wooden boat and it took an age until she was finally high and dry ashore.

We had reached Honduras and hauled out our boat straightaway, without even stopping for the usual formalities when entering a new country. We felt this deserved celebration and in the neighbouring village we found a restaurant which was also built out on poles over the water. Here, we filled our stomachs and it was already late when we walked back. On our way we passed a hut with loud music coming from it.

"That sounds just like a disco", Greg said at once.

"Fine", my brother agreed. "Let's have a look!"

"But only one last drink", I reminded them. "There's a lot of work waiting for us tomorrow!"

We entered the hut over an unstable catwalk. Inside, it was crowded with people, the music blared and several pairs were dancing, closely embraced. Water shone between the floor-boards and the bar was packed with wild-looking fishermen. They had been out fishing for lobster for weeks on end and we chatted for a while with one. "The lobster are caught on remote reefs. We use diving gear and have to dive up to three times a day. Decompression accidents are quite common, and it is dangerous, but well paid!"

Seafaring men, be they cruising sailors, fishermen or the crews of merchant or navy ships, have one thing in common. Their lives are dominated by extreme highs and extreme lows. The dangers at sea are mastered, but new challenges will come. Accordingly, they live their lives in harbour as if there were no tomorrow. Why not drink, dance and be merry with a woman as long as it lasts?

Stimulated by this atmosphere, we stayed for a second drink. And a third. And another one and then I lost count. In between we danced with the local beauties and my brother topped us all with a huge black lady.

"With her on board we'll heel over", Greg shouted into my ear. I then felt the floor move beneath my feet and looked around for my crew. Amy, Greg and Axel stood at the bar in deep discussions and with a certain amount of heeling themselves. "Let's go! Now or never!", I shouted at them, but it was easier said than done. The Cubra Libre had been quite strong and had apparently contained far more Libre than Cuba. Amy headed our little procession on our way back, while Axel, Greg and I staggered behind, arm in arm. The path was in utter darkness, as the village had no electricity save for the one hut which served as the disco. Our final hurdle was: how were we going to get back on board? The boat towered high above us on the slipway and the deck was about five metres over our heads. Greg, Amy and I just about managed to scramble up the steep ladder, but my brother had to be hoisted on board in a harness, using the main halyard. When we had all collapsed into our bunks, someone shouted: "At last we are high and dry!"

The Cuban rat

A rusty freighter was moored to the pier of the yard. It was called *God's Human Destiny*. Fred told us that this ship had arrived a while ago with a load of Cuban refugees. After we had launched *Ryusei* again, we went alongside the freighter and spent several days varnishing our deck. A wooden boat demands a lot of care and maintenance, especially in the tropics, where the wood has to be varnished at least every three months.

During this time we picked up a stowaway. Probably it was the last of the Cuban refugees from the freighter. At first, we did not notice our unwanted guest, but then we discovered half-eaten bags of rice and noodles in our provisions locker. We thought that a mouse had slipped on board.

"When a mouse or a rat comes on board it's a good omen. There are things to be found here and our boat is not yet sinking", was Greg's comment.

But then the incidents increased. Plastic tubs suddenly had holes in them. Electric cables and even the body of a torch were nibbled at. One night, a loud bang woke us and at first I thought that we had a burglar on board. In the end we found that our Hungarian sausage, which had been tied to the ship's bell, had been gnawed at and fallen down, where it crashed onto the plates and dishes beneath.

Only a rat could be this intelligent. "Rat, this is your last escapade!", we vowed.

Evaluating various strategies in our fight against the rat we spoke to a number of fellow yachties. One of them had a gruelling tale to tell.

"A rat is not easily caught. Especially on a wooden boat where it will find endless hiding places. I once had a rat on board. First, I tried poison. But after having tried a tiny amount of it, the rat never again touched it. Then I installed a trap. The trap collapsed but there was no rat inside and, from then on, the clever thing avoided both the poison and any type of trap. As the damage caused by the beast got worse and worse, I chose a desperate measure. I undid the exhaust from my diesel and let the engine run for two hours, after having closed all hatches and skylights. I had hoped to suffocate the thing in the exhaust fumes, but the rat proved to be virtually indestructible. In the end I tried all things at the same time. I installed the trap, put out poison and let the diesel run a whole afternoon. We went ashore for fear that the fumes might blow up the boat and, upon my return, exhaust fumes were coming from every crack in the boat. The next morning we opened up and aired the boat. It took a week to get rid of the last of the fumes, but this time it had worked. The rat had not been suffocated by the fumes but at least it must have been drowsy, so it ate some poison and was never seen again from then on. Only months later did I find the decomposed cadaver in the bilge!"

Another friend reported:

"During our Atlantic passage we noticed that we had a rat on board. The signs were clear. Everywhere we could see traces of things that had been gnawed at. Our strategy was simple. We laid a trail of bread-crumbs which led outside. We then tied a piece of string to the door leading out into the cockpit and pretended to go to sleep in our bunks. Soon, we heard the familiar rustling sound and we saw that the rat was eating her way along the trail. As soon as she was outside, we pulled the string and the door crashed to. The rat was now outside and the rest was done by the male part of the crew, with the scrubbing post!"

And he confirmed: "It takes the wit of a woman to deal with a rat."

"So we are lucky to have Amy on board", Greg and I replied. We borrowed a trap and prepared it with the biggest delicacies, strictly following Amy's directions. But our first try, with a large chunk of Swiss cheese, failed. The rat managed to steal the cheese without going into the trap. We then fell back on our secret weapon: Hungarian salami. Adjusting the trap to be as sensitive as possible nearly cost me my fingers, and the result was still negative. Only days later, when we had removed all edible things, did the trap finally put an end to this episode.

On the hunt for happiness

According to the history books, the Bay Islands have always been a magnet for foreigners. In former times, pirates and escaped slaves landed here. Today, mainly Europeans settle in these islands.

Why would people change their civilised world for such a remote place? There were of course numerous reasons. Love of nature, the urge for freedom, unemployment, evasion of taxes, love-sickness or simply fleeing from European courts of justice. One thing united them all, the search for a better life. Here they hoped to find happiness. This is made easier by the openness of the natives and the fact that in the islands, contrary to the mainland, English is the main language.

The first foreigner whom we met here was the American Fred Stone. He was one of the real characters of the islands. He did not look his age and despite his leg, which he had broken when falling off the slipway cradle, he was full of energy and limped around his yard with his crutch, keeping the workers on their toes. His wife lived on the mainland and once he returned from there very agitated.

"She hates this island and prefers to live on the mainland", he explained. "So I go and see her during the weekends. The night before last we were robbed by five armed gangsters. They tied us up and stole everything of any value from the house. And this has to happen to me, a former secret agent! My gun was out of reach when they burgled our house!"

I tried to pacify him. "Perhaps you should be grateful for that. Otherwise, after a shoot-out with five armed men, you might not be here now!"

The smaller islands off Guanaja were all private property. On one of them, Clark's Cay, the old pensioner Keith lived. With his wife, an architect, they had created a small paradise. Now, however, Keith lived by himself with his two dogs, as his wife had returned to the United States for health reasons. He, too, had originally arrived by boat.

"I learnt to sail on an old German yacht which had been confiscated after the war", he told us. "Here in Guanaja, I sold it back to a German, but stupidly he sank her in the anchorage by sheer carelessness."

Another of the small islands, the so-called Half-Moon Island, was shared by the Americans Jack and Terry. Both apparently had their reasons to choose early retirement on this island. One of them was a beauty surgeon, the other a stockbroker. Thanks to satellite communications gear, the broker could still work.

On 'Hugo Cay', we met Hugo. He had an athletic figure and was big, blue-eyed and blonde, so we dubbed him 'Adonis-Hugo'. He shared his island with his dog and, from time to time, paying guests. He lived the dream of many who flee from civilisation and he himself gave the impression of a gentle dreamer. But he loved his life. Apart from the house, he had a big salt-water basin in which, amongst other sea-creatures, turtles, prawns, lobster and sharks swam about. Like nearly all islanders, Hugo lived mainly independently of outside resources. Electricity was gained by wind generators and the rain water was collected in large cisterns.

We also got to know Jo. His former life must have been very stressful, as he had given his small hotel the name 'Stress-less'. After that, we stumbled upon the colony of Hanses. They were of course all Germans. To avoid confusion, their identical names were slightly modified. The one who was running the biological farm with his family was called 'long-haired Hans'. Another one was 'Bavaria Hans'. He was one of the former tenants of the Hofbräuhaus in Munich.

"I ran into some trouble with the tax people", he said. "So I gave up the business and went sailing with my wife, instead. In Guanaja we suddenly had the opportunity of buying an island, so we sold the boat and moved ashore." Sitting in front of his TV set, watching a German programme via satellite, he said: "This is just as good as home, but much more beautiful and, above all, freer!"

The youngest of all the Hanses was called 'Hansito'. Hansito had built up the Hotel Manati with a few partners. It was a three-storey building of wood. The construction had caused immense difficulties. To save some money, they had pre-fabricated the wood on the mainland but during the transport to Guanaja, the ship sank with the wooden cargo. Under truly adventurous conditions, the wood was retrieved and brought to Guanaja. The hotel was now managed by Hansito and a very nice lady from eastern Germany whose life in freedom had begun with the demolition of the Berlin wall. Another holiday resort was run by an Italian, and we also met a French couple who had also arrived by boat and had then been seduced by the beauty of this place. They were now working hard to build a house and a little harbour.

The Honduras Triangle

We shifted our anchorage closer to Hansito's hotel. We had originally intended to stay for three days and now we had already spent three weeks here. Friends of ours made fun of us on the radio: "You have changed from cruising sailors to cruising anchors. We will have to come and save your souls!"

A few days later, they arrived. They were Rudi with his wife, Admiral Gusti, on the Canadian boat *Ragnar II*. We had first met them on the island of Providencia.

"Just take a good look around!", I said upon their arrival. "The wooded mountains, the colourful lagoon with the small islets, and over there, Bonacca, the Venice of the Caribbean. But above all we are anchored here in the triangle between the Hotel Manati, a houseboat full of beautiful ladies, and one of the best watering holes in the entire Caribbean, the Bar Horizonte. This is the equivalent of the Bermuda Triangle. Who sails in here is invariably lost!"

The Hotel Manati was transformed into our social centre. Here, we would eat, drink, talk and spend our siestas in our hammocks. On the 19th of February we celebrated Greg's birthday, which turned into a rather turbulent evening in which many of the resident foreigners also participated. One of the hotel guests gave an impressive demonstration of his talents as a fire-eater and juggler. One of his most daring acts, juggling with five burning flares, was presented late at night and the alcohol must have handicapped the artist a bit, and from time to time burning flares flew around our heads. Hugo also had a special surprise for Greg and gave him a tin of biscuits. As we were about to try them, Hugo warned us:

"Careful, my friends, don't eat too many of them at one time. I made them myself."

Everybody seemed to know what the secret of these biscuits was, but I had to ask Hugo. "So what is so special about them?"

Hugo grinned. "They contain marihuana!"

Full of curiosity I tried one of them, but our friend must have made a mistake with the dosage. In contrast to the others, I felt nothing. The following evening we spent on Hugo's island and I laughed about his biscuits. He urged me to try once more and this time, the effect was undeniable.

Our personal Bermuda Triangle was filled with temptation, for example on board the house boat which belonged to the Hotel Stress-less. Jo had just about completed it, under a lot of stress. His first guests were three charming German holidaymakers. These ladies, Silke, Christiane and Reini, decided to stage a house-boat-warming party, which was a complete success. Everyone drank and danced as usual, and there was also a lot of flirting. Adonis Hugo found his match that evening, and Reini soon moved onto his island. The sad fact is that love makes blind, and months later I heard through the grapevine that Hugo had left his paradise for his love and followed her back to Hamburg.

The Bar Horizonte had a magical flair and had all that one could expect of a perfect Caribbean bar. It was built on the water and could only be reached by boat. One of the regulars here was Norman Taylor, an old fisherman who fascinated us with his yarns. It was also here that I got to know the marine biologist Sharon. She nearly put an end to my voyaging plans. She lived in a house which was similar to the bar, but had just split up with her Honduran boy friend and was about to return to the United States. Her house was consequently for sale. One glance was enough for me. Her dilapidated shack seemed like a palace made of wood. The view over the surrounding mountains and islands was superb, and the anchorage for the boat was just outside her window.

"How much do you want?", I asked her.

"10,000 dollars", she replied. "But I have already promised it to someone." She would have liked to sell her house to me, but it then transpired that the hut was officially owned by her ex-partner. Apparently she had forgotten that this was, despite all the charm, a land of freebooters.

In the bar, we also met the Americans Bill and Maureen Miller. They too had found an existence here. They lived in a nice house on the flank of one of the hills and they had found what they had been looking for after turbulent times back home. But Bill's career as a fisherman had found a premature end through storms and sabotage.

"Never try to go into competition to the local fishermen", he warned me. Once a year, they organised the visit of American veterinarians to the island. "There are countless dogs and cats on Guanaja, so we offer free treatment and, above all, sterilisation", they told us. Then Maureen asked: "We need an assistant. Wouldn't you like to give it a try?"

"Of course", I said. "I would actually have loved to become a vet by profession." So I volunteered. My job was to hand over medical instruments, hold down the animals and, above all, see to it that the doctors always had a fresh, cool beer at hand. The operation site was wisely chosen: it happened to be the disco where we had celebrated our first evening.

Tegucigalpa

"Do we need a visa to get into the United States?", I asked an official at the US embassy on the phone.

"Absolutely yes", came the answer. "Especially if you arrive by sailing boat. But you will have to pick up your visas personally from the embassy."

So the following day saw Greg and myself flying to Tegucigalpa. I was uneasy as the old plane lifted off the airstrip on Guanaja and remembered what Fred had told us: "I once tried to take off with an old private plane that was too heavily laden. I just managed to scrape over the hill at the end of the airstrip but lost so much speed that I crashed into the mangroves beyond. Dangling head first in the seatbelts, I noticed blood all over the windscreen. But I then discovered that I was not injured and that the blood came from a snake which had been chopped to bits by the propeller." However, our plane gained height and soon we were flying over vast banana plantations and an impressive mountain range.

In Tegucigalpa, the capital of Honduras, we took a taxi to the American embassy. The driver told us, amongst many other things, that Honduras was the second largest country in Central America and that six million people of Spanish–Indian descent lived here. "The Americans get too involved in our internal affairs", he also said. "That's why the old embassy has been burnt down by protesters!"

The new embassy building was more like a fortress. However, it seemed that the Americans could not be as unpopular as all that: a huge queue of people went the length of the street, and they were all waiting for their US visas. Greg and I went straight to the doorman and told him the name of the official with whom we had spoken on the telephone the previous day. We were ushered in instantly. Maybe our friend in the embassy secretly dreamt of cruising, to treat us to such a privilege as this. From the embassy, we took another taxi to a friend of Hansito's – the fourth Hans that we met in this country. Hans Brüchmann lived with his family in Tegucigalpa and had, without doubt, the very best restaurant in town. It was located on the top of a hill and offered superb views over the capital and the land beyond. He then invited us for lunch, and seldom have I enjoyed such spontaneous hospitality. "Chaps, you look as if you were hungry!", he exclaimed and proceeded to serve us a pile of German delicacies. It was only with an effort of will that we could manage all of it, and Hans joined us with a beer to listen to the tale of our adventures. One thing, though, irritated him: Greg's red ponytail.

"I'll be happy to treat you to a hair-cut", he insisted. "It'll cost less than half a dollar here!"

But my friend declined firmly. "The ponytail will not be touched. It belongs to the profession of boat-builder!"

While Greg returned to Guanaja that same day, I stayed overnight with Hans and his family, as our visas would only be ready the next morning – so I had the added pleasure of meeting the current Miss Honduras, who happened to be Hans' daughter.

Finale

The three days which we had originally planned for Guanaja had by now stretched to six weeks. "If we still want to visit Guatemala and Belize, my voyage to Europe will take another year longer", I complained. "So, fair enough, it would have been impossible to ignore Brazil and the Caribbean, and visiting all the places has so far been more than worthwhile. But now we have to skip a few, otherwise I'll never reach my goal!"

But doubts rose again when I heard that one of the islands off Guanaja was for sale for 50,000 dollars. For that price, one could not even buy a tiny studio in any of the European cities. Here, I could have had an entire island complete with a house on it. As luck had it, someone else was quicker than me, otherwise I might have ended up there for good. I had been told that all the countries of Central America were quite generous with visas and long-term permits to stay, especially if they were paid, or rather bribed, for.

Then Amy had to leave and this finally did start our preparations for sea. For three months she had been on board. Now, she said to me with laughing eyes: "Please deliver my man safely to our harbour in Maine!"

We were finally heading for northern latitudes. Generating electricity by solar panels, as we had done all along the way so far, would not be sufficient anymore, so I designed a shaft generator which was driven by a belt from the turning prop shaft. The parts were made to my drawings, and the generator worked – although we had to sail along at at least six knots before it produced any reasonable amount of electricity. Greg reassured me: "There's more than enough wind for that in the North Atlantic!"

We again took in the natural beauty of the place, both above and below water. However, the darker sides of this paradise are normally lost on the passing visitor. Before sailing north, we wanted to get rid of some equipment which had by now become nothing more than ballast. We were not surprised at quickly selling our windsurfer and parts of our diving gear. But we were surprised how quickly we found a buyer for our frightening shotgun. Apart from the ever-present danger of burglaries, there seem to be some bitter but hidden conflicts going on between the people living here. Even in such a paradise, one of the lowest human emotions apparently still reigns: envy. What good is it to leave your home behind and come here if you can only sleep with a shotgun under the pillow?

In the bay where we anchored was the half-sunken wreck of an old luxury liner. In the Bar Horizonte we learnt that it had been sunk there on purpose to be taken apart. Greg and I visited the wreck and found to our delight that the looters had not yet taken everything: the thick teak planks of the deck. We helped ourselves to as much as we could stow away on board, because sooner or later I would have to replace *Ryusei*'s deck.

Never before had a farewell been so bitter. But when we finally decided to sail, neither headwinds nor rough seas could stop us. Our German–Canadian friends on *Ragnar II* shook their heads. But with the words: "We prefer to face the devil than stay forever!" we set sail.

Piracy on Roatan

We reached French Harbour on Roatan well before darkness. In sharp contrast to Guanaja, this island was completely developed for tourists. But we did not mind this at all, as we were only going to have a very short stop here.

Greg was always on the look-out for work in the Caribbean. "Somewhere there has to be a classic yacht whose owner has the money to have her properly renovated", he would say. Since then, we had been looking for a suitable project. I often made fun of Greg – whenever we saw a rotting timber on some remote beach I would say: "Look here, all you need now is the owner with the funds to pay for a nice rebuild!"

But in Roatan we stumbled across a suitable project. It was a wooden boat, more than thirty metres long, which was going to have a complete refit. Just by chance I got to know her German owner in the bar of the yacht club.

When he told me about the rebuilding plans, I immediately asked him if he needed a professional boat-builder for the job. "I think so", he replied, "but it's the project manager's decision."

Back on board, we typed out an impressive-looking curriculum vitae for Greg, upon sight of which it was agreed that he could do the job. Indeed, he could have started at once as the whole project was going to be done under a very tight time schedule.

But after having inspected the boat, Greg said: "Whoever wants this ship rebuilt must be floating in money. I'm sure that the job will take at least twice as long as anticipated by the project manager. So I can easily sail to Maine with you and still return for the job later!"

Just to secure the deal I invited the owner and his designer for a short sailing trip. We beat against a fresh breeze with the lee rail awash. The owner enjoyed his spell at the helm and no doubt dreamt that his own boat would soon be ready again.

But luckily Greg's life took a different course. I later heard that this project was never finished. Allegedly, large sums of money had been embezzled by the project manager in Honduras. It appeared that piracy was still practiced in the islands of Honduras, as it had been since the times of Henry Morgan, albeit now in modern form.

Mexico and Cuba

The calm before the storm

Three hundred and ten miles still separated us from our next destination, the Isla Mujeres in the north-east of the Yucatan peninsula. As soon as the mountains of the Bay islands were below the horizon, the wind left us. "Is there a zone of calms in this part of the Caribbean?", we asked our friends on the radio. *Runaway* and *Compadre*, who were by now in the Pacific, assured us that this was not the case. They even warned us about the so called Northerly, a gale from the north-west which harasses this region at this time of the year. Towards evening the wind came back and swung to the north-east. The entire night, we sailed close to the wind. But then we once again drifted in complete calm. A dark front of clouds built up on the horizon. Greg, who has a reliable feeling for the weather, warned me: "This could be the calm before the storm. Let's take down the mainsail."

The wind then hit us with a surprising force from the north. Before we could react in any way, *Ryusei* was over on her side. We hove to and reefed the remaining foresail. Forty knots of wind is not that uncommon, but when it blows against a strong current, it creates hell. In a matter of minutes, the sea began to boil. Spray was flying horizontally and the waves broke over the deck. We could do nothing but struggle on under the small reefed foresail. Five long hours went by in this way until the wind swung around to the north-east and calmed down again. In the small hours we crossed latitude 20 degrees north. We were now highly conscious that we were heading towards colder climates. Then, another natural phenomenon had us on our toes. At a distance of about five miles, we saw the whirlwind of a tornado. Between the sea and the clouds was a spiralling column. Against our curiosity we only felt the urge to get away as fast as possible. Without the engine and a favourable current, this would have been difficult.

Mexico in 24 hours

As far as the largest country of Central America went, we were only interested in visiting the Yucatan peninsula. Here, we wanted to see the ruins of a fascinating culture. Chichen Itza, Tumal and Uxmal were the most famous remains of the Maya empire which once spread from Yucatan as far as Honduras. We intended to park *Ryusei* in the yacht harbour of the island of Mujeres for the duration of our land excursion. But we had reckoned without the Mexican immigration authorities. We were clearing in according to all rules in Mujeres, and all went well with the harbour master. But when we presented Greg's and my passports to the immigration people, we ran into trouble. As far as I could decipher from the rapid cascade of Spanish, they said: "South Africans need a visa. To enter without a visa is illegal and will result in prosecution!"

I immediately sensed that, this time around, the problem would not be solved by a little baksheesh, so I said "But we had not intended to enter your country. We are here because we had to divert from our course due to a bad storm and because we now need fuel. As long as my South African friend remains on board, we will not break the law."

"In that case you have to declare this to the harbour master. In the meantime, I will keep the passports here."

With an uneasy feeling, I left the immigration office and marched back to the harbour master. For a fee of thirty dollars he typed out a declaration that, according to the international law of the sea, we were permitted to stay here to take on fuel and water. Returning to the immigration officer with this document, I had a bit more success. However, the officer still insisted on keeping our passports until our departure the following morning.

"But we intend to sail very early in the morning, and your office only opens at ten", I said, fearing that he might come up with more aggravation before morning. I then patiently remained seated in his office and waited for the passports to be handed back to me, but this ploy failed. I left the office defeated, shortly before I would have been chucked out.

Greg and I decided that if we were not allowed to see the remains of the Maya culture we should at least have a good look around here, so we dived into the nightlife of the tourist resort of Isla Mujeres until the early hours. With the water and fuel tanks topped up, we left Mexico within 24 hours of having arrived there.

The boat is full!

No other destination filled us with so much curiosity as did Cuba. We met some very rough seas in the infamous Yucatan Channel, but the wind was ideal and the current was helping us along. According to the GPS, we often reached speeds of more than ten knots across the ground.

We did not sleep a great deal as we were now only two on board. Again I asked myself what drove people to singlehanded sailing. Is it a sort of euphoria once the forces of nature are faced entirely alone? When awake, the lone sailor must surely be very tired. When sleeping, he must be suffering from panic attacks and the fear of being run down or going aground somewhere.

So I was fearing the worst when I was woken up by a high-pitched whine early the next morning. In near panic I stumbled up the companionway steps. "What's up?"

"A plane nearly crashed into our mast. I think it might be the American coastguard. Here they come again!"

From the corner of my eye I could see a large propeller plane going through a wide curve and coming back towards us. I then heard a voice from the radio's loud speaker: "Sailing vessel, sailing vessel – this is the American Coastguard plane. Please identify yourself – over."

They asked me again before I could even answer, then I finally called them, first wishing them a 'good morning' as it was about 6 am, and identified us: "Coastguard, coastguard. This is the sailing vessel *Ryusei*, registered in Hong Kong, two people on board, one South African by the name of Greg Friedrichs and one German, owner and skipper, by name of Ralph von Arnim. Last port of call Isla de Mujeres, Mexico, heading for Havana, Cuba."

The answer was short: "Roger. Thank you. American coastguard, over and out."

So the watchful eye of the United States had already caught us. What does such a mighty nation fear that they even bother small, harmless sailing yachts at sea? Maybe it is the smuggling of drugs from places like Colombia. We had possibly been on the list of suspects ever since visiting Cartagena.

But there was also another, much more acute reason. During one flying visit back to Europe I sat next to an American TV journalist who was of Cuban descent, and she was participating in a UNESCO conference about refugees. She filled me in about the current situation. "Thirty years after Castro took over, the Soviet Union broke up and all help for Cuba stopped. The economic situation in the country, never really very healthy anyway, declined rapidly to an alarming state. Out of sheer need, a new wave of refugees was created. Thousands of Cubans went to sea in makeshift rafts, in the hope of drifting towards America. Most of them never made it, many drowned and only very few came through. The bulk of them were caught by the US coastguard and sent back to Cuba immediately. I've made a documentary about these refugees and their fate, which I shall publish soon."

As one example, she told me the gripping story of one young girl who had tried to flee with her parents and sisters on a rickety raft made from empty oil drums. As a sail, they used old bedclothes. But then the wind increased, the raft broke up and before her eyes all her family were drowned. Only she was rescued by the coastguard.

The journalist then implored: "Please promise me to rescue every refugee you might see drifting along at sea. Never mind about the orders of the coastguard who ask you to leave Cuban refugees to their fate!"

In those days, the strait between Cuba and Florida had a similar role to the formerly lethal border between East and West Germany, with the one difference that then, the western world welcomed every refugee from the east. But here, America obviously had enough of the Cubans. They must have believed that their own boat was full, and so turned the Cubans down and sent them back to their island.

On the following morning, still about 15 miles off the coast of Cuba, we suddenly saw an unlit patrol boat sneaking up in the dawn behind us. It then abruptly changed course for Cuba and vanished in a cloud of black smoke. Soon afterwards, we saw the skyline of Havana and hoisted the Cuban courtesy flag.

Welcome to Cuba

Following the instructions of the harbour master, we moored to the coastguard dock in the entrance of the Marina Hemingway. A uniformed gentleman stood on the pier and, as soon as our lines were fast, he introduced himself and came on board: "I am the inspector of the health authorities. Welcome to Cuba!" He then looked me straight in the eyes and asked: "How are you feeling?"

"Fine!"

"Perfect!", he said and went below decks with us where he started to fill in forms.

It was by now beginning to get hot, and I offered him a cool beer. Gratefully he accepted, asked us to sign the documents and left. But the next delegation had already been waiting ashore. Several gentlemen of the customs authority now boarded us. They had a good nosy look around and then settled in our saloon but were, like their health colleague, extremely courteous. I pulled another round of beer from the refrigerator and then the invariable question was asked: "Anything to declare?"

"No, nothing that I know of."

"Not even pornography?"

"Sorry, no."

"What a shame. We would have loved to see some!"

I had an idea. "We don't have pornography. But maybe you

might be interested in our collection of condoms?"

I opened our medical case and got out a small box which I had once bought in an American condomeria. All colours, forms and flavours were present. Our customs people were over the moon with delight. They had never seen such a variety before. Every one of them was allowed to choose one.

The rest of the clearing procedure now went very smoothly. But every time when one set of officials left, the next group was waiting on the pier. With the exception of the delegation from the coastguard, all of them were friendly and efficient. At the end of the procedure, we took stock: officials from seven different authorities had come on board. Health office, customs, immigration, coastguard, veterinary office, quarantine and agricultural office, and finally the marina administration. The Cuban authorities were beating all previous records and our ship's stamp was in permanent use.

"Welcome to Cuba! We would like to invite you to a Fiesta tonight! It takes place in the Hotel 'The Old Man and the Sea'. Two young ladies welcomed us with these words as we were berthing *Ryusei* in her allocated spot. They belonged to the hotel where the fete was going to happen, but Greg and I were delighted. Seldom had we been greeted like this before.

The Marina Hemingway dates back to pre-Castro times of the Batista regime and had been completely renovated not long before our visit. The service was perfect and a clear indication of how much Cuba was trying to attract visitors from abroad, although the lunch showed that tourists exist in another dimension here. For a chicken with salad we paid four or five times what it would have cost in Honduras, and at nearly ten US dollars this simple dish cost more than the average Cuban had as disposable monthly income.

Henry's Cuba

In the marina, Greg spotted a Virtue-class sloop, which was a small but beautiful wooden classic designed by Laurent Giles. *Lady of Spain* stood out among the many larger boats as very pretty and had a purposeful air about her. We got to know her British crew, Beth and Ben, who had been voyaging the Atlantic for two years but were now bound back home. We instantly found a liking for each other and so decided to explore Cuba together.

The Cuban Henry spoke excellent English and wanted to earn some money as a chauffeur and guide for us. He showed us the real, not the official, side of life in Cuba. "You must understand", he told us, "that doing this job is illegal for me. If we are stopped by officials, you will have to pass as personal friends of mine."

Once past the gates of the marina, we entered a different world. Ancient American cars cruised along and grandiose villas stood along both sides of the road leading to downtown Havana. But everything was run down and derelict, the scene grey, facades were crumbling and the streets were full of potholes. Electric cables dangled like spaghetti from the houses, and nobody seemed to be doing anything about it.

But in stark contrast to the run-down buildings, the people were colourful and lively. They defeated their drab surroundings by their liveliness, although we saw long queues in front of shops whose windows looked suspiciously empty. It was indeed a different world, impossible to describe here in a few sentences, although many aspects reminded me of my travels to other socialist countries like China, Hungary or Eastern Germany.

On the once famous shopping street 'Galiano' a lively trade was going on. "Look here – at last there is something to buy!", we said. "Yes", Henry agreed. "But this is the black market!"

When the time for lunch came closer, we had a choice. "Either we go into a vastly over-priced tourist restaurant", Henry said, "or we find an illegal, private place. What do you prefer?"

For us, there was no question at all. Soon afterwards, Henry parked in a quiet residential district. He then knocked on a door, which was opened just a little. Henry whispered something, then we were let inside. We were led through the house into a beautifully kept garden where we again seemed to be somewhere else, not in the Cuba we had seen this morning. The atmosphere was as pleasant as the service and the prices were adequate. For lunch, we had roast meat with black beans, rice, fried bananas and a salad. It tasted wonderful.

Afterwards we continued on our tour. We saw the square where Fidel Castro held his propaganda speeches; also a huge luxury hotel from the 1920s and finally the academy of arts. The architecture was sensational, although the state of the buildings was again no longer the very best. Henry told us: "Since the help from Russia has stopped, we are in a desolate situation. People vegetate with the absolute minimum and it is nearly impossible to survive on the standard rations for food that everyone is allocated. The money which we can officially earn to spent freely is about five

US dollars per month, so there is no real reason to work as the pay is so ridiculously low. So the black market and illegal work are flourishing. There are rapidly growing numbers of private restaurants, taxis, tourist guides, black markets and also increasing prostitution. This is partly tolerated by the government, but we all also live in fear of being caught."

We were impressed by what Henry had to say and he sounded more like a professor than like a driver or guide. "What is your profession?", Ben asked him.

"I was educated in Russia as an electronics specialist. I speak Spanish, Russian and English. But despite these qualifications and my relatively well paid job it is impossible to support my family just by official means. Like everybody else, I am dependant on this illegal side-job so that I can at least buy some food on the black market. I am now fifty, and for thirty years I was a follower of Castro. He can talk wonderfully. But sadly I have now realised that I have wasted my life in this respect. After his speeches, nothing ever followed. Instead of the promised improvements, there was oppression. The embargo by the United States is not a sufficient excuse for the state of this country, which went down and down while the party leaders led a life of luxury. I now think that capitalism cannot be worse. Only when people started to leave Cuba en masse did Castro relax the situation a bit by tolerating illegal jobs and the black market. I think he fears for his life. His appearances in public are now quite rare and he lives in fifty different places."

"How long do you think he can stay in power like this?"

"Don't be misled by what I say. He still has many followers. Otherwise he wouldn't still be here!"

The following day, we drove out into the countryside with Henry. We saw endless, swaying fields of sugar cane and tobacco. We then came to a mountain forest with little streams and cascades, and the beauty of this scenery pushed the dark aspects aside for the time.

The bottom line of all sins
In Cuba, the usual sins are readily available literally on every street corner: sex, tobacco and alcohol.

Cubans have a liberal view about sex. Before the revolution, Havana was the most popular brothel of the world. But looking at the attractive people and listening to their music it is easy to imagine what the norm rather than the exception was in the nightlife of those former times. Today, as in those times, it is less the fiery character than pure material want which has caused the oldest trade in the world to flourish again. We got ambiguous offers everywhere. In the yacht club bar, from balconies in town and above all in the bars and discos at night. Foreigners are there to be used, although the motives vary. Money, of course, but also the chance to flee from the grey surroundings for a while or even the wild hope of finding a long-term liaison with a tourist to enable the move abroad. The latter was nothing new for me. In China, where I once worked on a steel factory, we foreigners were even called "flight tickets" for this very reason.

Fidel Castro and Cuba cannot be imagined without cigars. Smoking cigars is a cultivated affair which demands respect and attitude. When we discussed this topic, I had an idea. "We all know that Cuban products are illegal in the States. How about if we were to boost our ship's income with selling Cuban cigars on Wall Street?"

So we decided to buy Cuban cigars on the black market. There was opportunity enough in downtown Havana. We were constantly approached by beggars. But once, a man came up to me, looked me in the eye and whispered the magical word "Cigars?" I nodded and followed him into a side alley where we discussed the products and the price. "Cohiba and Romeo & Julieta", I demanded. "But only first choice!" I was hoping of making the impression of knowing what I was talking about.

"Follow me, it is too dangerous here", the man said. Against all instinct, I followed him. He led me around many corners while the alleyways got increasingly darker and narrower. We ended up in the courtyard of a derelict building where we climbed the rickety stairs to a tiny flat right under the roof. It was obvious that a whole family was living in this small space. I felt uneasy and expected to be knocked down and mugged at any moment. But then a large cupboard was pushed aside and out came several boxes of cigars. I gestured at a box of Cohibas and demanded a quality test without having the faintest notion of how this was made. The man opened the box, took out a cigar and rolled it between his fingers to show that no tobacco was falling out. He then bent the cigar to a complete U without it breaking, and I thought: "Only good quality can withstand this treatment." So I bought several boxes, for 25 dollars each. In Europe, this would have been the price for a single cigar.

In the second attempt at buying, I asked the dealer to deliver the samples on board where I could pick and choose in easier surroundings.

All sins can be lethal. This is especially true for alcohol. Every year, more people are killed by excessive drinking than by any other drug except tobacco. I am sure that everyone knows at least one case of alcoholism in the family or circle of friends. One night, we were invited on Bob's boat and, on the question of whether we should drink the customary Cuba Libre on board or ashore, he answered: "I'd like to have a Cuba Libre without the Libre, which makes it a straight coke. I am an alcoholic and not allowed to touch a single drop anymore!" He proceeded to tell his life story, where alcoholism had cost him his job, his family and very nearly his life. "Alcoholics Anonymous has saved me, and sailing gave my life a new sense. Once you have lost your sense of proportion, you can never drink again!" At the same time, we experienced an active alcoholic on a different boat, and it was shocking.

This was reason enough for us to examine our own drinking habits. During our voyage, we went over the top on many occasions. Alcohol and cruising are close together, which is a real danger. But these negative aspects of alcohol nevertheless did not stop us filling our bilges with many different brands of rum. "Rum is life-blood in the extreme north", Greg argued. "Moreover, we should not forget the fact that we are honorary members of the Imperial Poona Yacht Club!" Still, we were sobered by the ancient realization that everything which is fun is either immoral or unhealthy.

Death in the disco
We used our time in the marina to thoroughly clean the boat, and for days on end we scrubbed and cleaned. After this feat, we thought that we had also earned ourselves some fun and dived into the local nightlife, joined by Beth and Ben. We went through a couple of bars and finally ended up in a discotheque under the open night sky. We were captivated by the sheer number of beautiful women and the Latin American music which boomed from the loud speakers. Soon, I went dancing with a fiery Cuban lady and was completely enthralled by the experience, so we did not hear the bangs at first. I thought it might be a fireworks display, but then we saw people fleeing from the disco in panic. Instinctively, we dropped to the ground and crawled behind a tree to find some shelter. From here I could see how a man, right next

to our table, had a drawn pistol and fired at someone from very close. The victim was then grabbed by a few rough looking men and dragged through the shocked visitors out into the street. The culprit followed unhindered, without being challenged by anyone. When all had quietened down again, I went back to my friends with Marie. Greg reported what had happened right next to them: "It began with a quarrel. One of them pulled a knife, the other a pistol. He fired at once, but luckily the shots did not go into our direction. The victim got at least five bullets in his chest from very close range. The dying man was then carried out into a waiting car which drove off with the criminal inside as well. However, there was great uproar out there; the car was surrounded by a large group of people who shouted and smashed all windows and lights of the car before they could leave."

My dancing partner apparently knew more. "Everyone here knew the victim. They killed him in cold blood!"

"Who are they?"

"The secret police!"

After this incident, the disco was closed, and we were not in the mood for fun anymore, anyway. So we returned on board, including my dancing partner who gave me an intensive course in Spanish over the next couple of days.

Blackout

I had been told that the batteries from Thailand would not even last one year. Now, two years on, it had happened. The four big lorry batteries had lost their capacity.

"It's due to the electrode sludge at the bottom of the batteries", the engineer of the sailing schooner *Lady Anja* told me. "You can save the batteries if you take out the acid and fill them with water. Then you rinse them with more water and finally top up with fresh acid. It works, we have done this once before with our own batteries. And with dollars you can buy anything in Cuba, even the battery acid."

Had we known how dangerous the handling of the acid was, we would just have bought new batteries. The new acid came in highly concentrated form and to dilute it down we poured some water into the container. This however triggered off a hefty chemical reaction and the acid went so hot that we feared the plastic container might melt away. From a safe distance we cooled the thing with a water hose. In the end, though, these efforts were successful and the batteries once more showed 13.1 volts. We reinstalled them on board and prepared for our departure.

A hundred miles lie between Cuba and Key West, which is at the very end of the Florida Keys. The wind was favourable and *Ryusei*'s keel cut swiftly through the water. I was on night watch, alone with my thoughts, when the alarm of the autopilot shrilled. "Low battery" said the display, which was confirmed by a glance at the voltmeter.

"What's up?", said Greg, wakened by my swearing.

"It seems that we have a short circuit of some kind. The batteries are nearly flat. I can see them plunging down on the voltmeter. The engine won't start, either. I have turned off all electrical systems but the batteries are still going down. We have a complete blackout!"

Nothing was working anymore. No autopilot, no navigation system, no echo sounder and no light. This was the nightmare of all cruising sailors.

"Don't panic", Greg said. "We have all that we need. Our boat is afloat, we have sails, compass and rudder. Instead of the navigation lights we can always show our paraffin lamp. The seafarers in former times weren't any better off!"

And he was right, we were far from helpless. We still had the sextant, although it was a long time since we had practised our skills with it. We also had our emergency kit which contained, among other items, a small hand-held VHF and a GPS. The latter helped us to find the entrance to the channel leading through the outer reef into the Florida Keys. The engine we then started with a simple trick. We waited until the sun had risen high enough to charge our solar panels, and at the same time changed course temporarily to increase our speed and thus the charging effect from our new prop shaft generator. Around noon we arrived on the anchorage of Key West.

United States of America

Applauding the sun

We checked in without any of the problems we had anticipated because of our visits to Colombia and Cuba, although the last of our fresh vegetables and fruits were confiscated for reasons of quarantine. Our contraband, in other words all our reserves of beer, rum and cigars, were luckily not discovered. All in all, everything seemed to be very laid back in Key West, which was mainly a holiday town with numerous bars and restaurants. We could not have chosen a better place to arrive on a new continent. One thing, however, was hard to get used to. The prices beat anything that we had paid so far.

Beth and Ben had arrived before us. Their boat *Lady of Spain* was anchored close to us. Together, we explored the village. Like everywhere in the Caribbean, the climate was tropical, so it didn't take too long before we settled down in a bar, which more resembled a wooden shack. While we enjoyed our first beer on the North American continent, Ben suggested: "What do you think about going down to the promenade at sunset. We've heard that every day at sunset there's a lot going on there."

It was packed with people. In between were many stalls

selling various things as well as jugglers, musicians and fire-eaters. But then the moment arrived when the whole crowd drifted down towards the beach. "What's happening over there?"; I asked someone, who laughed and replied: "The sunset!". Thousands of people had gathered here to watch the spectacle, and at the moment when the last ray of the sun vanished below the horizon, there was applause and tremendous cheering.

The American Dream

On the first of April, a new crew member arrived. Ben and Beth promised to keep an eye on *Ryusei*, while Greg and I took a hire car to pick up Gregor at the airport in Miami. I was surprised how much my brother's 15-year-old son had grown. He called me 'Uncle Ralph' and I protested: "Call me Ralph, skipper, or even Ralphman as Greg here does, but please forget about the uncle." We then jumped into the car and dashed off like a gang of teenagers towards Miami Beach. The contrast with all the countries which we had visited before was stunning: dense traffic, highways, skyscrapers, shopping malls and commercial centres. Here, one could probably buy anything – as long as one's finances allowed. We spent one day and one long night in the famous Art Deco district of Miami Beach.

As we passed a tattoo parlour, I said to Gregor: "Anyone who wants to go to sea must have a real tattoo. You can choose – an anchor, a naked woman or a dragon!" Reluctantly, Gregor went into the shop with me. The owner had tattoos all over his body, as far as we could see anyway, and I asked him: "Could you please show us what dragons you have?"

"No problem, we have more than enough of those", he replied and handed us a thick folder with numerous impressive dragon motifs. They came in all shapes, sizes and colours. The smallest one was the size of a penny, the largest extended over the entire body. Photographs of tattooed people further illustrated the catalogue.

"Tattoos and body-piercing are currently very much en vogue", the shopkeeper said. "You can have anything you want…"

But Gregor only wanted one thing – to get out of there as quickly as possible.

We also made an excursion to Fort Lauderdale, which convinced us that Florida is a land of yachts. The boats here were large and luxurious, and everybody seemed to live on some water's edge, with private docks at the bottom of the back garden apparently being the norm rather than the exception. This seemed to be the place where, for some, the American Dream had materialised.

Bahamas 'en passant'
Beth and Ben seemed more than a little relieved when we returned to Key West. "What's the matter?", I asked.

"Oh, nothing special", Ben began. "But just after you left a Northerly went through and *Ryusei* was swinging about on her anchor like mad, in acute danger of hitting the other boats. So I went across and chucked your stern anchor over board, in the panic not noticing, however, that the other end of the anchor cable was not made fast to the boat. But I was lucky that some divers were about who helped me to retrieve the anchor."

While discussing possible routes north, the subject of the Intracoastal Waterway crept up again and again. This is a system of navigable inshore canals which run parallel to the coastline as far as New York. But due to the small depth in the southern part of the waterway, we decided to sail outside after all. Also, *Ryusei* was still an ocean-going sailing vessel and not a paddle steamer.

We prepared for our onward voyage, but the weather situation remained unclear. But I was opting for leaving, arguing: "If we wait for the ideal wind we'll grow as ancient as all these hippie-pensioners in Key West!"

A fresh south-westerly then made the decision. As we left our anchorage, we saw an American fighting a large fish which he had hooked. As soon as he had the exhausted fish alongside his motor boat, he let go of the creature. It apparently was a tarpon, which is inedible. He bites quickly and fights hard, but cannot be eaten. We had to ask ourselves who of the two was more stupid – the fish or the fisherman? For us, fishing had always been strictly for the purpose of finding food.

Towards evening we anchored in the lee of the Looe Keys. Here we had one night's rest before embarking on the long passage north. At last, we were complete again: 'Three men in a boat', and Gregor had not even become sea-sick on his first day at sea.

As we headed north the following day, the wind swung around from SE to S and then further, to SW, W, NW and finally, during the following night, NE. This backing wind we took as an indication of bad weather and we were not surprised when we later heard a warning by the coastguard of thunderstorms and tornadoes. The night kept us entertained with lights above and ahead. Lightning went across the sky, while numerous ships were crossing our bows, culminating in the other-worldly sight of a fully illuminated oil platform in tow. This traffic and the unfavourable winds got on our nerves, and we looked for alternatives. One glance at the chart gave the essential tip. Only a slight change in course would lead us to the Bahamas, and around the break of dawn we reached shallower water. It was so transparent that we felt as if we were driving in some giant amphibian car over the ground. Shortly afterwards, we anchored in the shelter of the small island Piguet Rocks.

The place was perfect for snorkelling. Not as far as the corals were concerned, but the fish – never before had we seen so many, and such big, fish in one spot. They all gathered here: grouper, snapper, barracuda, parrot fish and many, many more. It seemed as if they were giving us one last farewell from the Caribbean.

After a quiet night at anchor, Greg and I were active early the next morning. Only our new crew needed some encouragement: "Hey, Gregor, you lazy bum. Get out of your bunk and into the water. And if you don't come into the ocean, the ocean will come to you!" The latter persuaded him, and we all swam a few times around the boat, just to wake up. We then had a substantial breakfast and up-anchored. We had thus visited the Bahamas which, with all the numerous islands, could well have kept us there for yet another season. The temptation was great. But even greater was my urge to sail on to Europe, at last.

Cape Fear

My urge to sail on did not impress the wind, which remained very light during the morning. When the breeze came through in the end, something else went. With strange noises, the boat veered off course and we knew what had happened. The autopilot was dying on us once again. Nasty reminders of the Indian Ocean crept up, where we had to steer by hand for over 2000 miles. But our next destination, Charlestown, was only another 400 miles away.

"Gregor, you can make yourself useful now. You'll have to steer while Greg and I try and repair the autopilot!"

This was Gregor's first sailing trip, so it took a while before we could leave him to keep the boat on course on his own. The rather heavy seas did not make it any easier for him. Then Greg and I disappeared below decks. The autopilot is attached directly to the rudder quadrant, which is of course hidden away in a most inaccessible corner of the boat. Once there, we could see at one glance that the autopilot was beyond repair. Luckily, we still had a spare unit on board, which was the older model we had used before. It did not quite fit, but we sawed and hammered until it finally did and the relief was great when we found that the old autopilot was still working after all this time.

Towering cumulus clouds and a fiery red sunset heralded bad things to come. As darkness set in, the sky put on an incredible show of lightning and flashes which Gregor thought was better than anything he had ever seen in a disco. After a while, the distant thunderstorm caught up with us with one cold gust and a downpour of such a force that we had difficulties breathing. Lightning and thunder were all around us now and Gregor had to take the helm once more as Greg and I went forward to reef the main. Under these conditions, this was dangerous and hard work, and we both put on our harnesses. The thunderstorm raged on for quite a while and we felt small and vulnerable. Nature showed us during this night what incredible reserves of energy she has and we were lucky not to have been struck by lightning.

The next days passed in a slightly more relaxed manner as the old sea-going routine set in. We were making good speed with the wind and the Gulf stream now helping us, so we decided to sail

on straight for Beaufort in North Carolina. We preferred to sail past the notorious Cape Fear than cope with the shallows in the Intracoastal Waterway north of Charleston.

As was to be expected, a front hit us just as we were off Cape Fear. The weather deteriorated within minutes, and then we were bashing to windward under heavily reefed sails.

Greg prepares for northern latitudes

The waves were short and steep and nasty, and we were soaked in spray. To make matters worse, the water temperature had fallen to 16 degrees Celsius – as opposed to the 26 degrees we had enjoyed in the Bahamas. We had finally left the latitudes of barefoot sailing and, for the first time, the foul-weather gear was used. The wind and an adverse current pushed us towards Cape Fear and the cape truly lived up to its name. Before getting too close, we started the engine and motor-sailed on. The last few miles to Beaufort were a protracted ordeal. It was around midnight that we finally reached the lit buoys which mark the entrance of the Beaufort Passage into the Intracoastal Waterway. But the lights were so numerous that we were completely baffled and in the end could not find our way along the narrow winding channel. In the end, we anchored close to one side of the channel and crept into our bunks.

Plague on board
Beaufort is a small town roughly half-way between Florida and New York. The harbour front with pretty, restored historic houses breathes an air of times gone by and for us it was a good place for a rest and to attack some urgent repairs and maintenance jobs.

This was also, for us, the beginning of our trip along the Intracoastal Waterway. We covered the 190 miles from Beaufort to Norfolk in three day trips. Our handicap was the draft of *Ryusei*. After the first lifting bridge, we ran into shallow water and had to wait for the tide. Once there was enough water, we carried on smoothly. It was a new sensation for us to be passing through a landscape of meadows, woods and little towns. Children played along the canal banks and sometimes we were chased for a little while by barking dogs. First, we were going along the Neuse River. Then we entered Pamlico Sound and finally reached Eastham Creek, where we anchored. It seemed as if we had somehow made it to a village pond. The shore was full of reeds and the trees and bushes full of the colours of spring, which were further enhanced by the setting sun. A beautiful picture!

But we were definitely getting further north. This was not only demonstrated by the later sunsets, but above all by the dropping temperatures. As soon as the sun was gone, the cold crept in. Below decks, we would gather around the still warm engine and try to find a bit of warmth there. My friends were freezing so much that they vanished into their bunks even before dinner.

"What's up with you?", I asked.

"I'm not feeling too good. Probably a flu", Greg replied from his berth.

"Me too", Gregor croaked from his bunk.

"Hey guys, you can't break down now!", I cried in despair. But nothing could persuade them to become fit again. Suffering, they were wrapped up in their bunks and they even lost their appetite. For dinner, they only wanted to have some tea and a few biscuits. I already feared the worst and thought that we had the plague on board.

Greg's condition worsened overnight, and he had very high temperature and was shaking with fever. Before sunrise, I got up the anchor and quickly motored the 20 miles to the next town, which was a place called Belhaven. We were lucky, in a way, as the hospital was directly on the bank of the ICW. With my ill crew in tow, I went to the clinic.

"How are you going to pay?", was the first question which was fired at us, even before we could mention why we had come in the first place. Then, Greg and Gregor got plastic wristbands so that there could be no confusion as to their identity. In the meantime, long questionnaires had to be filled in and finally, they were examined by a doctor. The diagnosis was for acute influenza.

With my weakened crew, I then continued the trip. A little later we reached the Alligator–Pungo River Canal. It was a warm and sunny day and Gregor tempted me to a round of backgammon.

"But I have to steer", said I.

"Oh, the canal is as straight as a ruler. Why don't we use the autopilot!"

And it worked better than I would have thought. We sat opposite each other on the main boom and put the game between us. Every few moves, I had to adjust the autopilot just a tiny bit. But then, I had a difficult move to make and I missed the right moment to check our course. Very smoothly, *Ryusei* slowed down as her keel slid into the mud close to the shore. Greg's head emerged from the fore-hatch, grinning: "You silly sods!"

At least he had found his old humour again. We were lucky to be able to get off the mud under our own power, as there was extremely little traffic on the canal due to the early season. We would have waited half an eternity for someone to tow us off, but with full throttle back and forwards and some frantic paddling with the rudder we finally managed to turn her bow towards mid-channel and come off.

The wind picked up and we could at last sail once more. In

the sheltered water of the Alligator River, we flew along with a hissing wake. Towards evening, we reached the Alligator Highway Bridge, which was operated by a friendly lady who waved to us as we passed. Beyond, we came out into Albemarle Sound and, as the wind was favourable, we continued through the dusk until we reached the other side, where we chose a spot just outside the channel and close to the shore in which to anchor. This was a mistake, as we instantly found out. A cloud of mosquitoes descended upon us and we fled below decks, closing all hatches as if we were about to weather a storm.

The following morning, I served my still weak and suffering crew a breakfast in bed and got under way. The channel was now winding its way through a wooded area, and nearly all the buoys and markers had the large nests of birds of prey on them. Then we were stopped by the coastguard, because Gregor, who had risen from his bunk, had settled down comfortably in the pulpit.

"That's very dangerous!", they told us. "If he falls over board, he could get caught by the propeller and be severely injured!"

The medication and, above all, the loving care of the skipper showed their effects and my crew regained their usual energy again. We were also nearing civilisation once more, which was obvious from the increasing number of bridges which we had to pass. For the night, we anchored in the harbour of Norfolk, immediately off the hospital, just to be sure and speed up their recovery.

On leaving the harbour of Norfolk, we passed America's largest naval base. Not only the number, but also the size of the warships impressed us. A whole fleet of nuclear submarines was moored in the harbour, and at the end of the pier were three aircraft carriers. The people on deck looked like ants in comparison to the size of their ships.

America's European Soul
The weather was as grey as the warships. It was raining and visibility reduced. I wandered back and forth from the navigation table to keeping a look out on deck.

"Something is wrong here", I finally declared. "None of the buoys are as the are shown on the chart!"

"You probably have an old chart", Greg said.

"No, it is as good as new!"

But the confusion was great and we just could not find the short-cut into Chesapeake Bay. Suddenly, we ran aground hard on a sand-bank and were lucky to get off again fairly quickly. But it was enough to make us choose the safer but much longer deep-water route and it was evening before we reached Yorktown in the state of Virginia.

Here, we met Frederic who had sailed with our friend Mike on *Aisa* from South Africa to Curaçao. He told us that it was here that, in 1781, George Washington defeated the British, after which the American colonies gained their independence and eventually got together to form the Untied States. The neighbouring village of Williamsburg was like a live museum for American history and reminded the visitor of the time of the European colonisation. Here it becomes clear that Europe is part of the American soul, and it is not without pride that the Americans refer to their European roots. Quite often, various European nationalities come together in one person: "On my mother's side, my grandfather was Irish and my grandmother Italian. On my father's side, my grandfather was Greek and my grandmother German", one American told us. In this sense, every American already carries in him the essence of their nation: The United States.

Chesapeake Bay

Under sail we headed for Annapolis. One look on the chart is enough to explain why Chesapeake Bay is one of the most popular sailing areas of the United States. Due to a lack of time we sadly had to ignore the multitude of beckoning anchorages. As darkness set in, the wind died and we continued under power. During Greg's watch I was wakened and, still sleepy, I crept from my bunk asking: "What's up?"

"I think that someone might be in trouble over there!"

Away on our starboard side, weak flashes of light were indicating something. We changed course and could soon make out the silhouette of a sailing yacht in the darkness.

"Ahoy there, we are in trouble!", someone called in broken English. "Our engine has broken down, our batteries are flat and there is no wind!"

Judging by the accent, I answered in French: "But that is no problem. Just drift on until the wind comes back!"

"We have lost all sails on the delivery from Martinique to here", the voice answered. "Now we only have a tiny storm sail left. The engine was last repaired in Norfolk, but now it's defective again and all the batteries are flat as well. Could you give us a tow?"

The boat was a 47-foot Tanyana which was being delivered under serious time pressure from Martinique to Annapolis to be sold there. So we acted as a tug for the last 30 miles.

In 1783, Annapolis had, for a short while, been the capital of the Untied States, but today it is one of the world's capitals of yachting. Every service one can think of is available for boats here and we grabbed the opportunity to make *Ryusei* fit for the onward journey. The mooring fees in the marina were shockingly high, but we quickly found a solution to that. Against a bottle of Cuban rum and a few cigars, the harbour master showed us to a remote corner of the marina and forthwith pretended that we were not there at all. In the end we only paid for two days, although we spent five days in the marina.

In the neighbouring town of Washington, now the capital of the US, the flags were flying at half-mast. America was in the state of shock. An administration building in Oklahoma had been destroyed by a bomb, and nearly two hundred people lost their

Along the coast to Newfoundland

lives in this attack. This act of sheer terrorism was instantly blamed on Arab extremists, but then the population was plunged into even deeper shock when it transpired that it had in fact been an American who had done this dreadful deed – out of bitterness with the state.

Greenwich

Before we sailed on, there was another change in *Ryusei*'s crew. Gregor had to return home to Germany and Amy, Greg's girlfriend, joined us once more. She was going to accompany us on their home run to Maine. We sailed on a light and sunny morning and after one night's stop in the idyllic Worton Creek we reached the Delaware Bay via the C-D-Canal. It was dusk as we found our way along the winding Cohaney River through reeds and flat marshes.

We anchored off the village of Greenwich; not on zero longitude, but on 75 degrees west. We were now on latitude 39 north and the cold was also felt by the cockroaches. We had not seen them for a long time, but now, in search of some warmth, they crept out of their hiding places. Greg cried out once as one of them wanted to snuggle up to him. Luckily we had met a yachtie in Annapolis who introduced us to the secrets of our diesel cabin heater. At last, we were able to heat our saloon to an acceptable level again and the last surviving cockroaches soon lost interest in us.

Greenwich is one of the most peaceful spots that I have ever seen. The old houses were embedded in a landscape of spring colours. The fields were in bloom and some trees definitely looked as if they were on fire. Along the shore, several wooden boats in differing states of decay were moored in the reeds. It was no surprise to meet a painter with her tripod here. Sally lived in Greenwich and her nature was as friendly as this place. She invited us to her studio, showed us her paintings and supplied us with sandwiches. She also told us that most of the people here belonged, like her, to the Quakers. For a long time we sat together and exchanged stories and as a farewell present she gave us a cooking book full of traditional recipes.

We came to this magic place by chance, but without a boat and our sense of adventure we would never have seen it.

Freedom

The contrast could not have been greater. It was cold and rainy when we closed in on New York's skyline. All seemed grey and menacing and the skyscrapers, on a Gargantuan scale, filled the horizon and reached into the dark heavy clouds.

One item however broke the grey atmosphere: the Statue of Liberty. The symbol of freedom and the magnet for millions of emigrants. As we sailed past her, we asked ourselves what this ever-cited freedom really was. Is it an illusion or a mental state? In our personal lives, we are subject to many constraints which vary from fundamental necessities to self-imposed pressures. Often we found how much we were envied for our freedom to go cruising. Conversation then frequently ended along the lines of "I'd love to do it as well but my career and my family keep me from realising my dream."

It was the need and poverty as well as religious and political persecution in their home countries which brought most of the emigrants to America. Here, they allowed themselves the freedom to steal from and persecute the native population. Freedom in this case was nothing more than the right of the mighty. And what is left of the Indian culture? Small groups struggling on the outer fringes of society. And the USA is the rule rather than the exception: similar fates were in store for the Incas of South America, the Bushmen of South Africa, the Aborigines in Australia. At least the realization that a lot of injustice has been perpetrated has created a democracy in this country which, on paper, guarantees "equality, justice and freedom".

As we were sailing out of season, we were allowed to moor free of charge in Manhattan's historic harbour, South Street Seaport. Part of the deal was, of course, yet another one of the Cuban bottles of rum.

We felt small and insignificant beneath the skyscrapers, but also the rigging of the full ship *Peking* whose masts towered high into the sky. We would have easily lost our bearings in the endless canyons of New York's busy streets, but a friend who lived here showed us around. The centre of New York, Manhattan, is on an island in the estuary of the Hudson River. In the short time we spent here, we managed no more than a superficial view of the usual sights: the World Trade Centre, Empire State Building, Rockefeller Centre, Museum of Modern Art, Fifth Avenue, Wall Street, Brooklyn Bridge and finally Central Park. We walked for miles and got extremely thirsty in the process. So we also included a pub in our tourist programme, McSorley's Old Ale House, which seemed more like the embassy of the old British Empire.

Devil's Gate

We left this western financial metropolis through Devil's Gate. This is a narrow and rocky part of the channel that leads to Long Island Sound. The tides cause whirlpools there which are similar to those in a mountain torrent. Without our engine we and *Ryusei* would have descended to hell there.

Before darkness we entered a harbour in Long Island Sound.

"The berth will cost you 20 dollars a night", the lady owner informed us frostily.

"And where are the showers, please?"

"Not available. There aren't any."

"But then, how can you charge so much money for one single night?"

"You either pay or you leave. Now."

We preferred to leave now and anchored in front of this inhospitable harbour off the village of Branfort. But we were even more enraged by what we found in Greg's famous butternut soup later that evening – a cockroach! It had probably wanted to warm up on the ceiling above the stove, fainted from the delicious smell of the soup and fallen in.

Mystic Seaport

In Long Island Sound began the world in which Greg and Amy were at home. This is the region known as New England. It consists of the states of Maine, Connecticut, Rhode Island, Massachusetts, Vermont and New Hampshire. New England is one of the birthplaces of the United States. It is here where the independence movement originated.

Greg had long told me that on our way to Maine, Mystic Seaport is a must. And he was right. As we sailed into it, I thought I had gone back in time. The small harbour and the village belonging to it seemed straight from the times in which sailing ships were still trading the world. Mystic Seaport had also once been a famous whaling port. The harbour museum has a fantastic collection of antique ships and other exhibits. The traditional crafts are shown in workshops, and there is no better place than this for anyone interested in the history of traditional seafaring.

The museum also has a large library. Greg suggested that this might be the place to find out some more about *Ryusei*'s history. Because of the conflicts when buying the boat in Thailand the former owner had withheld all documentation regarding *Ryusei*'s origins. All I knew was that she was a direct descendant of the yacht *Firebrand*, designed by Sparkman & Stephens, which had once won the Admiral's Cup. We spoke to the librarian about our research and he advised us to look up old copies of the magazine Yachting World. We did not have to look long, as between 1965 and 1968, *Firebrand* made the headlines:

Firebrand – Designed to win ...*Firebrand* has at least shown her power to windward and achieved her first offshore success in winning the Morgan Cup ...*Firebrand* maintained her remarkable series of victories by taking the Dinard Trophy ...Dennis Miller's *Firebrand* that won the day in a spanking breeze that gave everyone the sail of their lives ...*Firebrand* – most successful of the British Admiral's Cup team."

Dechamps & Daughters

"Return to Germany? I'm not even thinking about it!"

These were the words of my old friend when I asked him when he was planning to return home.

"We are so much better off with our four children over here. Everything is larger here: the land, the cars and the portions in the supermarket. When, for example, I buy milk I get it by the gallon here. The same applies to packets of cornflakes. And during the weekend, I can hammer in nails and mow the lawn without my neighbour complaining to the police about it. If anything, he would come round to offer his help. And anyway, taxes and social costs would have to be reduced dramatically in Germany before I'd even contemplate returning. The politicians can do what they like. One thing is clear to me – the higher the taxes over there, the better is business for us here."

This was quite a sobering assessment for someone like myself returning to Europe. Daniel was managing the American branch of a German company. His girlfriend had accompanied him to America. Now they were married and had two sets of twins, four daughters in all.

Daniel and his family visited us on board one weekend. Dechamps and daughters including their golden retriever were quite an impressive crew. Clad in lifejackets, the girls, aged two and four, with the dog, went through the ship like a typhoon. Only Nine, their mother, could half keep them in check. We had wished for sunshine and a light breeze for our little excursion from Mystic Harbour to Stonington, but we were met by drizzling rain and a fresh breeze so that, despite the reefs, *Ryusei* heeled far over as soon as we left harbour. Mother and daughters enjoyed themselves hugely, although father became quieter and quieter. His face soon assumed that unmistakable colour and the diagnosis was clear. While the dog lay down at his master's feet, the children disappeared into the front cabin where they shrieked with delight when the windows went under water as *Ryusei* heeled over. They were still speaking about this little trip months later and, who knows, maybe we have successfully planted the sailing bug in them?

Martha's Vineyard
'You must not miss out on Martha's Vineyard on your way north' was one of the things that I heard again and again. Now I know why. This island has a unique charm and, although it's close to some densely populated areas, life here is like on another planet. Vineyard's Heaven lived up to its name and Greg and I were euphoric when we saw that the anchorage was full of classic wooden ships. We made a tour in the dinghy to have a close look at these wooden beauties and ashore we visited an old boatyard. Wood is probably the most common building material in New England. Houses are made of wood and traditional ships are enjoying a huge renaissance. After a long walk through the village we ended up in the famous Black Dog restaurant. From our table here we could see out over the beach and eventually watch the full moon rise. It was nearly too kitsch to be true, and we later heard that this was one of President Clinton's favourite places whenever he came here on holiday.

The neighbouring island of Nantucket is known as the capital of the whalers. In former times, the women ran the town as the men were always away at sea. We thought this island to be even more attractive than Martha's Vineyard, as there was less tourism here. A large portion of the island is a natural park in which many animals, including deer, stags, hares, pheasant and geese live. Moreover, similar to us, thousands of migrating birds nest here every year.

The kingdom of Queens
Next morning the world had vanished. At first I thought that there just was a lot of condensation on the insides of our windows but, wipe as much as I wanted, it would not clear. I then opened the companionway hatch and put my head outside. The air hit me like a wet towel. Thick fog had swallowed up the world. Greg and Amy laughed at my stupefied expression.

"You'll have to get used to this. Fog is part of the life in New England. As soon as the moist air from the land goes over the water, the moisture condenses. With a bit of luck, the fog will lift during the day."

We felt like crawling back into our bunks, but following the line of "When the going gets tough, the tough get going" we started to get active. Visibility was less than 100 metres. Without our radar we would not even have found the way to the open sea. We could hear, but not see, the buoys. It was a weird atmosphere, with clanging and whistling everywhere, only interrupted once in a while by the loud booming of a foghorn. There was an object on the radar, probably a buoy. We could not be sure and the fog was so thick that Greg went to the bows as a look-out.

"Hey, Ralph, there's a buoy on collision course!", he then shouted at me. "Head over to starboard a bit!"

Seconds later the buoy materialised from the fog and slid past. Then the echo-sounder alarm rang out. We now had less than five metres of water between our keel and the rocky bottom. Choppy water indicated a strong tidal stream. We were now in the Pollock Rip Channel. Not so long ago, sailors only had their senses and a compass to guide them. How much easier was it for us! Very precise charts, various precision instruments, radar and echo sounder showed us the way. Also we had an engine which helped us along in a calm. But on this calm day, there was another danger. The seabed was literally covered in lobster pots, each with its buoy floating on the surface. We tried to avoid them as best we could, fearing that we would otherwise catch their ropes in our propeller. With a water temperature of only 8 degrees Celsius it would not have been much fun to dive and cut loose the prop.

We then rounded Cape Cod and arrived at a place of which our pilot said: "Provincetown is easy to enter in any conditions. The town is the honky-tonk example of the best and the worst in summer resort commercialism."

Greg and I wanted to find out what this meant. Amy remained on board, and in the dusk Greg and I wandered along the main street of Provincetown. There was a higher density of souvenir shops and restaurants than anywhere else.

"Something's wrong here", Greg said after a while. "Have you noticed?"

"What? Apart from bars and women, everything is here!"

"Exactly. Did you see the last few couples walking past? They were all men. And what sort of men! Just have a closer look!"

Greg was right. There were no mixed couples here. Most of them were dressed extravagantly but at last I thought I spotted a hetero couple. They stood in the doorway of a house. We went up to them and asked: "Could you tell us where we can find a nice bar around here?"

The man answered in a high-pitched voice: "Sure, sure, my children! Right here, in our massage salon! Do come in, my dears!"

His corpulent partner with long red hair danced about in anticipation, smiling hugely. I then saw her hands and realised that she was a transvestite. Embarrassed, I declined the invitation. "We're only thirsty sailors looking for a good place to drink!"

The transvestite shook herself laughing and answered in a deep voice, describing the way to a bar, but not without looking Greg up and down with a certain longing. The bar was called 'Old Colonie' and was the meeting point for the fishermen and some eccentrics like us. Here we also had it confirmed that Provincetown is the kingdom of Queens.

Boston's Chinatown

We decided that this was not our kind of place, and set sail at the crack of dawn. The weather punished us. It was cold and foggy and it drizzled constantly. We also had to beat upwind, as the breeze was coming from the north-west. Even the birds seemed to have their problems with this kind of climate. Two of them landed on board, utterly exhausted, and flew inside the cabin to warm up before continuing on their way. Our mood was appropriate to the weather. Things only livened up a little when we sighted the oldest lighthouse of America, which has shown the way into Boston for 279 years.

I have always felt that one of the advantages of a big family are the cousins, even if they are only very distant ones. Boston was shown to us by a very attractive young female cousin of mine, Julia. She was a talented artist and had left Germany to settle here. Full of enthusiasm we met on the very pier which had been the scene of the famous Boston Tea Party in 1773. She could hardly believe that I had gone to so much trouble and sailed all the way from Asia to Boston. "I would never go through all the hassle of travelling to Asia", she said. "There's no need, Asia is in Boston, anyway."

"How do you mean?"

"Follow me and I'll show you!" She then led us through

downtown Boston. At one point we turned a corner and found ourselves in a street which came straight from another world. This was Boston's Chinatown. Chinese people hurried past, and all around me I heard the familiar sounds of the Chinese language. Red and golden signs with Chinese letters dangled above the shop entrances and dragons and lanterns were everywhere. The entrances to the restaurants had all the elements necessary for a flourishing business: cramped hallways with water basins to keep bad spirits out, mirrors in strategic positions so that all is in order and small altars with little presents for the deceased ancestors. This was Chinese culture in its purest form. Julia led us to a Cantonese restaurant. We sat down around a round table, but the cold neon light and hard chairs reminded us of the fact that we were here to eat, not to linger around. Only when the clients change quickly will the business make money.

Julia was right. Why should she travel? Boston had it all. A booming economy, many different cultures, museums and galleries and some of the best universities. There could hardly be a better place for an artist.

As I knew that I would soon be needing fresh crew, I asked her about sailing to Europe with me. But she flatly refused: "Back to Europe? No thank you!"

Gloucester's tragedy

Greg and Amy had already chosen our next destination. In brilliant sunshine we sailed 25 miles north to the harbour of Gloucester. What Nantucket and Mystic Seaport were for whaling, Gloucester was for the fishing industry. It was here that the famous schooners had been built, which sailed out for the cod to the Grand Banks off the Newfoundland coast. It is said that over 10,000 Gloucester men have died while fishing these notoriously stormy waters. A bronze statue of a fisherman serves as a reminder of this tragedy.

In those times, nobody would have even thought of going to sea without economic necessity – unlike us, for example. Pure need was the motive to go to sea. And today, a trip from A to B would be far easier, cheaper and quicker in an aeroplane. Did we know what we were doing?

I did. I wanted to find some distance from my former life. Also, I wanted to realise my long-held dream of tasting the cruising lifestyle. The decision to return to Europe from Asia gave me the opportunity to do this. In time, the voyage turned out to be a mixture of fun and adventure, of romance but also of apprehension. My horizons had been widened and the voyage had helped to better understand foreign cultures. Cruising under sail has become more of a vocation for me. Why, I thought, should any person go only in one direction all his life? For 15 years, I was a metal expert and played with fire there. Why shouldn't I now play the next 15 years with water (while cruising) and then, maybe, another 15 years with the earth? The cycle of life would then be almost complete – fire, water and earth.

The inscription on the statue reads: 'They who go down to the sea in ships.' A man disappears without trace. No body is found, no explanation. Only the mystery and diffuse hope remains. My American friend Melanie, with whom Greg and I had spent many happy hours in Durban, had gone to sea in November 1994 from Borneo. "Disappeared at sea", was the official version. How can a Swan 57 with an experienced crew of four disappear just like that? Had it been pirates or drug traffickers, or was it simply a reef or a floating container or possibly a collision with a large ship? We will probably never know. The torture of uncertainty stays with us. And there are more examples. The son of my parents' friends in Mauritius has been missing for many years. Arnaud du Rosnay, one of the world's best sailors, wanted to sail on a surfboard from China to Taiwan, alas without the permission of the authorities. Had it been nature or maybe the navy which has caused the young sailor to disappear completely? We can never know.

Springtime in Maine

We passed Cape Ann and reached the outlying Isles of Shoals. But the natives of these islands did not want to know about us. A religious group lived on the first island. As soon as we were within earshot in our dinghy, we were turned away politely but unmistakably. On the neighbouring island, we were again unwanted. Here, a colony of sea birds was nesting and they chased us away with loud cries. On the third island, Smuttynose, we decided that we were not going to be chased off as easily as on the first two, although we had to tread carefully ashore, as the ground was covered in birds' nests. The sea gulls tried to intimidate us with mock attacks. The breeding season was nearing its end and the little ones had either already left the egg or were about to break free from it.

Now we were nearly in Maine and it was only another day's trip to Portland. This started off relaxing enough in an easy breeze but, as we came nearer to Portland, the wind piped up. Spray flew from our bows and *Ryusei* behaved like a horse on its way to the stable. As we passed the lighthouse of Portland, we were exhilarated and overjoyed. The rush however abruptly stopped when we ran aground in the entrance to the marina. Amy's parents had organised a free mooring for us but due to our large draft we could not use it. Luckily we then found another berth close to the centre of town.

Amy's family knew well what cruising people long for: eating and drinking. Their house was in a romantic location on the shore of a lake, and we had the traditional Maine mussel soup and a mountain of lobsters. The preparation of the lobster found our particular interest, and the recipe is as follows:

For each lobster to be cooked, one glass of beer is poured into a big pot and heated up. Then the lobster is turned on his head, the claws are held back and the bone above the nose is rubbed until the lobster is completely quiet. When the beer boils and the pot is full of steam, put the lobster in head first. This is supposedly the most humane way of killing a lobster! When the lobster turns red, after 10 to 15 minutes, it is ready. The lobster now has to cool off a bit as it is eaten with the hands. Some butter sauce rounds off the dish nicely.

While we enjoyed our lobsters, I learnt some things about Maine. This is the largest state in New England. The rugged coast with many outlying islands is similar to the West Coast of Scotland, although the shore of Maine is more wooded. There are also countless lakes, ponds, rivers and streams. The inhabitants of Maine are mostly nature loving. Amy's father explained: "We love our freedom and would never hesitate to defend it with a weapon in our hands. In the United States, Maine had the lowest rate of criminality. The reason is that we also have the highest rate of private weapons. Criminals have to beware here!"

Tough practice, as harsh as the climate. The cold part of the year is extremely long and sometimes, so we heard, spring would change to autumn directly. "Sometimes, the summer only lasts one day here!", people said.

On our way north we were enjoying a prolonged spring. Even Maine was in full bloom. And coming from the tropics, we experienced this season much more intensely. For me, the voyage along the American east coast was like eternal spring.

Maintenance and repair

Once in harbour, the cruising sailor usually spends his time with maintenance and repairs on his ship. This one time, we broke with tradition and decided to start with ourselves. Greg had been complaining about toothache over the past weeks, and Amy said to him: "My cousin is a dentist. He'll treat you as soon as we're in Portland." However, neither Amy nor myself had ever reckoned with the fact that I, too, would become her cousin's victim. Fate was especially hard to me and I lost my wisdom teeth. The pain was one nuisance, but worse was the fact that, for a while afterwards, I had to decline all offers of steak and lobster.

In contrast to Greg, who was growing his long, red ponytail, I had my hair cut from time to time. This was always a fun experience, as barbers, just like taxi-drivers, love to communicate and often tell good stories. There was a small barber shop near the yacht harbour.

"Today is not possible, but come tomorrow at seven", the barber said.

"In the morning or the evening?", I asked.

"In the morning, of course!"

"Are you serious?"

"As much as I am standing here!"

Yachties have a good sleep once in harbour. Especially in the early mornings. So I was still a bit sleepy when I entered the shop.

"Ah, here is our new victim!", the barber called out, obviously in good humour. "Sit down and be comfortable, it will be your turn very soon now!"

To my surprise, the salon was crowded, despite the early hour. I squeezed into the last remaining seat and instantly regretted having stayed. But not for long, because Bob the barber and his regular clients excelled in jokes and humorous banter.

"How much is it?", I asked when it was my turn.

"I am a racist", Bob replied. "Elderly persons like my friends and myself pay five dollars, everybody else six!"

I had to admit that the entertainment alone would have been worth more than that. I noted that the seniors only had their hair trimmed by the millimetre, if they still had any left at all. In this way, they could enjoy the show more often. When I left, my stomach ached from laughing. As I closed the door behind me, I read the sign on the door saying: 'I survived Bob'. This was motivation enough for me to turn my energy towards my ship once again.

Crew

My fear was confirmed in Portland: "I'd love to sail on to Europe with you, but it won't be possible", Greg told me. "For two reasons: Amy and my visa. My current visa is still valid for a few months. But if I leave the States now, they won't let me back in later."

"So Amy has asked the one important question, has she?" But the answer was obvious. From this moment onwards, we were looking for a new crew for me. I posted a notice on the board at the yacht club, and a young man answered the advert. But Greg and I at once sensed that this man and I would never get on with each other. I then asked the editor of the magazine Ocean Navigator which has its office in Portland. The members of the editorial staff would have jumped at the chance to sail with me, as none of them had actually ever crossed an ocean. "We dream about it, we write about it, but sadly we have no time to do it", they complained.

At least one of the editors could give me a piece of advice concerning storm tactics. "Would you recommend the use of a storm anchor?", I asked.

"No", he replied. "They are expensive and are seldom used, if ever. We have long-term weather forecasts today. If a front with a storm passes your way at sea, you usually have enough time to leave the critical area under sail. So a storm sail is worth much more than a storm anchor. In a real emergency, a storm anchor can also be improvised with what you have on board!"

One day I met a friend of Amy and Greg. She visited us on board. Then we met again for dinner. I was a bit late and when I arrived I found Greg and her deep in conversation. As I sat down, Greg said: "Ralph, congratulations. You've found your first crew member. Malley here has decided to sail with you!"

"Are you sure?", I asked. I could not believe what I had heard, as I happened to know that she was engaged and also had a regular job. But she smiled and answered: "I need a change. A passage at sea would be just the right thing. I will just take six weeks special holidays from work and fiancé!"

"And what about your experience?"

"I've worked one summer's season on one of the Rockland sailing schooners."

So we agreed that she would join the boat in Camden.

Greg's harbour

Greg and I sailed on alone as Amy had returned to her work in Seattle. The Casco Bay off Portland is like a labyrinth of islands and channels. We thoroughly enjoyed the trip, even though we had to use the engine for lack of wind. In a tight space between two islands, the shrill alarm of the diesel sounded. We quickly found the reason: the cooling water was boiling, as the cooling water hose had a leak. The tide was setting us ashore, so we had to change the hose in record time. Just about in time we were able to start the engine again.

We had prepared *Ryusei* for the Atlantic crossing in Portland. Everything we could think of was tested and repaired. The engine had been checked by a specialist and so the breakdown came, as usual, completely unexpectedly and in the worst possible situation. And apart from the cold, another phenomenon made life difficult for us: the tides. The further we sailed north, the stronger they ran. Especially along the coast of Maine. Planning our route demanded a lot of care, if we did not want to end up on the rocks or waste our time trying to stem a foul tide.

Nevertheless, we reached the estuary of the Kennebec River on the ebb. Four knots of adverse tide was simply too much. So we anchored and put in a siesta. Soon after, a gurgling noise woke me and one glance outside was enough to put me in a state of panic. "Greg! Quick! We're rotating!", I shouted. The next moment we were on deck. The tide had formed a maelstrom and we were in the centre of it. *Ryusei* was spinning around like a merry-go-round and the next instant we hit a motor yacht which also lay at anchor. Luckily we had seen it coming and managed to fend off with our big fenders, and like a tornado the maelstrom suddenly moved on and died down. Soon afterwards the tide turned and we went upriver on the young flood. The river wound its way through a hilly and densely wooded landscape.

Before darkness we reached Bath Harbour. This is the place where, up to 1920, the largest clipper ships were built. Schooners with up to six masts were constructed and launched here. The marine museum of Maine is built on the remains of the shipbuilders Percy & Small. Years before, Greg had served his apprenticeship as a boat-builder in the workshops of the museum. Greg was over the moon at meeting his old friends again and in the evening he led me to the most expensive restaurant in town. We were greeted warmly and had a fantastic meal – free of charge. "How did we earn this?", I asked Greg. He whispered to me: "The owner of the restaurant once was, for one long cold winter, my girlfriend!"

Now I knew: this was Greg's harbour.

The treasures of Maine

Maine's coast and islands are a unique sailing area. There is a choice of thousands of anchorages, but Greg luckily knew the best ones. After Bath, we went to the island of Damariscove. This place had been of some importance at the beginning of the colonisation. It was close to the fishing grounds and also afforded some shelter from the native Indians. The ships came from Europe to fish and used the bay in which we now anchored as a base. An old wooden sailing ship, on which lived a lobster fisher with his wife and child, was also here. Every day, he went out to his lobster pots in an old motor boat and, when he had enough lobster, he brought them to the mainland. He told us that in Maine, about 15,000 tons of lobster are caught each season. "To keep the lobster grounds alive, fishing is now only allowed in season. We are also only allowed to catch lobster from a certain size upwards."

In Portland we had heard that the current season had been better than any before; there were lobster in abundance and so they were even sold at McDonald's. I then asked the old fisherman: "There are so many lobster-pots here in Maine. How can you be sure that no one else empties yours?"

"Very simple", he replied. "Poachers are shot. So we have no problem with them!"

For days on end, the weather forecast had promised us some sun. On the morning after our arrival in Damariscove the sun finally showed up. The shallow angle of the sun's rays and the clear, northern air gave a special tint to the scenery.

For reasons unknown to me, Greg kept pushing to sail on. We passed hundreds of places in which I would have loved to spend a night.

"You'll see", Greg said. "But we have to hurry so that we are there in time!"

The pilotage between all the islands, shallows and narrows was rather demanding, but with the last light of the fading day we came to a bay called Pulpit Harbour. In this idyllic bay was a whole fleet of the finest sailing schooners that I had ever seen.

"Here we are. Did I promise too much?" Greg was excited. "These are the traditional schooners from Rockland and Camden. They are chartered and every Friday, before going to their charter base for the weekend, they anchor here."

But that was all I could find out on that evening. Greg had sighted an old friend, the captain of one of the schooners. As soon as our anchor was set, our dinghy flew into the water and Greg disappeared off towards the schooner *Wendameen*. I enjoyed the sudden peace and quiet, the nature around me and the wonderful sight of the schooners. These were the treasures of Maine: Nature, sailing ships and lobster.

The captain's dream

I was about to get to know another treasure: Maine's female sailors. In Pulpit Harbour, Greg returned with the news that his friend Niels Parker, owner and skipper of the schooner, had recommended someone for my Atlantic crossing. "I know her", said Greg. "She's a nice girl. I once worked with her on *Wendameen*.

"I should like to meet your friend before I decide anything", I replied.

The schooner captains gave an impressive demonstration of their skills the following morning. One big schooner after another up-anchored and left the bay under sail. I cannot say to this day how they managed to sail through the narrow entrance without running aground.

"Experience is what counts", said Greg. "They always sail along the same routes and know these waters like the backs of their hands. Originally, these schooners were used as transport along the coast. They are all sailing vessels without engines. In an emergency and for tight manoeuvring they have a tender with a small engine which can be used like a miniature harbour tug."

Most of them we saw again in the harbour of Camden. We found a berth, hired a car and drove to the next harbour, Rockland, where I met Niels and his ship. *Wendameen* was a gaff-rigged Alden schooner dating back to 1935.

"What a shame we didn't meet earlier", Niels said. "Elizabeth was here a week ago to ask if I knew anyone who could give her a passage to Europe. She's a good sailor and a woman full of energy. If you don't mind her singing, then she's the perfect crew for you!"

The assessments of both Niels and Greg were near identical, and nobody could hope for better references. "Where can I get hold of her?", I asked.

"In New Mexico. She's studying there. That's at the other

end of the United States!"

A long telephone call followed. Three days later, Elizabeth arrived in Camden, escorted by her mother who wanted to see which dangers her 21-year-old daughter was going to be exposed to. Malley arrived at the same time and so the new team was complete. Two women and the skipper. Was this an old dream come true?

Maiden voyage

On the trip to Camden I noticed that one of my alternators was defective. The repair was more expensive than anticipated, because we happened to pass by a second-hand car dealer on our way to the workshop. There, we spotted an old Volkswagen Golf diesel and, out of curiosity, we enquired about the price. After my departure, Greg wanted to travel to see Amy in Seattle. But the flight was too expensive for him, the train went through Canada and so he would have left the States, and the buses were booked solid for weeks to come.

"Keeping the hire-car for the next two weeks would cost me 200 dollars. I could just as well give you that money to buy this car, although you'd have to pay the difference in price. This way we'd have a car until I left and you can then drive in your own car to Seattle", I suggested. So we not only returned with a repaired alternator, but also an ancient car for which we had paid 500 dollars.

The next leg to Mount Desert Island, Greg drove overland while I sailed with Elizabeth and Malley. This was a completely new feeling. Greg had wanted to sail with me for two weeks, and these turned into one-and-a-half years. The voyage with all its adventures had welded us together but now the inseparable team separated. The unavoidable day had finally arrived and I felt as if the pilot had left the ship. Greg was a far more experienced sailor than I was and, although I was officially the skipper, it was always his judgement which counted.

Our maiden voyage was a roaring success. Wind and weather were perfect as we sailed through sheltered waters between the islands. We all had the urge to just sit on deck and take in the beautiful scenery which passed by. But the pilotage demanded full concentration – one mistake and we would have run aground on rocks. There are more than enough of these in Maine, and it was only close once, after we had missed a buoy.

Elizabeth and Malley knew each other from Portland, so the

new team was not entirely unfamiliar with each other. My new shipmates explored *Ryusei* full of energy and curiosity and wanted to know every little detail – especially Elizabeth, who insisted on being familiarized with every safety item on board. But in view of our planned Atlantic crossing, this attitude was entirely correct. For me, it was a new experience. Greg and I knew our boat so intimately that we instinctively made nearly all manoeuvres without speaking one single word. Now, every move had to be explained beforehand. This was the only way to avoid confusion.

Greg was waiting for us on the pier of Southwest Harbour in Mount Desert Island. With him was his old friend David. They had done their apprenticeship in Bath together. Although we had only sailed a day's trip, Greg and I welcomed each other as if we had been separated for weeks. Greg had already been a bit worried about us. He knew the rock-infested waters between Camden and Mount Desert Island only too well.

A great day

Summer finally caught up with us on Mount Desert Island. The temperatures of 35 degrees Celsius in the shade reminded us of former times. The beer went down as smoothly as never before. The choice of beers was fantastic in Maine, but the brands 'Sea Dog' and 'Shipyard' remained our favourites. We wanted to have one last sail together. David accompanied us and, for Malley and Elizabeth, it became a training sail. We experimented with all different sails and, running under main and spinnaker, *Ryusei* nearly took off. We sailed like hell until we finally anchored off Roque Island which had the shape of an atoll with a long, sandy beach. It was quite similar to the tropics, until I poked my toe into the icy cold water. The temperature was freezing and I changed my mind about swimming. We then tried to fish for our dinner, but without any success and in the end we had to buy the ingredients from a fishing boat which was anchoring close by. Elizabeth and Malley then prepared a fantastic New England Clam Chowder, which is made as follows:

Sauté two large onions in butter. Add four large potatoes, cut up, and water. Before the potatoes are cooked, add half a litre of cream and an adequate amount of clams. Keep simmering on a low flame. Add a portion of sweet corn and spice with chillies according to taste.

In northern latitudes, dusk hovers for a long while. There is nothing as pleasing as anchoring after an active day sailing, especially in these beautiful surroundings.

Answering my question of what kind of experiences he had had with women on board, Niels had said: "Women on board can be either excellent or disastrous!"

For us, it had been a great day and the women on our boat had contributed considerably.

Nudism and a crash-landing

The summer days on Mount Desert Island drifted past, and again and again we invented reasons for postponing our departure. Once it was a bathing excursion, then a sundowner trip, then a barbecue or even rock climbing.

The hypocrisy of prudish America was demonstrated to us during our bathing excursion to a remote lake in the woods. The last bit from the car park to the lake had to be walked along through the forest, and we were a little bit surprised when we met completely naked men and women on the way. Apart from the complete absence of any clothing, they behaved perfectly normally and with friendly greetings. The same happened at the lake; everybody jumped around naked. It seemed to be the Eden of nudists, and anyone insisting of wearing bathing clothes would have caused embarrassment.

Only a few days before, Greg and I had sat on the shore near Camden when suddenly, two policemen came crawling out of the undergrowth. "Hello", we said, "what are you looking for?"

"Nudists!", they replied. "Be warned. Nudism is strictly forbidden in Maine!"

Elizabeth told us that people were now and again rebelling against this moral straight-jacket. "My sister is a lawyer", she told us. "Last week she made the news in Portland. She informed the press and walked across the busiest bridge in Portland – topless. When the police wanted to arrest her, she pointed out the clauses in the American Constitution that guarantee equality. She also threatened a scandal. In face of the press and the Constitution, the police had to give in and retreat!"

David was the one who suggested climbing. Elizabeth was instantly taken in by the idea and the rest of us went along. "I love climbing", I said, "but so soon before our sailing date?"

Soon we found ourselves standing beneath a sheer rock face. David and Elizabeth, both experienced climbers, went up first – David climbing first with Elizabeth belaying him, then David belaying from above and Elizabeth following him. I was dizzy from watching, and then the inevitable question came: "Who next?"

"The skipper! The skipper!", all cried out in unison.

Climbing was one of my stronger points, but I had no climbing shoes. I wore sneakers instead and managed to make my way up the rock face with great effort. Then Malley followed. She was about two metres from the ground when she fell. The rope slowed her fall but it stretched so much that she crash-landed on the ground. She cried out in pain and clutched her foot. We had to carry her down the steep path back to the car and in the hospital her foot was X-rayed and it was clear that it had been broken. The pain was one thing, but Malley suffered more from the notion that she might not be able to sail with us.

I tried to soothe her. "Don't worry. We'll organise a waterproof plaster!"

In fact, she was strapped up with a plastic boot which was removable, instead of being plastered in completely. The following day she was able to hobble about on crutches.

"If anybody speaks to my fiancé or my parents, this accident must not be mentioned!", she implored us. "If they knew about it, they'd never let me sail!"

The big day arrived on the 28th of June. *Ryusei* was fully provisioned and as ready as she could be. We managed to finish the officialdom in the record time of thirty seconds. We hugged each other one last time and slipped the mooring lines.

On that day I wrote in my log:

'Look ahead and go, before getting sentimental!

'One-and-a-half years together at sea is a long time. Greg is what one calls a sea dog. A man who has his senses tuned for the ship and nature. He introduced me to the world of wooden boats and its traditions. Together, we have been a great team. Our positive spirits led outsiders to judge *Ryusei* a happy boat!'

Canada

Lunenburg & *Bluenose*

As we headed out to sea, we could not deny a certain nervousness. None of us knew what was ahead. Nova Scotia, Newfoundland and the Northern Atlantic were all new. The turbulence ashore and especially Malley's accident had welded us together, but we still had to get used to each other. At least the question of who slept where on board was easily resolved: Malley with her plastered foot occupied the front cabin, Elizabeth got one of the two saloon berths and I slept in the quarter berth next to the navigation table.

We again went through the emergency equipment. Life jackets were allocated and tried on. We then made an inventory of the grab bag in case we had to abandon ship and go into the life raft. It contained a VHF, GPS, compass, torch, flares, thermo-blankets, knives, emergency food and drink rations. "What do we need that for?", Liz asked and held up a can of beer.

"That's the last drink for us in case everything goes wrong", I replied.

We then checked the EPIRB and the radio. We also ran through the man overboard procedure and manoeuvre. The first try went completely wrong; this we blamed on a whale that surfaced in a critical moment and distracted us.

"What do we do if the skipper goes over the side?", Liz asked. "The chance that Malley and I will sail a successful man overboard manoeuvre is slim – especially in heavy weather!" Of course she was right, as my two new shipmates yet had very little experience in handling *Ryusei*. But to go overboard was, in these low water temperatures, nearly always lethal anyway, so we made a point of wearing our harnesses all the time while on deck, even during the daytime.

Charles Darwin once said that 'if there were no sea-sickness, then everybody would go to sea.' But as it is, nearly everybody suffers from this illness. Some more, some less, and most of the time it goes away after a while at sea. There are countless medicines but one of the most effective is to busy the sick person with some task on board. Malley got hit by the illness, and tablets and activity helped. But more important were her will and courage.

With the last light we reached the harbour of Lunenburg. After our 200 mile passage, we jumped ashore happily. Half an hour after arriving, we found ourselves in the pub to celebrate the first successful leg of our voyage. My lady shipmates had already shown a level of routine which Greg and Guy had taken much longer to achieve.

In the darkness on our way back we could make out the silhouette of a mighty schooner. The ship lay alongside the pier and drew us like a magnet. We wandered over to have a close look, when Liz suddenly cried: "But that's *Bluenose II*. It was on this ship that I sailed for the first time in my life!"

In the light of the following day, we fully appreciated the fine sight that this ship presented. She was the replica of the legendary Newfoundland schooner which was launched here in Lunenburg in 1921. For a long time, she had been the fastest sailing ship in the world. We got to know the navigator of *Bluenose II*, who showed us around the ship and also gave us some valuable hints about the weather patterns in Nova Scotia.

The history of Lunenburg is closely connected to the fishing and shipbuilding industries. In the early years, this little village with the pretty wooden houses was a new home for many immigrants from Germany. The rather eccentric ship broker and antiques dealer Bruce gave us a taste of the past when he welcomed us into his shop with ancient German military music which came from an original gramophone. He also offered us various ships and wrecks which were for sale, and in the end he wanted to sell us his entire shop with all that was in it.

"I would like to move and marry once more. The lucky one

is 19 years old. It will be my fifth marriage", the seventy-year-old said with a long look at Malley. I had the distinct impression that he was already noting her down for his sixth round.

But Bruce knew this part of the world like the back of his hand and he recommended us some of the nicest spots along the coast.

Halifax

As we left Lunenburg, we saw *Bluenose* under full sail. She made a truly majestic impression, especially on this day which was the day of Canadian independence. Soon after, we were swallowed up by the fog and the wind went asleep. Without the engine and the radar, we would never have reached Halifax. The whole town was decorated with banners and flags, but not in our honour: the world summit had just ended.

How far this part of the world is still conscious of its maritime heritage is documented by the many maritime museums. Each of the larger towns north of New York has its own, and Halifax of course is no exception to this rule. Normally, we would have been allowed to moor at the museum dock but, due to the summit, this was entirely taken over by the navy. In the end we found a berth near the deep-sea tugs. We then asked the captain of one tug where we should go to for the clearing procedure. When he heard how little time we were staying, he said: "Don't worry about checking in, the officials don't take leisure boats very seriously here, anyway!" He then invited us to have a look around on his brand new tug instead. Moreover, he pulled from the drawer in his navigation desk a chart of the coast of Newfoundland which we were still lacking and gave it to us as a present.

Bras d'Or Lake

Sunshine was enough incentive to get moving again. We had heard a lot about the magnificent Bras d'Or Lake, both in Lunenburg and in Halifax. "You must not miss that under any circumstances", people had told us. So the temptation was great and we decided on the detour. As was usual for this time of year, we were wrapped in thick fog as soon as we had reached the open sea. The look-out just watched the radar screen. Once, an object which turned out to be another sailing boat came close. Like a ghost ship, it emerged from the fog only to disappear again moments later. My entry in the log shows how we felt about navigating in the fog:

'Wet, cold and noisy (engine) morning. Zero visibility and a chart with too small a scale for coastal navigation. Islands on port side were unexpected. Luckily they showed up on the radar. We could not see them, but passed so close that we could hear the breakers. Scary! How did the old schooner captains sail this shore without engine and navigational electronics?'

With our eyes glued to the radar and the echo-sounder, we sailed into a gulf. Suddenly we felt a warm wind. The next moment, the fog lifted and the rain stopped. St Peter came in sight. This is the place where a lock gives access to the largest salt-water lake in the world. Soon after having passed a lifting bridge and a short canal, we moored in the lake. The difference in temperature compared to the open sea was considerable – 24 degrees Celsius seemed nearly tropical, so we rigged our hammocks and held a siesta. Sailing is exhausting, after all!

Along the shores of the Bras d'Or lake live the descendants of the original Scottish settlers. On a stroll through St Peter and a visit to the pub we could not fail to notice how open the people were here. Completely different from the large cities: everyone here seemed to be genuinely pleased about new visitors.

Jerry MacDonnell, the pharmacist, saved us. He gave us what the bank had just declined: money, or rather, cash on my credit card. "We accept Visa, but not Mastercard", they said in the bank. Jerry found an easy way to help. He just let me sign a sales slip, as if I had bought something in his pharmacy, and paid out the cash instead. He also presented us with the sailing pilot for the lake and gave many tips for good anchorages. Jerry dreamed of cruising and would have loved to join our ship there and then but, with his family and his business, he was not independent enough to do so.

We were. Furthermore, this was the 4th of July, the day of American Independence from Europe. With the unusual sail combination of genoa and hammocks we sailed off onto the lake, helped along by a warm and gentle breeze. We sailed past densely wooded shores until we reached a small island by the name of Scots Island. Here, we anchored and went swimming, although the water was icy cold. But then I found the trapped lobster and my hunting instincts were alive again. Although the lobster pot was in deep water, I managed to extract the lobster and attach a thank-you letter with a bank note in a plastic bag inside the pot.

On the remote pier of Marble Mountain we celebrated the catch and the day of independence which was so important for my shipmate friends. Earlier, we had wandered around the small village with the typical wooden houses and a small church which we entered. Liz sat down and played the organ and sang with a voice which would have made Ella Fitzgerald green with envy!

For her 21 years, Liz was highly talented as a musician, a sportswoman, hungry for more knowledge and full of an incredible energy. Malley was older and had an inner calmness which was another ideal contribution for our team. She also had the best eyes and ears of us all. Liz could not see well but heard very acutely, whilst I don't hear brilliantly but can see very well. The three of us complemented each other perfectly, for example when finding our way through the fog.

Another day we spent in Baddeck, the one-time home of Alexander Graham Bell who revolutionised the world by inventing the telephone. We, on the other hand, nearly sank our boat here when filling the tanks with fresh water. Stupidly, we had forgotten to close a valve so that, for a while, we filled the bilges instead.

Seldom have I enjoyed days as much as those spent on the Bras d'Or lake. The temperature was flt for summer, the sky and the water were incredibly translucent, the light and the colours were extraordinary. We sailed along in smooth water between wooden hills and islands.

Petites's troubles

We left the lake and sailed overnight to Port aux Basques in Newfoundland. Here, we only stayed one night, as we were bound further east along the coast. The harbour of Petites is tucked away behind the rocks and impossible to find without local knowledge, but luckily a fisherman came to the rescue. With hand signs he motioned us to follow his boat. "Look! He wants to lure us onto the rocks!", I shouted when his boat disappeared ahead between the rocks. I went into neutral and let *Ryusei* drift towards the rock face slowly. Suddenly we saw an opening in the rocks, just where the fishing boat had vanished. The tiny village is along a short canal-like crevice in the rocks, which is lined on both sides by jetties and huts. The village looked like a world in miniature, and our pilot gestured towards the small wooden pier.

We could not turn around in the tiny harbour, where the feeling of intimacy and shelter was overwhelming. An elderly man on the pier took our lines and we invited him on board for a welcome drink. Before we had finished, a whole load of children stormed up the pier and fired many questions at us. Liz and Malley took good care of them.

Within an hour of our arrival, we had already met 11 of the 14 school children who live in Petites. The two young daughters belonging to the teacher couple were particularly attached to us and we soon got to know their parents. Immediately, they proudly showed us an old sextant and oil paintings of a wonderful fishing schooner which had belonged to one of their grandfathers.

The old fisherman who had helped us with the lines came by again towards evening and told us: "We live in our little world of predicament here. The only connection to the rest of the world is by ship, but at last there is the telephone. We generate our own electricity. The population has gone down from 70 to 55, and of these 14 are school children. About ten work as fishermen, two are teachers, two run a small shop and one is a boat builder. All the young people go away, and why should they stay? We are all unemployed since the government closed down the local fishery two years ago. Once, fishing was so profitable that a new boat would pay for itself within one single season! So everyone went fishing, but modern techniques and no control had catastrophic consequences. The big drag-nets not only get the cod, but all living creatures who are essential for the biological balance of the sea. The fish were simply eliminated. As a last concession, we are still allowed to catch a few lobster at certain times of the year. And even this is poorer than it's ever been: in 150 pots we now maybe get 30 or so lobster. Newfoundland's fishermen are out of work and many remote villages will sooner or later be deserted."

Only the children did not seem to share the worries of their parents; they still lived in the wonderfully intact world of childhood.

Storm in the harbour

During the night, the forecast front went over Newfoundland. The wind howled in the rigging and rain drummed on deck. *Ryusei* kept us on our toes, as the wind and an undercurrent in the harbour pushed us on to the pier. We doubled up the mooring lines, used all our fenders and rigged a fender board. All through the night we went on deck in turns from time to time to check if all was well and to try and tame the halyards which were clanging against the mast like mad.

We stayed in bed for the entire morning, with thick fog and rain making the outside world miserable. Only when the still strong wind killed the flame of our diesel heater, so that a cloud of soot drifted through the boat, did we get up.

The boat-builder Norman showed us his workshop. Here, he built the traditional dories as they were used for fishing. These are seaworthy little boats, clinker-built.

After that, we wandered through the village with him. We passed the hut of the fire brigade and what allegedly was the oldest church in Newfoundland. From the coast we had a fine view over the rugged cliffs, which shimmered in shades of pink while the ocean waves crashed against them to explode in a shower of spray. The romantic landscape suddenly made me want to stay here. On our way back, Norman invited us to his cabin where we warmed up with hot coffee while he told us of snowmobiles, of the hunt for moose, and of the legendary salmon river which was close to his hunting hut. He also told us of a lucrative second income, the smuggling of alcohol from the French island St Pierre to the mainland.

"Nearly every fisherman does it at least once in his life, myself included. On our way back, a friend and I were going to load our contraband, most of it in rum, in the shelter of the fog onto the boat of the buyer. But we managed to get the one, clear, sunny day of the summer! With a lot of luck we managed to hide the booty in a remote bay without being caught, but after this trip I was a nervous wreck. I will never again take that kind of risk!"

As Liz, Norman and I returned to *Ryusei*, we found Malley entertaining half of the village children on board. They were overexcited and had never before seen a sailing boat from inside. We then cooked a nourishing hot soup, and combination of the many people on board, the cooking and the heater transformed our boat to a sauna. But spirits were high and it was not before eleven at night that the troops began to leave. "Now the curfew for children and husbands begins", Norman grinned as he, too, left.

The wind had died down until the next morning, but thick fog was wrapped around the village. Looking out of the companionway, I was struck by a romantic image. Straight across from us was a wooden hut built on stakes over the water. An old man sat in the open doorway and stared into the fog. Was he dreaming about the times when there were so many fish in these waters that, as they said, they slowed the passing ships down by the friction of their bodies against the ship? We could not even guess what went through his mind. But one thing is for sure: the human being was the biggest enemy. He, and nothing else, had destroyed the once so abundant and plentiful fishing grounds of Newfoundland, which had been the richest in the world.

Grand Bruit

Nothing is more pleasing than to spend a storm in harbour. We now thought that it was over, although the sea was still very rough. But as soon as the fog had swallowed Petites, there was no turning back. It was a small miracle that we managed to make it to Grand Bruit without shipwreck, and Norman had even warned us: "The entrance to Grand Bruit is just as difficult to find as the one here!"

This woke me from the daydream, in which I had lived through my voyage once more. Here, on the cliffs near Grand Bruit, I forgot my promise to stay in harbour a long time. The final leg to Scotland was waiting and the weather seemed right. Let's go!

PART III

The Atlantic

Promises made at sea are soon forgotten in a quiet harbour.

Feeling the rock

*R*YUSEI SLIPPED OUT OF THE BAY of Grand Bruit in a complete calm. As always, a thick layer of fog lay on the sea. We could only see the receding coastline on the radar. For the entire day we motored due east and then, after reaching a previously set position, turned towards the coast once more. Like a curtain, the fog lifted and majestic scenery unfolded in the soft glow of the setting sun. Sheer rock faces rose vertical from the sea, some up to a height of 400 metres. We motored up a fjord which cut deep into the land. At the very end, we anchored beneath a waterfall that seemed to come straight from the heavens. All this natural splendour had us stunned, but Liz recovered first and said: "Let's bring the inflatable over the side. I want to feel the rock."

"You want to do what?", I asked.

"Feel the rock. Touch it. Mountaineers do it before they attempt to climb it."

"I hope you don't want to climb it, otherwise we might all end up with plastered feet!"

But she insisted that she just wanted to feel it. So we rowed across in the dinghy, as the rock seemed quite close. However, after half a mile we were still far off and had to turn back as darkness was by now setting in.

The entry in the log of that evening says a lot of our mood: 'The moon rose and showed us its full face. The scenery under the illumination of the moon and the sound of the waterfall was an unforgettable experience. I even climbed the mast and sat on the spreaders to be closer to the moon and get a better view of nature's show.'

The next morning, the sun shone and helped us to become active. Liz and Malley put me ashore in the dinghy and while they rowed off again I climbed the mountainside to take some photographs. At first I only wanted to get a little bit higher up, but then something came over me and I just had to carry on. I climbed and climbed until I was on a high plateau, breathless from the ascent and the view. I was able to see along the entire length of the fjord. But the warm summer temperatures had also woken up other creatures. Mosquitoes attacked me and made me begin the descent again. Liz and Malley had already started to worry about me being away for so long; in answer to their questions about where I had been I answered, slightly embarrassed, "On the summit, to feel the rock."

14th July on St Pierre

We went to the fishing harbour of Grand Bank to top up provisions. A taxi brought us to the supermarket but it ended in embarrassment when we came to the checkout till with our fully laden cart only to hear that they did not accept credit cards. I then took another taxi to the bank but got another rebuff: "Sorry, we do not accept Mastercard here, but there is another bank which does, about 80 kilometres from here in the next town!"

"Everything is going wrong today", I muttered as I returned to my waiting friends in the supermarket. But the taxi driver disagreed: "It can't be too bad. There is something to celebrate, after all. It's my 64th birthday today and there is a great fete on the nearby island of St Pierre!"

I wished him all the best for his birthday and then asked what the fete on the island was all about. My only excuse for not knowing is that, when in cruising mode, we are free of the dates of the calendar – otherwise it would have shamed me, as a French person, not to have know: it was the 14th of July, the French national holiday. "The island goes crazy on this day", the driver assured me.

Malley's emergency funds saved our shopping. While she took the taxi to fetch the money from the boat, Liz and I planned to sail to St Pierre, despite the bad weather. "We can't miss this thing – especially if the skipper happens to be half French!"

The harbour master was not surprised to see us sail. "Ah yes, the 14th of July", he said knowingly. "They really know how to celebrate over there. Alcohol is much cheaper there, too. It pays to sail there – good luck!"

But the 15 miles to St Pierre were decidedly uncomfortable sailing, beating into an icy cold wind in a short, choppy sea which sent the spray flying aft. Once in harbour, however, we found shelter and soon recovered. Due to the close proximity to the fishing grounds and the sheltered natural harbour, French fishermen arrived here centuries ago. Today, St Pierre and the neighbouring island of Miquélon belong to France and are a 'Département outre-mer', just like Guyana and Réunion.

St Pierre was decorated with flags and banners. The centre of town had been transformed into a giant fun fair. A band played and there was a considerable amount of drinking and dancing, the latter however mainly to stave off the cold. In the 'Ile de France' restaurant we experienced how a meal is celebrated in France. The menu was endless and we needed an equivalent amount of wine. A firework display rounded off the evening and, after all this activity, I was longing for my berth. But Liz and Malley were far from tired and said: "You can't give up now! Let's go to the disco!"

We nearly drowned in the sea of human bodies. Malley was cheered when she decided to dance despite her foot which was still in plaster. It was in the early hours when we finally found our way back on board.

We felt as weak now, the morning after, as we had been fit the night before, but wandering around in the crisp, clear air soon brought us back to normal. Along the harbour front were warehouses, a reminded of former times. Fishing had been the main activity on St Pierre until the fateful day in the year 1920 when the sale of all alcoholic drinks was forbidden in America and Canada. The geographical position of this French island ensured that this was to become the most important place for storing and importing rum and whisky into the prohibited zones.

St Pierre prospered. In a flourishing illegal trade, the so-called rum-runners brought their cargoes ashore to the mainland, and a true war between the customs people and the smugglers soon raged. In the end, Prohibition crumbled in the face of trade which was far too profitable for business people and gangsters.

Fishing

Rain and strong, gusty wind forebode bad weather. With strongly reefed sails, we beat up the bay of Trespassy, where we finally found a sheltered pier. Everything is so much more troublesome in northern latitudes! The cold, variable weather, fog, rough seas and strong currents made life difficult. How easy it had been in the tropics! The curve of the barograph clearly shows the difference. In the tropics, the air pressure was an easy steady sinus curve. Here, it was a ragged irregular zigzag. Luckily, we were in constant contact with Herb Hilgenberg, the weather supremo of the North Atlantic. He had made it his hobby to interpret the weather situation for us cruising sailors. He knew our intended route and the main details of our boat, and we were one of many boats who were going to cross the North Atlantic this summer, although very few chose the northern route which we were taking. "This is only a small front passing through", Herb said. "Best stay put somewhere snug and wait until it's past!"

Luckily, a second yacht arrived. On *Spirit of Joshua*, a wooden yacht from Lunenburg, we could at least warm up, as our diesel heater was always extinguished by strong winds. (This only improved after we had modified the flue pipe.)

As soon as the wind abated, we set sail. We saw some whales as we were passing the famous cape of the north, Cape Race. They surfaced, blew and disappeared again, displaying their mighty flukes. Towards evening we sailed into the bay of Fermeuse and moored at the pier of the village of the same name.

Some locals instantly arrived to offer help. One of them was particularly engaging. His name was Bob Ryan and he told us about the life of the Newfoundlanders. Originally, he had worked in the fishing industry. "But when the government closed down the fishing, we lost our jobs overnight and had to learn something new!" In one of the last harbours, we had met a former fisherman who now worked as a helicopter pilot. Bob, in contrast, was studying history. Although he had great knowledge about the eastern provinces of Canada, we were mainly interested in the practical aspects of fishing. "We've sailed all along this coast without catching one single fish", we complained.

"You must be using the wrong bait", Bob replied. Back at his place, he showed us a bait which he called a 'jigger'. It was a piece of lead in the form of a fish which had a ring at the tail end and two large hooks coming from its mouth. "These are the bait which our forebears used", Bob explained. "You let it down on a line to the ground. Then you pull it sharply upwards, repeating several times until you have a fish."

I doubted this: "How could a cod bite on that huge hook?"

"They don't always. The form and the movement of the bait fish attracts many other fish. They swim past the bait so close that when it is pulled up the hook catches the fish somewhere in the side. Making these jiggers is an old tradition, and these are cast from a model which my grandfather used."

"Before we cross the Atlantic I should like to catch a few

cod. Whereabouts do you think we can still find some?"

"A while back they were everywhere. Off the coast of Newfoundland is a shelf with a depth of 20 to 160 metres. These are the famous Newfoundland Banks. The Grand Banks are the best known of them. They extend for about 500 miles to the south-east from Cape Race. It's here that the cold water of the Labrador Stream hit the warm waters of the Gulf Stream. This is why we are hidden in fog most of the time. But the nutrient-rich Labrador Stream has made the banks incredibly rich in fish. Fishing has been the reason for settlers coming to Newfoundland. For centuries, the fishing schooners came from everywhere and anchored on the Grand Banks. They swarmed out in small dinghies on both sides of the ships, fished by hand and came back, fully laden, in the evenings to the mother ship. As soon as the holds were full, they set sail and raced each other home. Whoever arrived first got the best prices, but it was competition to the death. The schooners were incredibly hard pressed – they always sailed over-canvassed and overloaded. Some of them were so old that people used to say they were held together by maggots holding hands! As soon as there was heavy weather, many of them were lost. However, that is all history now! With modern fishing techniques, the fish reserves have been all but wiped out, so the government has stopped all fishing in our territorial waters until the population of fish gets back to normal. Outside the 200-mile zone, though, fishing goes on as ruthlessly as ever while here even angling with a jigger is forbidden. Even having one is illegal. Anyone caught fishing risks having his boat confiscated!"

Slightly worried, I asked: "Does this apply to a private sailing boat as well?"

"In principle, yes. But don't worry. I'll show you a place on the chart where you are guaranteed to find plenty of fish!"

Blood on Virgin Rock

We visited the capital of Newfoundland, St John's, by bus. The place had the character of an old-fashioned English town and showed many traces of the former prosperity through trade and fishing. We found all we needed: shops, restaurants and bars. In the centre, we spotted two chaps cycling along on antiquated penny-farthings, wearing the clothes of that era. By chance, we met them again later in an Irish pub. They turned out to be two Englishmen who were doing their unusual bicycle tour for charity. In the end they surprised us with an invitation: "If the weather keeps you here until then, you are welcome to join the Governor's garden party, next Wednesday!"

But the forecast had given us the green light to leave on Friday. This immediately started a heated discussion.

"Impossible. We can't sail on a Friday!", said I.

"Why not?"

"It brings bad luck!"

"Nonsense! Pure superstition!" In the end, we found a compromise. "As long as we sail on the Friday only to fish on the Grand Banks, then our voyage proper only starts with leaving Canadian territorial waters!"

"Long may the big jib draw!", father and son shouted after us as we left on Friday. The fish factory in Aquaforte, on whose dock we had moored and spent our last night in Canada, belonged to them. The wind blew 20 to 25 knots from the SSW. Bob had given us our course: "Ninety miles off the coast is a shallow spot on the Grand Banks. The legendary Virgin Rock, the Mecca of cod!"

However, we were worried by an iceberg we had seen floating past the coast a day before. We preferred to meet obstacles such as these in the daytime, so we sailed early in the morning and arrived at our destination shortly after midnight. The GPS had shown us the way, and the echo-sounder and the short, steep waves conformed that we were now in the vicinity of the Virgin Rock. The pilot warned us that in bad weather the seas would be breaking here. Fog and a cold drizzle reduced visibility and the waves seemed threatening. A prudent mariner would have sailed on at once. But who has the chance to catch some illegal fish on the Grand Banks more than once in his life?

The temptation was greater than the fear. We took down all sails and anchored in 20 metres of water. Although we let out all the chain, it took a long while until the anchor was set. What we then experienced is best compared with a ride on a bucking bronco. The waves pounded *Ryusei* with incredible anger and force. Everything which was not securely tied down or bolted in place was thrown back and forth, including ourselves. Once in a while, a wave would crash on deck. Liz, Malley and I could do nothing but close the hatches and wedge ourselves into our bunks as best as possible. All loose things on the boat rattled and clattered. Sleep was impossible and we impatiently waited for the morning.

"It's getting light! Into battle!", I shouted as the first light dawned. But only Malley was roused by my battle cry. Liz, who was normally game for anything, declined. "I can't bear the thought of how you are going to kill the poor fish", she said.

It was a real effort, both physical and of will, to get out on the dancing deck. We had our doubts at first that we could catch anything at all in these wild seas, but Malley was not deterred, even with her plastered foot. She stood on the stern and used a hand-line with the jigger which Bob had given us as a farewell present. I did the same at the bows. As soon as the jigger hit the ground, I pulled in a bit of the line and gave a couple of sharp tugs. Not one minute passed before I felt the jerk. "I've got one!", I shouted, and seconds later Malley's shout came back: "Me too!"

Shortly afterwards, we heard Liz: "That's enough!"

"Why? We're only just getting going!", Malley countered.

"Four of the poor cod are enough for us", Liz replied. And she was right, so we ended our fishing and cleaned the fish in the cockpit. Malley, who was usually subject to sea-sickness, had cheeks red with excitement, while Liz, our tough cookie, seemed unusually pale. "What's the matter?", I asked.

"I can just about stomach the sea, but the fish blood is too much!", she replied.

All hell breaks loose

When conditions are bad, you just concentrate on staying afloat –
Gary Cain

As soon as the anchor was up, *Ryusei* was not held back any longer. Under sail once more, things were stabilised a bit on board and life became bearable, at least temporarily, because a cold front passed over us during the night. The wind swung round from south to north-west and increased. With difficulty, we reefed the main. Then the wind piped up to gale force and the sea was transformed into a boiling hell. Our heavy ship surfed down the short and breaking seas and reached new speed records. All this in fog, at night and in the summer temperatures of the North Atlantic: six degrees Celsius! Below, it was icy cold as our heater did not work in these conditions.

At this time of the year, the Labrador Stream sends broken-off pieces of icebergs on their way south. This was the end of even a mighty ship like the *Titanic*, which hit an iceberg and sank on the southern tip of the Grand Banks in the year 1912.

"How can we avoid hitting one of those monsters at night and in fog?" we had asked Bob in Newfoundland.

"The weather stations regularly broadcast ice reports which

contain the positions of icebergs. They also show up on the radar. Even without this help, you would sense an iceberg before actually hitting it, as the temperature drops sharply in its vicinity. In former times, foghorns were also used. As soon as an iceberg was around, the echo of the foghorn would warn the crew of the ship!"

After 15 hours the wind died down and soon the world was as peaceful as if nothing had happened. Even the sun showed, which was particularly good for our morale. As we sailed over the Bonnet Flamment Shelf, we passed through mighty fleets of fishing vessels. In every direction we saw these nasty, threatening things. These were the floating factories with which the seas of our earth are plundered of all life. The statistics are shocking. Every year, these 37,000 modern ships catch about 40 million tons of fish. The traditional fishermen did not even pull half as much as that from the seas. I saw these huge ships not just here, but also in the Indian Ocean. They use vast drag nets, whilst others have endless long-lines and drift nets. The oceans of this world are plundered and so destroyed with no thought for future generations. Luckily there are still a few who dare to stand up against this gross idiocy.

We should not have left Canada on a Friday. The gods of the sea had obviously not accepted that, by anchoring on Virgin Rock, we had actually postponed our true departure until Saturday. They now gave us a thrashing. The wind turned around to the south and a nasty cross-sea was the result. "If you follow the great circle route to Scotland, the distance will be shorter but you will be closer to the centres of the passing lows", Herb said to us on the radio. "I would recommend that you remain south of 48 degrees North until you reach 30 degrees West. From there, you can head straight for Scotland on the rhumb line, if the wind allows you to. If you follow my advice, you'll have moderate winds from the north-west."

"What is moderate?", I asked.

"Oh, not more than 30 or 40 knots of wind!"

On this piece of news we at once got active in the galley. Malley brewed us a pot of 'storm soup', enough to last us for three days, and I started to prepare a fish curry à la Mauricienne, using our freshly caught cod. "As long as the weather permits, we should eat well!", I declared. I also added more than double the spices which I normally use for this dish, with the result that we were nearly on fire after the meal. "But we have to warm up somehow as long as our stupid heater does not work!", I claimed.

Thankfully, the temperatures rose as we reached the Gulf Stream. The difference was remarkable. In a matter of hours the water temperature rose from nine to 16 degrees Celsius, but at the same time the weather deteriorated. The barometer fell and fell. The sky darkened. Wind and waves increased. It cost us a lot of energy to take down the last remaining bit of the mainsail and to reef the genoa. We should have changed from the genoa down to the much smaller jib number four but the wind was by now too strong for that. My entry in the log speaks for itself.

'We began the night with the triple-reefed genoa' (We had roller-furled the genoa such that only 1/3 of the sail area was in use.) 'Frequently the waves smashed on deck and made the cockpit area wet and unsafe, so the watch was held inside in front of the radar screen. To generate the electricity for the radar and the hard working autopilot we kept the shaft alternator running, causing a grinding noise. Combined with the other noises and the violent movements of the boat this was the most intensive display of sea forces I have ever experienced. Sometimes the boat shot up like an elevator to subsequently surf down the crest of the wave at hair-raising speed. Several times the yacht broached in front of a breaking wave. Three times the Genoa backed with such violence that it sounded like thunder. Malley and Liz remained remarkably calm and handled the scary night with a lot of courage. We were scared but did not loose our sense of humour. At least Malley's soup saved our souls!"

The weather fax showed that the eye of the low was passing directly overhead. "I did warn you to stay further south!", Herb said when we complained about the weather, "but it seems you just can't wait to get to Scotland! And take care, the next low is creeping up on your backsides already!"

For six days and six nights we sailed on in gale-force conditions. It was incredibly cold and wet on board. The accelerating forces were often brutal. There was nothing we could do about it and it became one endless stretch of suffering. We tried in vain to ignore this awful situation and we were lucky that the boat kept us too busy to succumb to real fear.

At least we were sailing along downwind. Only after the ninth day at sea did the situation calm down and Liz made a fantastic chocolate cake, decorated with balloons, to celebrate this fact. She really excelled under such circumstances and during the entire storm she was always ready for work above or below decks. Even in the most miserable hours she was still able to produce hot meals in the galley.

But how pleasing that the weather is like life itself – every low is followed by a high. After the gale, we found peace. The wind died down and the temperatures rose. For the first time we could relax a little and begin to actually enjoy ourselves.

For several days, we had heard a clap of thunder twice a day. This confirmed that we were on track for Europe – it was the supersonic thunder of Concorde breaking the sound barrier! This plane takes just 3 1/2 hours to do the distance which we would cover in three weeks – if we hurried! "Those guys up there don't want to waste any time, but they're missing their lives", we agreed.

Herb's last forecast for us was "A new low is forming west of you. This could bring north-easterly winds in the next few days. As long as it remains possible, you should sail directly for Scotland. You might end up beating against the wind very soon. Good luck!"

Herb Hilgenberg, the amateur radio operator and meteorologist from Canada, had been a good pilot for us. With his calm voice, he gave advice and courage to us and other sailors out in the Atlantic. At the time, there were only two other boats in the North Atlantic apart from us who were in contact with him. One was about 300 miles behind us and the other was near Greenland. Everybody else sailed much further south.

The wind swung around as Herb had prophesied and soon we were pitching upwind through rough seas against 30 knots of wind. It now came from the direction in which we wanted to go. "Navigation is quite simple, really", a very experienced sailor had once remarked, "you just beat upwind and you will eventually get to where you are going!"

But that is, of course, much easier said than done. We had at last changed the genoa for the jib but even this we reefed down and sailed as close to the wind as we could. Again we were thrown about by the waves, but now they came from the side. One sea broke with such force against the ship's side that I could actually hear the planks creak. These were terrible moments in which I feared that my old wooden ship would break apart. Countless times, we checked the water level in the bilge. We made more water than usual, but that was to be expected under these harsh circumstances. The seas were high, but not mountainous enough to really threaten *Ryusei*.

Europe

Dingle

North-easterly headwinds forced us to make a landfall in Ireland. This created a problem which I had not reckoned with. My chart for Ireland was much too large-scale and was useless for coastal navigation. In the end, we made do with a pilot book and a road map which I found on board quite by chance. We then chose Dingle as our first harbour.

Long before the green mountains appeared in the hazy morning sun, the air was filled with the scent of land. The feeling of finally closing in on the land once more after all the past hardships was indescribable. Ireland's highest mountain was to starboard, the Dingle peninsula to port. As we were marvelling at the scenery, our fishing line went taut with a bang. We hauled at the line and were amazed. Instead of a fish, a large sea gull had been caught. Wearing gloves, we freed the poor creature from the hook and were glad to see that it was apparently unharmed. We then slowly and carefully inched closer to the coast, apprehensive because of our inadequate charts. Not far outside the bay, a dolphin appeared and performed a few somersaults for us. What a welcome!

Ireland greeted us with sunshine and fine summer temperatures. At last, we had our feet on solid ground once more – although this ground seemed to sway. With rolling gait, we staggered along the harbour front to a café, where we indulged in a huge breakfast and the latest newspapers. "This is the life!", my companions enthused – especially when we learnt that there were 52 bars and restaurants scattered around this small village. We felt that we could not have chosen a better harbour for our first European landfall. One of the best watering holes was in the shop of a shoe-maker, immediately opposite the church. Another bar we frequented was owned by an 80-year-old lady. It seemed as if we were drinking in her sitting-room. Dingle made us dizzy with elation, not only because of our successful voyage. On this day we proved once more that alcohol is to sailors what water is to fish.

Arran–Asia

Scotland was beckoning, so we left the harbour of temptations on the evening after our arrival. In a magic night under millions of stars we sailed northwards over a smooth sea between the Blasket Islands. Another night we spent at anchor in the bay of Inishbofin. Although the island is usually peacefully deserted, it was now the scene of wild partying. A group of yachts had just finished their race here and had taken over the pub. Together with the only other cruisers, a Scottish family who were circumnavigating Ireland, we dived into the celebrations. In the later stages, Ian MacLeod, a professor from Glasgow university, accepted a challenge from the Irish for a bagpipe competition.

As they left the bay on the following morning, he piped the Scottish national anthem from the deck of his boat. This put us in the mood for Scotland, and we hoisted the St Andrew's Cross before up-anchoring ourselves.

A mere 300 miles were now between us and our final goal and we could not wait any longer. But the green hills of Ireland seemed to be glued to the horizon and slipped past in tantalising slow motion. As the sun rose on the morning of the 8th August, the moment had finally arrived. The Mull of Kinytre sat on our port side, Northern Ireland was to starboard and the conspicuous island of Ailsa Craig loomed ahead. Then, the familiar hills of Arran rose from the early haze.

Shortly afterwards, we sailed past Pladda, Arran's southernmost lighthouse. My emotions threatened to overwhelm me. I was in a state of complete exhilaration. I had known Arran since my childhood. It was here that, over the years, my bonds with the sea had developed. Now it was here that my voyage from Asia would end.

The weather could not have been better. A light south-easterly enabled us to fly the Dragon, our cruising spinnaker. We then dressed our ship with all the flags that we had on board, amongst them of course those of all 26 countries that we had visited. The voyage from Asia should have taken one year. Two years and 22,000 miles had now passed, a voyage in slow motion but a life in the fast lane. Reason enough to pop a champagne cork. "Our arrival will probably be quite turbulent", I prophesied. "Let us enjoy our last moments of peace!" With this, we sat on the foredeck and drank the champagne to toast our shared adventures.

Scotland was, at the time, baking in a heat-wave. The sun was hot enough for us to sail in bathing suits. Then we passed a small island which I remembered well from times long past. It is called Holy Island and has a Buddhist monastery on it. Tropical temperatures and the culture of the Far East: Arran meets Asia!

Whisky Galore

Oh times are hard in Barra,
You'd hear the Botchas cry,
No food to feed a sparra,
And every bottle dry.

"Ahoy there! You are already expected on the pier!", the crew of a passing yacht called out to us. Then my old friend Howard Walker came to meet us in his motor-launch and escorted us in to the mooring off Lamlash. His offer to take us ashore we however turned down. We had sailed this far and now we were going to swim the last few metres. To the sound of cheering and bagpipes, we jumped overboard and swam to the pier. They had all come: my father and our best friends on Arran, Lady Jean Fordes and Howard's family. For days and filled with growing anxiety, they had waited for us. We nearly drowned in hugs, compliments and champagne.

We had now reached Europe and Arran. But our main objective was still waiting to be fulfilled: to retrieve the hidden bottle of whisky in Glen Sannox. Lamlash is in the south of Arran,

Glen Sannox in the north. On this last trip, we were accompanied by my father and his friends. So as to leave no doubts about our mission, we had hoisted the flag signal 'Whisky Galore'. The weather remained sensational: sun, warmth, light winds. Out came the Dragon once more. This was sailing at its best and our guests cheered us with delight. Despite these thousands of miles, our old wooden ship was in great shape. Arran's mountains slid past as we came closer and closer to the world's most beautiful valley, Glen Sannox. In the mouth of the little stream bearing the same name we anchored and went ashore in the dinghy, circled by a suspicious basking shark. We were in a festive mood and celebrated with a barbecue ashore.

As the sun fell towards the horizon, Malley, Liz and myself marched off for the finale of our voyage, in search of the whisky. For several kilometres, we wandered uphill over rough terrain. I was on a sharp look-out for any hints of the place where I had buried the whisky ten years ago, under a conspicuous rock. My companions began to have doubts: "There are thousands of rocks around here. How can you identify the right one?"

"I might be a little forgetful", I replied indignantly, "but not when it comes to whisky. Trust me!"

They were both impressed when, at the end of the valley, I led them to a large rock and dug out the bottle from the soft earth underneath within minutes. Alas, this joyous moment was only too short. We had just taken a first sip from the bottle when we were attacked by millions of angry midges. We took a quick photograph and fled down valley from the tiny beasts. It was a hot and sticky night, and the stream was beckoning. At one point we threw off our clothes and jumped in. Moments later, a solitary wanderer came past. Stunned by all this nudity, his eyes nearly popped out on stalks.

It was only down by the shore that the midges left us in peace. As darkness grew and the stars rose above, the whisky helped to launch wild thoughts.

I was pondering basic questions. I had only wanted to come home to Europe and had now turned into a cruising sailor – one who fears no cost and no trouble to be in a position to sail the world's oceans, who is crazy enough to forfeit a secure existence, to share a tiny ship with other people, to expose himself to wind, cold and wetness. No material things can motivate for this. It is the experience in itself. I was motivated by the challenge and satisfied at having achieved a goal, both alone and in a team. Time and space were filled with new dimensions for me. Problems of our day-to-day lives, be they of a private nature or related to jobs and businesses, shrink to near-meaningless in comparison. I had found entirely new perspectives for my life.

"We have reached Scotland. We have salvaged the whisky. What are we going to do now?", I asked.

"I've lost my job in the meantime", Malley announced, "and if I don't return very soon, I might also lose my fiancé. I would like to fly back home. As quickly as possible."

"I want to travel to Africa. But before that, I would love to sail a bit more around Europe", said Liz and then asked me: "and what are your plans?"

"I shall sail on until I find a harbour. Somewhere in Europe I shall swallow the anchor, start a new career and, who knows, maybe even a family. But that is for the future."

EPILOGUE

AGAIN AND AGAIN I was asked the smug question of how the trip had really been, with two wonderful and attractive young ladies alone on a small ship. Everybody suspected romance, but none of us wanted this. Nature had enough adventures in store. Once in a while, we feared for our lives. But our team was as strong, if not stronger, than any male crew before. No other leg of my voyage had put us to such a hard test as the North Atlantic. And in the eyes of nature we are all equal. The only thing that counts in the end is how we cope together.

What has become of us, after all these adventures?

• Guillaume Felisaz returned to France and settled down in Marseilles.

• Luke Raubenheimer stayed in South Africa only temporarily, and went cruising again.

• Guy Hammond has, after a short intermezzo in South Africa, married and settled in England.

• Greg Friedrichs has married his girlfriend Amy in America. They now live on their wooden sailing boat in Seattle.

• Maryallice Weber (Malley) married her fiancé on Diamond Island in Maine. Today she works as an artist and helps her husband to run the 'Liberal Cup', a brewery/pub.

• Elizabeth Trice went travelling in West Africa after our voyage and has now decided to study music back home.

• The skipper, his wife and son are currently at anchor.

Glen Sannox – journey's end

APPENDIX

Travel data

From – to	Nautical miles	Non stop
THAILAND – SINGAPORE	550	
SINGAPORE – MALAYSIA / Tioman	355	
SINGAPORE – INDONESIA (August 93)	520	
INDONESIA – CHAGOS	2031	16 days
CHAGOS – MAURITIUS	1226	
MAURITIUS – REUNION (incl. Race)	376	
REUNION – SOUTH AFRICA / Durban	1460	12 days
Durban – Cape Town	1032	
Cape Town – NAMIBIA	491	
NAMIBIA – ST. HELENA	1309	9 days
ST. HELENA – BRAZIL / Natal	1749	13 days
BRAZIL – FR. GUYANA	1270	7 days
FR. GUYANA – TOBAGO	609	3½ days
TOBAGO – PANAMA / San Blas Islands	2258	
PANAMA – HONDURAS / Guanaja	628	5 days
HONDURAS – USA / Florida	736	
USA / Key West – North Carolina	760	
North Carolina – New York	558	
New York – Maine / Portland	493	
USA / Maine – CANADA / Virgin Rock	1372	
CANADA – IRELAND / Dingle	1788	12 days
IRELAND – SCOTLAND (August 95)	416	

Total distance (nautical miles): 21,987

Technical specifications

Name	*RYUSEI* (Japanese: 'Dragon Star')
Type	Sloop
Design	Sparkman and Stephens (*Firebrand*)
Builder	Kato Boat, Japan
Year built	1966
Length overall	44 ft 13.41 m
Lwl	34 ft 10.36 m
Beam	11.6 ft 3.51 m
Draft	6.9 ft 2.06 m
Displacement	13 t
Ballast	4.9 t
Hull material	Wood
Mast	Aluminium
Sail area	approx. 90 m²
Engine	Yanmar Diesel, 44 hp
Fuel	470 l
Water	580 l

Hull
Burma teak (32 mm) – Carvel planked on laminated frames of Japanese elm – keel and backbone of solid teak – bronze fastenings – deck supports, mast support and chainplates from stainless steel (#316).

Deck & Equipment
Deck partly covered with teak – Doghouse with sprayhood – fixed bimini over the steering position – selftailing sheet-winches (Maxwell) – electrical anchor-winch (Muir)

Sails
Main, Genoa (130%), Jib No. 4, Cruising Chute, Staysail, Storm jib, Trysail

Engine/electrics
Yanmar diesel, 4 cylinder, 44 PS
Hydraulic gearbox, ratio 3:1, fixed propeller
Two alternators (90 and 30 amps); six solar panels, 42 watts each. Four batteries, 150 amps; inverter–charger, 300 watts, 30 amps)

Interior
Interior clad in mahogany, floor boards from Japanese cherry wood; berths, one double in the forepeak and three singles in the saloon; shower in the fore-peak; head (Lavac)

Equipment

Refrigerator	155 l with cool-box, 12 Volt (Adler Bodour)
Stove	Three-burner gas stove with grill and oven
Heater	Diesel (Dickenson)
Water pumps	Two (fresh water, salt water)
Bilge pumps	Two electrical, 1 mechanical, 1 manual
GPS	MAGELLAN NAV 5300 DX
Sextant	TAMAYA
Radar	FURUNO 1621
Weather Fax	KODEN FX 7181
Instruments	B&G Echo-sounder, Speedometer, Water temperature, Anemometer
Autopilot	AUTOHELM 6000 with interface to GPS and B&G AUTOHELM 5000 Complete set as backup
Radio SSB	ICOM HF Transceiver IC-731 with antenna-tuner AH-2
Radio VHF	Stationary: STANDARD
Hand-held: ICOM IC-M7	
Life raft	AVON for 6 persons
EPIRB	Two systems: ACR, LITTON
Man overboard Equipment	includes lifebelt, light and signal buoy
Emergency steering	Emergency tiller
Burglar security	Electric cable with 7000 volts
Code flags	Complete set
Anchor chain	10 mm/85 metres
Main anchor	CQR 22 kg
Stern anchor	Danforth 15 kg
Storm anchor	Bruce 35 kg with 15 m chain (10 mm) and 130 m nylon warp (24 mm)
Dinghy	2.6 m inflatable with rigid hull/SEA NOMAD
Outboard engine	MERCURY 15 hp
Stereo	Radio, Cassette, CD
Diving gear	Compressor: NAUTICA MCH-6
Three diving bottles with aqualung	
Spare parts	
Tools	

DESIGN BY SPARKMAN AND STEPHENS

Firebrand

DESIGNED TO WIN IN TWO KINDS
OF RACING

L.O.A.	...	...	43.20ft	Draft	6.68ft
L.W.L.	...	...	30.00ft	Displacement ...	10 tons
Beam	...	...	11.26ft	Ballast	5 tons
	Sail area (main	100 per cent foretriangle) 725 sq ft			

PRESSURE on designers of offshore racing yachts has been steadily increasing since the late 1930's when yachts were first built with the principal purpose of racing offshore, and every year new yachts appear where designers and owners have been even more ruthless than their predecessors. All the time the trend is away from the leisurely "Solent yachting" approach to design and nearer to the type of dedicated efficiency which is expected in a racing car or an aeroplane, but, until recently, has not been expected in a sailing yacht.

Since their early, overwhelming success in offshore racing with *Dorade*, Olin and Rod Stephens have steadily established themselves to the point where they are known and respected throughout the world of yachting as the men responsible for some of the finest yachts ever built. Coupling this background of experience with the drive of Dennis Miller, who has been part owner of *Clarion*, the winner of the Fastnet Race in 1963, was bound to produce an interesting result.

Firebrand is 30ft on the waterline and, thus, a likely contender for the British Admiral's Cup team and it is in this combination of the needs of offshore racing with the special requirements of racing round the buoys in the Solent that she can be said to have broken new ground.

Below the arrangement is aimed solely at offshore racing with large chart table and galley amidships, and the offwatch crew comfortably tucked into permanent berths where the motion is least. From the construction point of view *Firebrand* follows modern American practice with laminated frames, wood floors on every frame in the ends and a fabricated metal mast step structure. The ballast ratio is almost fifty per cent with a sail area/displacement ratio of about 161. The engine is so low that it must have needed a shoe horn to get it in despite the unusually slack bilge section.

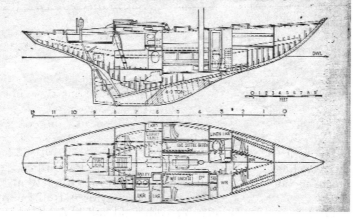

Ryusei's sistership, Firebrand